TRIX

Trix

The Other Kipling

Barbara Fisher

https://www.openbookpublishers.com

©2024 Barbara Fisher

This work is licensed under an Attribution-NonCommercial 4.0 International (CC BY-NC 4.0). This license allows you to share, copy, distribute and transmit the text; to adapt the text for non-commercial purposes of the text providing attribution is made to the authors (but not in any way that suggests that they endorse you or your use of the work). Attribution should include the following information:

Barbara Fisher, *Trix: The Other Kipling*. Cambridge, UK: Open Book Publishers, 2024, https://doi.org/10.11647/OBP.0377

Copyright and permissions for the reuse of some of the images included in this publication differ from the above. This information is provided in the captions and in the list of illustrations. Every effort has been made to identify and contact copyright holders and any omission or error will be corrected if notification is made to the publisher.

Further details about CC BY-NC licenses are available at
http://creativecommons.org/licenses/by-nc/4.0/

All external links were active at the time of publication unless otherwise stated and have been archived via the Internet Archive Wayback Machine at https://archive.org/web

Any digital material and resources associated with this volume will be available at https://doi.org/10.11647/OBP.0377#resources

ISBN Paperback: 978-1-80511-152-8
ISBN Hardback: 978-1-80511-153-5
ISBN Digital (PDF): 978-1-80511-154-2
ISBN Digital eBook (EPUB): 978-1-80511-155-9
ISBN HTML: 978-1-80511-157-3

DOI: 10.11647/OBP.0377

Cover image: Kennet, William Morris, Morris & Co., Birmingham Museums Trust, https://unsplash.com/photos/white-blue-and-green-floral-textile--KfLa4I4eTo

Cover design: Jeevanjot Kaur Nagpal.

*To the Memory of my Son, Andrew Fisher Williamson
and to the Future of my Son, Douglas Fisher Williamson*

Contents

Acknowledgements	ix
Introduction	1
1. The House of Desolation	9
2. Macdonalds and Kiplings	33
3. Rescue	43
4. The Family Square	57
5. *The Heart of a Maid*	93
6. Wife of Jack	103
7. *A Pinchbeck Goddess*	121
8. Breakdown	145
9. Psychic Research	167
10. Relapse and Exile	197
11. Recovery and Return	213
Select Bibliography	233
Index	241

Acknowledgements

My first thanks go to Shirley Seigel, who generously gave me her sister, Dorothy Adelson's unpublished manuscript 'Kipling's Sister' to explore and expand. Dorothy's beautifully written manuscript was my original inspiration. Shirley's generosity was matched by the uncommon kindness of Lorna Lee, whose *Trix: Kipling's Forgotten Sister* was invaluable through all the research and writing of this book. Lorna not only shared her knowledge, but also invited me into her home, accompanied me to Bateman's, the Kipling home, and arranged for me to visit Helen Macdonald, daughter of Trix's first cousin, Julius. Helen Macdonald had preserved many of Trix's papers and personal possessions, including her egg-shaped crystal ball and her fan, and she generously shared these with me. These letters, photographs, and memorabilia were auctioned in 2014 and are now mostly at the University of Sussex, in Brighton. Some, including Trix's fan, are at the Beinecke Rare Book Library at Yale University in New Haven, Connecticut.

On my several visits to Brighton, I was helped by the librarians at the Rudyard Kipling, Trix Kipling, Lockwood Kipling, Baldwin, and Macdonald Papers located in the Special Collections of the University of Sussex. The librarians at the British Library in London, at Texas A&M in College Station Texas, at the Berg Collection at the New York Public Library, the Houghton Library at Harvard University, the Beinecke Rare Book Library at Yale University, the Library of Congress in Washington, D.C., and The Society for Psychical Research in New York have all been generous with their time and knowledge. I am especially grateful to Professor Ralph Crane of the University of Tasmania who shared with me a huge and heretofore unseen cache of Trix's letters to her friend Maud Diver. My thanks go to Mary Hamer and Andrew Lycett who have not only shared their research and writing with me but have helped and encouraged me. David Alan Richards, Kipling's bibliographer and the donor of the Kipling Collection to Yale University, has been generous in sharing his vast knowledge of the works of Rudyard Kipling and all things Kipling. I am grateful for the support of the Kipling Society in London where I presented a piece of this biography in 2011. With the editorial advice of Janet Montefiore, 'Trix: The Other Kipling' was published in *The Kipling Journal* in September 2014. I was encouraged in my work to be on the short list for the Tony Lothian Prize of the Biographers' Club in 2013.

I have been especially fortunate to be a member of a small biography writing group, which included Pat Auspos, Betty Caroli, Ruth Franklin, Dorothy Helly, and Melissa Nathanson. The close attention of this group has been extraordinarily important in the writing of this book. Women Writing Women's Lives and BIO, the Biographers International Organization have been warm and welcoming.

Lastly, I thank my husband Jack Resnick who supported me through the research and writing of this book and travelled with me on numerous occasions to Southern England, Scotland, and India to locate the places where Trix lived.

Introduction

A tiny old woman, wearing a long woollen coat and a dark straw hat decorated with bright silk flowers, paces in front of the hippopotamus pool in The Edinburgh Zoo on Corstorphine Hill. She is surrounded by children who gather near her and, at a greater distance, by curious but wary Scots. She has large, prominent, sapphire-blue eyes, and a sharp nose that sniffs the air as her fingers clutch at it for emphasis as she speaks. Her several necklaces and many bracelets make clinking sounds as she finds the right spot near the pool. When a sufficient crowd has gathered, she addresses Maggie, her hippopotamus friend, in Hindustani, the hippo's native tongue. She has compiled a private glossary of Hindustani words, which she consults when conversing with the hippos. Maggie responds to her high-pitched commands as she raises her head from the murky water, her tiny ears alert and twitching.[1] When she moves purposefully on to the elephant enclosure, the children clamber after her. Once she locates her favourite baby elephant, she pulls herself up to her full height—barely five feet—and stands confidently before him. In piercing, pedantic tones, she orders the little elephant to bow low in a salaam. When he drops to his knees, the children cheer. She bends down to the children and, in a confidential soft voice, says that it is beyond her powers to get the elephant to say 'please'. The children squirm and giggle with pleasure at this private confession. The adults keep far enough away to show their disdain for an eccentric character but stay close enough to observe if the elephant will follow orders.[2]

---

1   Margaret Macdonald, 'Memories of Trix Kipling', in *Trix: Kipling's Forgotten Sister*, ed. by Lorna Lee (Kent: Pond View Press, 2003), p. 112.
2   Colin MacInnes, *England, Half English* (London: MacGibbon & Kee Ltd, 1961), p. 114.

This is Trix Kipling, the younger sister of Rudyard, in old age, performing winningly on her last stage. In many biographies of Rudyard Kipling, Trix makes her final appearance at the Edinburgh Zoo, and she is portrayed not as a cunning old charmer and an accomplished performer but as a lone madwoman, gesturing and jabbering in Hindustani to the uncomprehending elephants. This image of Trix as flighty and fey at best, incompetent and insane at worst, has persisted unchallenged for decades.

While Kipling's biographers properly identify Trix as Rudyard's sole companion during his miserable childhood and as one side of the 'Family Square'—the pet name for the four Kiplings happily reunited in Lahore—they lose sight of her when she turns twenty-one. They delight in Trix's beauty and wit, which captivated the Viceroy's son, and they ignore her once she marries a dour Scot ten years her senior. She surfaces in Rudyard's life now and again as an inconvenience or an embarrassment.

When I tried to discover how this unfortunate view became established, I recognized that by the time Trix married at twenty-one, Rudyard was already famous and traveling the world, never to return to India, while Trix remained on the sub-continent. The two were rarely in the same country or even on the same continent, although they were both in England during the onset of Trix's two periods of mental collapse (in 1898 and 1911). Thus, Trix was especially present in Rudyard's life and thoughts during her periods of extreme mental and marital distress. Disliking Trix's husband, Jack Fleming, and disapproving of Trix's participation in psychic research experiments, Rudyard distanced himself from both. He (correctly) held Jack largely responsible for Trix's first breakdown, and (incorrectly) blamed the Society for Psychic Research for Trix's later mental troubles. Trix's years of contentment and creativity seem to have passed Rudyard, and his biographers, by.

Trix may also have been overlooked because her poetic talent, which blossomed early (in her teens), also faded early (in her thirties), never developing into mature art. While her beauty, her wit, and her 'reverent irreverence'[3], lasted a lifetime, they were appreciated only by a small local audience. Her story is one of resilience and reinvention, not one

---

3   Lance Thirkell to Sheila Wilson, 30 January 1988. Private collection of Lorna Lee.

(like her brother's) of precocious gifts resulting in fame and fortune. Trix fought to turn her many talents into personal satisfaction or worldly success, and she was hampered not only by the expectations of her family and the restrictions of her time, but by her own inhibitions. It goes without saying that stories of struggle, compromise, and defeat are less satisfying to tell or hear than stories of struggle, perseverance, and triumph.

Thus, most of Trix's fascinating life is unknown. In telling Trix's story, my primary intention is to rescue her from the misrepresentations, trivializations, and outright neglect of Rudyard's many biographers.

Here, for the first time, is the story of Trix's life, beginning with the terrible childhood she shared with Rudyard as a Raj orphan living with cruel strangers in the south of England. I follow her through her calm adolescence and describe the six happy years she spent back in India, being spoiled by her parents and being encouraged by her brother to write parodies, poetry, and stories, which were regularly mistaken for his. I trace her marriage to a stiff British officer stationed in India under the Raj from its hopeful beginnings through its childless, cheerless middle to its ultimate uneasy accommodation.

I correctly locate and attribute all of Trix's short fiction, poetry, and journalism, giving special attention to her two ambitious but flawed novels. I explore Trix's participation as a writer of automatic scripts for the Society for Psychical Research, describing the society's rigorous methods, serious purposes, and extremely modest claims and placing its activity in the context of nineteenth-century scientific thought. Finally, I discuss the causes for Trix's two periods of mental illness and the efficacy of the treatment routinely prescribed for her and for most female mental patients at the end of the nineteenth and the beginning of the twentieth centuries.

Most importantly, I give a voice, a mind, and a heart to a misunderstood, misrepresented, but indomitable woman.

At about the same time that Trix, aged seventy, was charming children at the Edinburgh Zoo, she wrote to old family friend Edith Plowden describing the circumstances of her birth. The harrowing description serves as an explanation for how Trix became an exceptional performer and an unforgettable presence. In order to survive, she made herself first into a clever little show-off and later into a fascinating fabulist.

Here is how Trix began the story of her birth:

> I was born June 11th 1868—Mother was sent home by doctors—that she might not run the risk of a second long agony—such as she had when Ruddy was born—As it was she nearly died poor darling—& I was still born—with a black eye & broken left arm—Aunt Georgie picked me up from the hearthrug where they had put me—practically dead—as I hadn't breathed.[4]

The central character here is Alice, the mother who 'nearly died'. The damaged newborn, also 'practically dead', is reported almost as an afterthought. Casually, it seems, Aunt Georgie retrieved the baby from the cold floor. She patted the baby's back with her tiny hands until the busy doctor found 'a minute to spare' from attending to Alice to give the baby a good pounding. This revived the lifeless infant. Although the baby survived, its dangers were not over. Georgie carried the infant into her husband's painting studio and laid it carelessly on an armchair. A stout art dealer, visiting on business, came into the studio and prepared to seat himself on the silent, swaddled bundle.[5] Georgie, busy welcoming the important guest, rushed over, snatched the child in her arms, and carried it away from the danger. The baby, 'a poor scrap of humanity', is almost thrown away, forgotten, and left to die discarded on the floor. She is saved, almost on a whim, by her aunt—who rescued her because, according to Trix, 'I looked so like a Blake baby—as I sprawled on the floor-big & white'.[6] The doctor noticed after delivering the baby that its arm was broken, but he didn't bother to set it until several days after the birth, when the child had shown it 'meant to survive'.

Survival, she was being taught at birth, was her own responsibility. She had better learn this lesson quickly and well.

That Alice Kipling insisted on giving birth back in England and not in India, where she had been living, and that a daughter was born to her on this date in the home of her sister Georgiana Burne-Jones, is known. But the pathetic descriptions of a bruised and broken child left to die on the floor, then almost crushed by a fat visitor, and finally neglected by the doctor, are featured only in Trix's version of the story. In this telling,

---

4   Trix Kipling, letter to Edith Plowden, 7 October 1936. University of Sussex.
5   Ibid.
6   Ibid.

Trix imagined her infant self as injured, unseen, and unloved, and thus liable to be ignored. She depicted the adult world as powerful, selfish, and careless, liable to discard or destroy a helpless, damaged child. Thus, a child had better make itself seen and heard—and fast. The story serves as an explanation for Trix's character and her most memorable qualities. Trix was a performer, a girl and a woman whose dramatic presence and extravagant speech were always noticed.

Alice returned to India when her new baby was several months old. Her husband, John Lockwood Kipling, had stayed behind when Alice returned to England for the birth of her child and only met his daughter when she had already developed her own infant personality. When the baby was placed in his lap for the first time, she displayed her playful nature. She 'insisted on playing Bo Peep & tried to pull his beard out'.[7] He responded to her antics by calling her 'a tricksy baby'. Although she was named Alice Macdonald Kipling after her mother, she was, after that, never called anything but Trix or Trixie. The name stuck, presumably because all members of the family agreed that it fit the high-spirited infant. Trix always gave credit to her father for the invention of her name.

Fig. 1 Trix as a young child in 1872.

---

7   Ibid.

If Trix had not absorbed the lesson of self-preservation at birth, she was given a second chance when she was three years old. As a toddler living in India with her parents, she was suddenly sent, along with her brother, to live with strangers thousands of miles away from home, without explanation or preparation. Bewildered by her banishment and fearful of more neglect, she worked to make herself seen and heard. Fortunately, she was very pretty to look at and astounding to listen to. She had an especially keen memory for written and spoken impressions, and she practiced improving these natural gifts. After hearing a poem or song one time, she could recall and recite it perfectly. She soon became an eager show-off and an accomplished performer. Before she became a writer, she was an actress, a singer, and a prodigious reciter of verse.

When Trix was not performing for an audience, she invented stories to amuse and console herself. Alone much of the time, she rehearsed her favourite plots, featuring the rescue of innocent children in peril and the dreadful punishment of neglectful or cruel guardians. With her sole companion, her brother Rudyard, she created imaginary worlds which only they could enter and invented imaginary languages which only they could understand.

As Trix matured, she easily spun stories, wrote verse, and composed clever parodies. In her twenties and early thirties, she published her many stories and two novels; she created characters and plots focusing on what she knew, imagined, and feared—imposture, miscommunication, misunderstanding, detachment, betrayal, and abandonment. She created women who suffered from the loss or lack of children, who struggled with their own baffling anger and malice, and who were often the architects of their own unhappiness. She composed these unusual fictions mindful of the strictures of her society and careful of her personal modesty. Still later, she wrote automatic scripts for psychic research experiments, in which she expressed her feelings of longing and distance, disguised (even from herself) as messages between the dead and the living.

As a slender and winsome woman, Trix combined her story-telling gift with a theatrical delivery, making her an exceptional presence. She was recognized by everyone who met her as an enthusiastic and expansive talker. She peppered her conversation with quotation, long memorized passages of verse—especially Shakespeare—and enthralling stories, historical, personal, and imaginary. Among true believers and credulous admirers, she was known for her ability to flashback in time, to call forth ghosts, and to see visions in a crystal. One of Trix's friends concluded, 'She was easily the most remarkable woman I ever expect to meet, and to listen to her stories, was well-nigh to expire of assorted excitements and interest'.[8] This is the impression she put effort and energy into making. She liked to have an audience and knew how to play to a crowd. She demanded and commanded attention. She did not want to be neglected or forgotten, and, by those who met her, she rarely was.

---

8   Rachel Ferguson, *Royal Borough of Kensington* (London: Jonathan Cape, 1950), p. 32.

1. The House of Desolation

When Trix told the story of her birth, she strung together an almost comic series of close escapes from death. When she told the story of her childhood, she found no humour in the long years of lonely banishment. Overcoming abandonment and neglect, she outfoxed infant exposure. Later, and with difficulty, she outlasted childhood horrors.

In early October of 1871, when Trix was three years old and Rudyard was not quite six, they were awakened one cool autumn morning by their mother and readied for a short journey. They left the large and comfortable home of their grandmother at Bewdley in Wolverhampton, where they had been visiting, and, with their mother, took the train south to Hampshire. Rudyard was a sturdy boy with a solid stance, a steady gaze, and a sure sense of himself and his place in the world. The trip posed the prospect of another day of exploration and adventure for the curious child. Trix was a softly pretty, blond, and blue-eyed little girl. Too young to have a sense of herself or her world, she set out on the journey as on any other day, reassured in her changing surroundings by the familiar presence of her mother and brother.

Recently accustomed to train travel, the children sat comfortably and contentedly next to their mother. After the train journey, they rode in a hired carriage past fields of brick-mounds and wide expanses of barren heath. The carriage rolled on through the sandy streets of the shabby town of Southsea, stopping at a newly built, three-storied building at the end of a bare road. At number 4 Campbell Road, Havelock Park, they entered a dim and narrow entryway and were introduced to an older couple, Mr and Mrs Holloway. Mr Holloway walked with a limp to greet his guests, bending down to shake hands with the little boy. He had a pleasant face covered by a short beard. Mrs Holloway was a thin, bespectacled woman with a wide smile stretched to expose large teeth held by gleaming wires.

The children had been on an extended holiday in England, having travelled with their parents from Bombay. They had arrived with their parents in Southampton on 13 May 1871, after the long voyage from India through the newly opened Suez Canal. They had proceeded to London and then on to the Grange, the large and luxurious home of their aunt and uncle, the Burne-Joneses. For five months, they had moved about England, paying visits to other relatives of their mother—to their grandmother Hannah and Aunt Edie Macdonald at Bewdley; to Aunt Louisa, her husband Alfred Baldwin, and son Stanley at nearby Wilden. They also travelled to meet their father's mother and sisters at Skipton. The children had made several more visits with their parents to the Burne-Joneses and had been treated to a seaside holiday at the coastal town of Littlehampton. During the long family vacation, no mention had been made of any special plans for the children's future. Nor had any explanation been given to the children for the long ocean voyage, except for a chance to visit with relatives back in England. Their only expectation was for a long holiday abroad. They had not been told the chief purpose of the trip—to leave them indefinitely with strangers.

Having spent several months being introduced to their parents' friends and relatives, they were comfortable travelling and staying with new people. There was nothing unusual in being taken to visit an elderly couple in an unfamiliar place, but this place was more than unfamiliar—it was unpleasant. It had a musty smell. The rooms the children could see from the front parlour, where they had been deposited, were small and dark. While Mrs Kipling talked with the Holloways, the children stared and sniffed about. After inquiring about the plan of the house, Mrs Kipling was given a tour of the lower floor and the back garden. The children could hear footsteps as the Holloways, speaking in low voices, showed Mrs Kipling around the house. Then all was silent, and their mother disappeared. She was simply gone.

I can see Trix standing there in the parlour beside her brother Rudyard, waiting patiently for her mother to return. After a while, growing uneasy, she turns herself around, searching for the familiar warm folds of her mother's heavy skirt and reaches up for her mother's extended gloved hand, but they are not where they should have been. The reassuring swell and swish of her mother's presence are gone. Trix looks about her, trying to understand where she is and how she had come to be there. She recognizes nothing except Rudyard, standing stiff and still beside her.

Rudyard assumed at first that their mother had momentarily forgotten to take them with her, or had been called away on some errand and would soon return. Waiting and watching in the gloomy room, he assured Trix that there had been some slight misunderstanding or some easily remedied mistake. Rudyard had expected that after the short visit, like many others they had recently paid, they would be leaving with their mother to return to the home of their grandmother or their aunt and uncle. Having been told nothing, given no warning of the abrupt change that was about to occur, neither he nor Trix had any way to understand where their mother had gone. They could not believe that they had been purposely left behind. Given no explanation or farewell, the children were utterly confused to be alone in an unfamiliar house with people they had only just met. Rudyard looked about with distaste and scorn at the dark cramped rooms, while Trix looked to Rudyard for some clue, some words of explanation.

After a while, the children were forced to accept that they had been abandoned, although for how long they had no idea. For days, weeks, and months after, they waited, with hopes steadily dimming, for the return of their parents. Before giving up hope completely, they invented fantasies of running away through the streets, across the heaths, and up the sandy dunes to the sea (which they could hear from the house) where they would overtake their parents boarding ship for Bombay.

Many years later, Trix came to understand that their parents,

> doubtless wanted to save us, and themselves, suffering by not telling us clearly before-hand that we were to be left behind, but by so doing they left us, as it were, in the dark, and with nothing to look forward to [...] As it was, we felt that we had been deserted, 'almost as much as on a doorstep,' and what was the reason? [...] Mamma was not ill [...] Papa had not had to go to the wars; [...] they hadn't even lost their money [...] But there was no excuse; they had gone back to our own lovely home, and had not taken us with them. There was no getting out of that.[1]

---

1   Alice M. Fleming, 'Some Childhood Memories of Rudyard Kipling', *Chambers Journal* (March 1939), p. 171.

Whatever the justification, the result was that Trix, having been left 'as much as on a doorstep', felt like an unwanted parcel.

The children struggled to invent an explanation for having been handed over to strangers and consigned to the mean little house, appropriately named Lorne Lodge. Their greatest difficulty was that 'we had had no preparation or explanation; it was like a double death, or rather, like an avalanche that had swept away everything happy and familiar'.[2] In time, they understood that Mrs Holloway—who commanded the children to call her Aunty Rosa—Mr Holloway who was to be called Uncle, and their twelve-year-old son, Harry, were to replace their family, and that Lorne Lodge, with its small bare patch of garden, was to be their home.

Mrs Holloway, with what they soon recognized as her typical cruelty, told the children that they had been left because they were tiresome creatures. The kinder Mr Holloway assured them that she was only joking and that they had been left in England because the climate in India wasn't good for little people. But this did little to enlighten the baffled children about the utterly unexpected and inexplicable change in their lives. They had only their imaginations to make sense of their startling new situation.

Slowly, they became accustomed to the bleak house and shabby neighbourhood. Lorne Lodge was a narrow house of three stories at the end of an undistinguished street lined with similar houses.

> It was a small house of six rooms, not counting the greenhouse, which only Aunty Rosa remembered to call 'the conservatory.' It wore a shabby stucco pinafore, and had a front garden about the size and shape of a Persian prayer carpet, where nothing grew except a bank of St John's wort, which sloped down to the playroom window in the basement. That playroom was always chilly and smelt of mushrooms even in the summer, and any toys put in the wall cupboards [...] turned blue with mildew after two or three days. At the back of the ugly brickwork a mean little scullery and coal shed suggested architectural dermatitis and deformity.[3]

---

2   Trix Kipling, 'Through Judy's Eyes', in Lorna Lee, p. 362. Punch and Judy were the names used by Rudyard for the two bereft children in his story 'Baa Baa, Black Sheep'. Trix in her memoir of childhood 'Through Judy's Eyes', written much later, used the same names.

3   Trix Kipling, 'Through Judy's Eyes', p. 346.

There was a dining room with 'a big sideboard with funny bits of looking-glass where you didn't expect them, and where they chiefly reflected people's feet'[4] and a big, polished table used for both meals and lessons. The drawing room, like the dining room, was dark and dreary with a musty smell the children found disagreeable. Trix shared a bedroom as well as a bed with Mrs Holloway. She delighted in the few pretty feminine touches in the bedroom—a skirted dressing table, a red satin and white lace pin cushion, red and white glass scent bottles.

Rudyard shared a bedroom with Harry in the dark, low-ceilinged attic. Having lived in the warmth and luxury of India with servants to wait on him in brightly decorated rooms, wide airy verandas, and gardens planted with fragrant flowers, Rudyard was amazed and appalled by his new surroundings. He remembered the parks in Bombay where tall pink oleanders blossomed, green parrots perched in the trees, and striped grey squirrels—tame enough to eat from one's hand—scampered about. Trix remembered little of India after having been away for six months, but she trusted Rudyard's descriptions of pastel-petaled flowers and brightly feathered birds.

As the children became accustomed to the house, they became acquainted with the Holloways—Mrs Sarah Holloway, Mr Pryse Agar Holloway, and their son Henry, called Harry. Mrs Holloway, 'a puritanical, narrow-minded Evangelical', was a sharp, bony woman with 'frowning eyes, grinning lips, long yellow teeth, and soiled widow's cap'. 'She was [...] early old, with pepper and salt hair in lank loops above large ears [...] Her lips looked dry and chapped even in summer, and never hid the large front teeth and the gleaming gold wires that fastened the back ones, and her throat was long and skinny ("Just like poultry".)'[5] The father of the foster family—Pryse Agar Holloway, a retired Navy captain—was softer by nature. He treated the little boy kindly and protected him from the bullying of twelve-year-old Harry. He told Rudyard stories and took him on walks. Little girls held only slight interest for him.

Rudyard, who had been pampered and spoiled back in India, was cocky and talkative, and accustomed to lord it over his devoted ayah and the other servants. Friendly servants told him local folk tales, taught

---

4   Ibid.
5   Ibid., p. 351.

him Indian songs, carved toys for him out of fruits and nuts, and took him to Hindu temples. Rudyard felt entitled to pull his ayah's hair and even bite her. Throwing stones at the younger servants was permitted. Mrs Holloway was determined to discipline the imperious, arrogant, and impertinent little boy.

Trix had only one memory from India—a scary story she had been told or perhaps a dream resulting from the story, of a savage pantomime featuring a tiger skin rug. She was terrified of this image which haunted her dreams. No other images of India stayed with her. Trix was a sweet-natured, adorable, fair-haired toddler, who was easy to love. Mrs Holloway loved her for herself and also, Trix believed, because 'She had always wanted a daughter and her happy heart engulfed [Trix] as much as the somewhat fastidious child would allow'.[6] Trix longed to be loved, and Mrs Holloway did love her.

The first years at Lorne Lodge were sad and lonely for Trix, but not frightening. She was favoured and pampered by Aunty Rosa, who taught her to read and write and to behave and speak properly. She encouraged the pretty child and praised her efforts.

Three years into the children's captivity, when the gentle Captain Holloway died (29 September 1874), the situation worsened. Mrs Holloway felt free to indulge her bad nature and encourage the worse nature of her son. Most of Rudyard's and almost all of Trix's memories of Lorne Lodge date from after the captain's death, when Mrs Holloway along with Harry made life a misery for the two children stranded in her desolate house.

Harry, fifteen at his father's death, became the children's chief enemy. Trix and Ruddy hated and feared Harry, who was nine years older than Trix and six years older than Rudyard. Trix watched helplessly as Harry openly taunted and tormented Rudyard with questions, ensnaring him in lies and confusions. After trapping Rudyard in contradictions, he reported them back to Aunty as intentional lies. Aunty punished lies severely, often with beatings, which Trix could hear and see but do nothing about.

Trix herself lived in terror of Harry. She listened for his comings and goings, sensitive to the sound of his footfall on the stairs and his approach to the door. When she heard him come home from school,

---

6 Ibid., p. 364.

she tiptoed away to hide herself. When Mrs Holloway was at home, she hid behind her ample skirts, but Mrs Holloway was often out or busy around the house. And Harry was especially crafty in seeking Trix out when his mother was not around. Harry cunningly manoeuvred Trix into crannies and corners where he touched, teased, and threatened her. Trix searched for whatever protection she could find and was grateful to find Jane, the maid of all work. Jane 'was very quick and clever in helping her to hide from him; and did not tell where she was even if Harry twisted her arm and thumped it'.[7] But Jane had work to do and an employer to please and could not be a completely reliable shield. Trix knew that Harry was a tattletale and a liar, both a bully and a toady, with 'a crow's quickness in finding a wound to pick at'.[8] He could easily get Jane sacked and get Trix into trouble.

Trix didn't simply hate and fear Harry, she was physically repelled and disgusted by him. She felt sickened by the smell and shine of his over-pomatumed black hair, and she distrusted his shifty narrow eyes, set too near together. He tortured and frightened her in subtle and surreptitious ways, often just by his large and looming physical presence. She shuddered with fear and revulsion just thinking about him.

Trix came to understand that Aunty protected and indulged her only child. She allowed him free rein to bully Ruddy and, when she was not present, gave him tacit permission to bother her. As well as his mother's permission, Harry had his society's acceptance of bullying male behaviour. Little girls were sport, small creatures to be teased and toyed with. Trix sharpened her wits plotting to evade, repel, and defeat Harry. Trix later recalled that, 'Up until the age of eleven I hated Harry so wholeheartedly that I have only disliked a few people, in a mild, tepid way, ever since'.[9] Trix knew that it was dangerous to protest or resist him. He was quick to feel a slight and quick to return one. Afraid of worse punishment from Harry, Trix never complained. Instead, she learned how to run away quickly and hide herself securely. When Trix was a pretty six-year-old girl, Harry was an oily fifteen-year-old.

Aunty often promised Trix that if she were a good girl, one day she would marry Harry. Harry, privy to his mother's romantic fantasy, thus considered Trix his own property, to tease and touch. Trix never accused

---

7   Ibid., p. 363.
8   Ibid., p. 358.
9   Alice M. Fleming, 'Some Childhood Memories of Rudyard Kipling', p. 169.

Harry of misbehaviour, sexual or otherwise, but she may not have understood nor had the language to express his interference as sexual. His attentions to Trix may not have been sexual, but it seems likely that greasy, pimply teenage Harry touched Trix in ways she did not like. She found him physically loathsome.

When, at the age of twenty-three in 1888, Rudyard, a gifted artist, illustrated his autobiographical story, 'Baa Baa, Black Sheep', he drew Aunty Rosa with sharp angles and dark lines as a furious, accusatory figure. She points a long bony finger as she furrows her brow. 'Devil boy' Harry has horns and a forked tongue. Trix, in the three pictures in which she appears, is a little girl with cropped hair and bangs. She wears 'a short-sleeved blue frock and white pinafore, white socks, and bronze shoes with soft soles rounded like biscuits'.[10] In all three pictures, she is cowering behind Auntie's skirts. In two of them, she looks out from behind Aunty's skirts with a wide-eyed and wary gaze, and in the third, she is tiptoeing away from the scene, partially hidden by Aunty's dress. She can only be hiding from and hoping to escape from Harry. In Rudyard's pictures, Trix appears to be about six or seven years old, the age when her memories first came into focus.

Fig. 2 Rudyard's drawing from 'Baa Baa, Black Sheep'.[11]

---

10 Ibid.

Fig. 3 Trix, always behind Aunty's skirts in Rudyard's drawing from 'Baa Baa, Black Sheep'.[12]

Every day, Trix watched as Rudyard and Harry packed up their books and went off to Hope House School in Somerset Place, while she stayed behind. At home, Trix was taught by Aunty, a careless mixture of religion, music, and manners. Aunty served as Trix's sole teacher, companion,

---

11 From Rudyard Kipling's, *Something of Myself*, ed. by Thomas Pinney, pp. 167–68. The illustrations accompanying this reprint of 'Baa Baa, Black Sheep' are by Kipling in a holograph of the story now in the Berg Collection of the New York Public Library. In his *Rudyard Kipling* (London: Weidenfeld and Nicholson, 1978), pp. 27–28, Lord Birkenhead reports on the Kipling parents' reaction to Rudyard's story, 'Baa Baa, Black Sheep'. It was a grievous blow to the Lockwood Kiplings when they read these savage outpourings in cold print, and, unwilling to recognize their own contribution to this suffering, they tried to make Trix say it was all exaggerated and untrue, but even to comfort them, she could not pretend that they had ever been happy'.

12 Ibid.

caretaker, and nurse. Jane, Trix's protector from Harry, was Trix's only other possible companion throughout the long days. But as a servant in the household, Jane was shy of becoming Trix's friend, although Trix longed for her closer companionship. 'There was so little scope for love in her narrowed life that it was natural for a starved, sensitive nature to long for praise, or at least for notice. She was absolutely without companions, or the chance of making little friends'.[13] When she was seven, Trix briefly attended Sunday school and dancing classes, and there she tried to make friends. But Aunty discouraged friendships and made visits with other little girls impossible. Trix's time with Rudyard was limited by his own need to study and by Aunty's strict rationing.

Every Christmas beginning in 1873, Rudyard went away for a month to spend the long holiday with aunts, uncles, and cousins in London and in the country. He spent most Christmas vacations with his aunt Georgie, wife of the painter Edward Burne-Jones, at the Grange, in an exciting bohemian, intellectual atmosphere where frequent guests included John Ruskin, William Morris, and Charles Eliot Norton. Trix was not invited on these excursions. When Rudyard went off, she wept with resentment and confusion. She was hurt that she was not invited for the holiday parties and tried to find reasons and made excuses for the insensitivity and unkindness of her relatives. The aunts and uncles, who were in the habit of entertaining Rudyard alone when Trix was a toddler, failed to notice that, over the years, Trix grew old enough to be a proper guest. Christmas holiday was therefore an especially bleak time, as Rudyard was gone for a month of celebrations, which Trix could only imagine and envy. Not once during this period was she ever invited to visit her many aunts and uncles. She bore this slight without explanation or complaint. Trix also suspected that Aunty Rosa, not wishing to be parted from her during the holidays, protested against her being included in the family celebrations away from home. Trix had one brief holiday to Brighton with Mrs Holloway during her six years at Lorne Lodge.

Aunty did love Trix, and Trix, starved for attention and praise, needed and wanted her love. But being Aunty's favourite was double-edged. By arousing and accepting Aunty's tender feelings, she felt she

---

13   Trix Kipling, 'Through Judy's Eyes', p. 357.

compromised herself. Aunty Rosa often compared Trix to Ruddy, her good behaviour used as a stick to beat Rudyard with. Thus, as Trix curried favour with Aunty, she risked putting Ruddy into even greater disfavour. Winning love from one person important in her life necessarily meant hurting someone else even more important. She hated Aunty for putting her in this position and hated herself for encouraging it. Rudyard suffered more blatant tortures. He was baited, bullied, and beaten. But he recognized and sympathized with Trix's more subtle dilemma and forgave her for what she considered betrayals.

In all comparisons and competitions, Aunty favoured Trix over Rudyard. While this might have weakened the bond between the two, it never did. Rud and Trix stuck close together, sharing stories and keeping secrets. They were protective and proud of each other. Rudyard firmly maintained for himself and for his sister his sense of Kipling superiority over all Holloways. Rudyard defended himself and his sister against Aunty's humiliating and demeaning treatment by holding her birth, breeding, manners, and education in complete contempt. This was a particularly raw spot for Sarah Holloway, a woman of lower-class origins, whose husband was of a higher class and whose young boarders had connections and expectations far above her own or her son's. Rudyard remembered the fine home, polite conversation, and refined manners of his parents in India and spent long holiday vacations with his wealthy and cultured aunts and uncles. Although Trix had no direct experience of this, she trusted Rudyard's conviction that Aunty was of a much lower caste than Papa and Mamma. He often told Trix that she did not need to mind what the 'no-caste' woman did or said. The two mistreated children created a special bond over their sense of social superiority. It served them well against Aunty's frequent demoralizing words and actions.

Brother and sister formed another bond as co-conspirators—protectors of each other's lies and subverters of Aunty's rules. Aunty considered reading books an improper pastime for the children, and when she discovered Trix or Rudyard reading instead of playing with their toys, she reprimanded them severely. To avoid her interference, they each invented tricks to deceive her. Trix often seated herself on the damp playroom floor, lined up her dolls in a neat row opposite to her, and ordered them to sit properly and attend. Then she happily read her books aloud to her assembled audience, pretending she was a teacher instructing a class. In this way, she wasn't lying when she reported to Aunty that she had been playing with her dolls. Rudyard devised a clever although cumbersome method for confounding Aunty. He lay on the floor reading, holding his book with one hand while manipulating the unsteady legs of the table with the other to make a thumping noise. Thus, he disguised the silence of reading with the pounding of play (see Fig. 3).

Much of Mrs Holloway's teaching focused on her strict religious beliefs, which she impressed on Trix and which Trix adopted. Always a gifted mimic, Trix easily learned to imitate Aunty's pious attitudes. But over time, Trix began to understand that producing the outward signs of godliness and piety was not the same as feeling godly and pious. The feelings that actually arose from her heart were feelings she recognized Aunty would find unacceptable. Thus, she learned to disguise her real feelings and invent substitute thoughts that could be acceptably expressed. Small and specific lies expanded into large-scale deception and invention. Trix later wrote of one of her fictional heroines, 'One of the most wearisome necessities of her life had been the constant fabrication of thoughts, or, rather, of substitutes for thoughts, such as she could share with her aunt'.[14] Trix assigned this wearisome and wounding work to her fictional character, but she clearly knew of it first-hand. Trix was especially sensitive to adjusting herself to what the adults around her wanted from her. Eager to please and assuming that causing displeasure could mean expulsion, Trix expressed only those thoughts and feelings that were appropriate and proper. She made herself into what she thought Mrs Holloway wanted her to be: a good, grateful, obedient, God-fearing, Christian child.

Trix could be herself only with Rudyard and with Jane, the housemaid, but her time with Rudyard was strictly limited and her comfort with Jane was never perfect. From Aunty, whose pious model recommended strict Christian goodness, and Harry, whose unwanted attentions required flight, she learned the crucial survival skills of running away, hiding, and lying.

---

14 J. M. Fleming (Alice M. Kipling), *A Pinchbeck Goddess* (New York: D. Appleton and Co., 1897).

When she was alone, which she was most of the time, Trix relieved her loneliness by inventing fantasies and dreaming. At the age of four, Trix learned to read, remarkably before Rudyard learned to read. His education in India had oddly not included the alphabet. Once they were both fluent readers, they devoured whatever books they could find and asked for more to be sent to them.

Trix was required by Aunty to read the Bible, and she knew it well, but she also read *The Arabian Nights, Sidonia the Sorceress*—a racy German tale—and the fairy tales of the Brothers Grimm and Hans Christian Anderson. Instead of following orders to play, she read story books, and, by the age of five, she was reading for her own pleasure, despite Aunty's disapproval. Books and magazines were sent to the children, mostly to Rudyard, by the parents, Uncle Alfred Baldwin, and other relatives. Whatever was sent to Rudyard he shared with Trix. They both read *Robinson Crusoe*, the novels of Walter Scott, poetry by Wordsworth and Tennyson. Later, despite Aunty's prohibitions, Trix read Shakespeare's plays and eighteenth- and nineteenth-century poetry and fiction. Dickens's novels were her favourites. While Aunty's lessons were her only formal education, she read from books brought home by Rudyard, sent from India by their parents, and from a small library in the house. (When she was finally sent to school, she was found to be 'absolutely ungrounded, curiously ignorant, but singularly well-read'.)[15]

Reading books of brutality, sensuality, and magic, Trix developed her own violent imagination. She loved playing with words and invented her own private language by transposing letters of the alphabet. Trix and Rudyard made up stories for each other and shared outlaw fantasies. 'We had a sort of play that ran on and on for months, in which we played all the parts. I'm afraid there was generally a murder in it; or we ran away to sea and had the most wonderful adventures'.[16] Rudyard and Trix together nursed rescue and revenge fantasies, which they spun into complicated tales. Having read the same books and lived in the same bleak circumstances, the two children could elaborate on each other's stories, continue each other's trains of thought, and almost read each other's minds.

---

15   Alice M. Fleming, 'Some Childhood Memories', p. 170.
16   Ibid.

Even later in life, they could complete each other's thoughts, sentences, and stories. (As teenagers, when they started writing for publication, they collaborated effortlessly. Trix's stories and poems were indistinguishable from Rudyard's.) The story-telling gift, shared by both, was a form of consolation as well as a means of survival. From the various tellings and retellings of incidents, both Ruddy and Trix were liable to confuse fact with fiction or embellish fact with fiction. Charles Dickens' *David Copperfield*, which they loved, became a touchstone for them both. Orphaned and sent from home, David suffered deprivations, hurts, and longings similar to their own. Like them, David pondered his life's central mystery—how a gifted child like himself could have been so easily thrown away. Rudyard and Trix not only shared David's miseries, they savoured his triumphs—revenge on his enemies and early success as a writer.[17]

Mrs Holloway had no fondness for books in themselves, one book being of equal value to any other, but she understood that reading books and sharing stories were pleasurable activities she could control and curtail. As punishments, she often confiscated books from the two children, isolated them from each other, and enforced silence between them.

Trix and Rudyard were strongly discouraged from what Aunty called 'showing off'. Very early on, Trix revealed herself to be a facile talker and a prodigious memorizer, reciter, and imitator. Most of the time, she was praised for her performances, but, inexplicably, at times, she was criticized for exhibiting these same talents. Rudyard was

---

17 David Copperfield endures a miserable childhood but is eventually rescued. He grows up to be a writer. His life story was similar enough to Rudyard's and to Trix's to give them great comfort and sustain them through many years. David, like Rudyard, had been pampered and praised as a child and found his fall from grace unaccountable and unacceptable. (In chapters X and XI of *David Copperfield*, David describes his childhood unhappiness. 'All this time I was so conscious of the waste of any promise I had given, and of my being utterly neglected, that I should have been perfectly miserable, I have no doubt, but for the old books. They were my only comfort, and I was as true to them as they were to me, and read them over and over I don't know how many times more'. 'I know enough of the world now, to have almost lost the capacity of being much surprised by anything, but it is matter of some surprise to me, even now, that I can have been so easily thrown away at such an age. A child of excellent abilities, and with strong powers of observation, quick, eager, delicate, and soon hurt bodily or mentally, it seems wonderful to me that nobody should have made any sign in my behalf'.) Rudyard as well as Trix wondered how they too could have been 'so easily thrown away' and how nobody seemed to notice or care.

positively punished for showing off, one of his major crimes. His chatter often resulted in his being accused of inventing, pretending, or lying. He was regularly beaten with a cane for showing off as well as for lying. Trix witnessed Ruddy's canings and ached to protect him. But she was helpless to do anything except fantasize furious, bloody scenes of vengeance.

Aunty never caned Trix or rapped her over the knuckles, but she enforced one punishment which terrified Trix at the time and haunted her ever after. One day after committing an infraction of one of Aunty's many rules, Trix was ordered to stand upon the highly polished dining room table. When Aunty lifted her onto the table as a punishment, Trix thought, at first, it was a game and laughed. Standing on the table seemed like no punishment at all, until Aunty reminded her that she should be ashamed of her naughty behaviour. When the punishment was repeated several days later, Trix felt its full terror. Balancing on the high table, she felt as if she were exposed atop a high tower. Her soft-soled shoes slipped and slid. She grew dizzy and faint and imagined she was about to fall over the edge and be dashed to pieces on the carpet far below. Half-way through the punishment, she felt the floor sinking farther and farther away, while she grew colder and colder, and a funny noise, like a boiling kettle, sang in her ears. Rudyard offered his long hair as a lifeline and then his sleeve, but Trix was forbidden to accept his help. She was afraid of moving even a little for fear of upsetting the inkstands or the slates. The punishment only lasted five minutes, five minutes more if she whimpered, but it seemed an eternity.[18]

Standing high up on the table, she felt exposed and afraid. (Drawers were not always worn, and when they were, they had an open seam at the crotch.) Never before had she felt so dizzy and cold. Never had she heard a steady, squealing ringing in her ears. Standing on the table, Trix was exposed to the loathsome Harry's curious gaze, and possibly she was explored by his probing fingers. Trix reasonably felt afraid of falling

---

18 Virginia Woolf's sexual abuse as a child of six by her half-brother has been well documented in her diaries and letters. It is only a coincidence that the first experience of abuse narrated by Virginia closely resembles this incident described by Trix. Like Trix, Virginia was ordered to stand up on a high shelf and there was molested by her half-brother Gerald. 'I still shiver with shame at the memory of my half-brother, standing me on a ledge, aged about 6 or so, exploring my private parts'.

or fainting. But unreasonably and inexplicably, she also felt ashamed and disgusted at being exposed and exhibited.

One day, the doctor came to the house while Trix was standing unsteadily on the table. Seeing the child shivering and as white as a sheet, the doctor took her straight off the table and placed her onto his knee to comfort her. Trix tried not to cry, as the doctor took Aunty to task. Despite Aunty's explanations of her 'wise handling' of the children, the doctor reprimanded her. 'You must remember that you can't treat a china cup, egg shell china too, as if it were a tin mug,' said the doctor. Behind Aunty's back, Rudyard danced his 'special war dance'.[19] Trix was never again forced to stand on the table, but the punishment remained a well-remembered source of terror and shame. The doctor became her hero.

Only once did Trix seriously protest against Aunty, and it was on Rudyard's behalf rather than her own. Towards the end of their stay at Lorne Lodge, when Rudyard had been bullied into submission and Trix had been outraged into rebellion, she heroically came to her brother's defence. After Rudyard recognized that bringing bad reports home from school resulted in beatings, he formed the habit of destroying the reports before reaching the Holloway door. For quite a while, he successfully kept Aunty ignorant of his poor grades, but he was eventually found out.

Aunty discovered the ruse one Saturday morning and was enraged, more at the deception than at the poor marks. As a punishment, she shut Rudyard up in his room without food or water for two days and called him a 'moral leper'.[20] All through the weekend, Trix longed to help her brother, but she was banned from going near his door. When Monday morning arrived and it was time for Rudyard to go to school, he was allowed out of his room. Trix was awake and downstairs, listening for some sound from Rudyard's room, when she heard his steps descending from his attic room. Aunty ordered Trix to go to the drawing room and practice the piano, without moving from the stool, for forty-five minutes. On her way to the drawing room, Trix asked to see her brother. She was told that Rudyard was still in disgrace and could not be

---

19 Trix Kipling, 'Through Judy's Eyes', p. 356.
20 Lord Birkenhead, *Rudyard Kipling* (London: Weidenfeld and Nicolson, 1978), pp. 25–26.

disturbed on his way to school by his silly sister. Harry added that she might never see her brother again. As she entered the drawing room, Trix heard Aunty storming at Rudyard with more than her usual shrill fury. Hoping to drown out the hateful noise, she sank down on the piano stool and, as ordered, pounded out the scales she had been practicing. Trix listened for Aunty's rage to subside, and when she heard Rudyard leave the house, she crept to the window. Believing herself alone and unobserved, she drew back the oily lace curtains, peered out, and saw Rudyard going down the small garden path, walking like an old man. A placard covered the whole of his back. It was made of strong cardboard. Neatly printed by Harry in big block letters were the words: KIPLING THE LIAR. Trix tiptoed out into the hall, silently opened the front door, slipped out, and ran to catch up to Ruddy. When she reached him, she grabbed at the placard and tried desperately to tear it from his back. It was so thick that she couldn't even bend it. It was neatly and tightly sewn to his little blue overcoat with string so strong she couldn't rip it. Reaching into Ruddy's pocket, she found his pen knife and tried with its short blade to pick the stitches out, but Ruddy protested weakly, 'Don't, don't dear. Leave it alone—it's no good—she'll only beat you too'.[21]

While Trix hung on, desperately pulling on the placard, Ruddy crept on to school, broken down at last. Eventually Trix gave up and ran back, her long hair whipping her face, to meet Aunty, who, brandishing a cane, resembled a scarlet-faced virago. Aunty had never used the cane on Trix, but it seemed, in this instance, she might. Trix screamed at Aunty, 'You are a wicked woman. I'll never speak to you again. How dare you sew that wicked placard on poor Ruddy'.[22] She threatened to tell the authorities of Aunty's cruelties.

'You don't know anyone to tell' retorted Aunty.

'Yes, there's the doctor, and you can't stop me telling the vicar. I'll stand up in Sunday School, and I'll tell the postman and the policeman on the corner of Palmerston Road. She threatened me with the cane, and I said; that's right, thrash me as if I was Ruddy. You know how I bruise and when I'm black I'll go the police and show them and have you punished'.[23]

---

21 Ibid.
22 Ibid.
23 Ibid.

Confronted with Trix's unusual fury, Aunty backed away, loosened her grip on the cane, and blinked back her tears. Tender-hearted Trix felt sorry for making the poor woman cry, but Ruddy needed her protection. When she was fighting for Rudyard, she felt righteous and bold. Ruddy was too broken by fasting and beating to defend himself. The story of the LIAR placard was also told in much abbreviated form by Rudyard in his story, 'Baa Baa, Black Sheep'. In the story, when the child is ordered to wear the placard, he, with uncharacteristic recklessness, defies Aunty and refuses to wear it. When Rudyard told the story again much later in his autobiography *Something of Myself*, he reduced it to one sentence and omitted his defiance. There, he accepted the punishment and actually wore the hated sign through the streets of Southsea. Only in Trix's tale (as told to Kipling's biographer Lord Birkenhead) does she play a heroic part. Hers is a revenge story—how she came to Ruddy's defense, finally stood up to Aunty, and prevailed.

All three versions of the story resemble an early incident in *David Copperfield*. After David bites his hated stepfather, Mr Murdstone, he is sent away from home to a school where he is forced to wear a placard tied like a knapsack on his back, reading 'Take care of him. He Bites'.[24] Both Trix and Rudyard knew *Copperfield* well, but it is unclear exactly how their stories came to resemble Dickens's. Perhaps something similar actually happened to Ruddy, and the children embellished the facts of the incident by borrowing from *Copperfield*. Perhaps they so identified with David that they confused what had happened to him with what had happened to them, perhaps this was a common form of punishment, or perhaps there is some other explanation.

From Trix's story, whether true, embellished, or invented, it appears that she felt she had a few friends she could turn to if she needed help—the doctor and the vicar. Should she ever alienate Aunty by acting on her vengeful fantasies, she had reckoned her possible allies. On an earlier occasion when Aunty threatened to whip Rudyard, Trix pictured Aunty's severed head, 'with its frowning eyes, grinning lips and long yellow teeth, and soiled widow's cap' rolling on the floor.[25] Trix often played out in her imagination scenes of violent retribution.

---

24 Charles Dickens, 'Chapter 5', in *David Copperfield* (London: Bradbury & Evans, 1850).
25 Trix Kipling, 'Through Judy's Eyes', p. 353. Jane Gardam's novel, *Old Filth* is loosely based on Rudyard Kipling's childhood as a Raj orphan. The young boy of the novel

Trix's more immediate annoyance from Aunty was not her cruelty but her constant affection. What bothered Trix the most was Aunty's physical nearness, which she had no choice but to accept. During the six years when Trix shared Aunty's bed, she had to tolerate falling asleep with Aunty's bony arm around her. Trix often woke in the night from a recurrent nightmare of the Indian tiger skin. When she cried out, it was Aunty who was there to reassure her. Aunty's presence in the bed calmed her nighttime terrors, but Aunty's unwanted consoling words and constant physical affection made her uneasy. Trix 'always hated being hugged by anyone but her own family, and wished more than anything, except going back to Bombay, for a bed of her very own'.[26] Trix was a fastidious child, uncomfortable with physical affection. For years, she longed for the privacy and safety of her own space.

Whatever mistreatment the children endured, it was never spoken of or written about to their parents or other relatives. They did not complain of the difficulties of their lives or ask for relief. These were simply the facts of life, how it was, how it would continue to be. Both Rudyard and Trix wrote regularly to their parents in Bombay and later in Lahore, but their letters were strictly censored and often dictated by Mrs Holloway. Rudyard, who had the chance to complain to his aunts and uncles with whom he visited on holidays, never did. When Aunt Georgie asked him later why he never told anyone how he was being treated, he explained, 'Children tell little more than animals, for what comes to them they accept as eternally established. Also, badly-treated children have a clear notion of what they are likely to get if they betray the secrets of the prison-house before they are clear of it'.[27]

During Rudyard's Christmas visit to the Grange in 1876, his aunt noticed that he was having trouble with his eyes. She also sensed that there was something strange in his behaviour. He reported seeing things that weren't there, things that frightened him. Aunt Georgie, concerned about Rudyard's well-being, wrote to Alice, urging her to come to England to check up on her boy.

---

lives with two girls, who share between them many of Trix's qualities. The three children are cared for by a woman who mistreats and beats them. Together the children plot to kill the evil woman. It is one of the girls who suggests murder. Trix, in shared fantasy with Rudyard, often rehearsed Aunty's violent murder.

26 Ibid., p. 348.
27 Rudyard Kipling, 'Chapter 1', in *Something of Myself* (New York: Doubleday, 1937).

Alice did not respond with immediate action. She had considered visiting England the year before but she had postponed the trip, unwilling to leave Lockwood—who, in April of 1875, had taken on a new post, as the head of the Mayo School of Industrial Art and curator of the Lahore Museum. This was a far more substantial, varied, and interesting position than his old job as teacher at the Bombay art school. Alice was pleased to find her husband advancing in his career and was hopeful that the move from Bombay to Lahore would prove professionally advantageous for Lockwood and socially advantageous for the whole family. She felt confident that Lockwood could fulfil his new professional responsibilities, but she believed that he needed her help to settle him in his new post and introduce him to the new society of Lahore.

By early 1877, Alice felt confident in Lockwood's place at the museum and in Lahore and was willing to leave him. Responding to Georgie's alarming report about Rudyard, which she had received many months earlier, she determined to return to England to find out what was troubling her son. Her daughter's health and happiness had not been reported to her by her sister, who had not seen the child for years. In April 1877, five and a half years after she had left the children without preparation or explanation, Alice reappeared without warning at Lorne Lodge.

When she stepped from her four-wheeled carriage in front of the dismal house, Rudyard recognized her immediately but hung back, uncertain how to react and afraid of being accused of showing off. Trix had no memory of her at all and had no idea how to react. Seeing this beautiful woman for what seemed like the first time, Trix was simply amazed. She could not believe that this lovely creature, who declared herself to be her mother, could actually be her longed-for Mamma. She ran to her mother's open arms. Drawing away to take in the dazzling vision, she was surprised by her mother's pale smooth skin and bright blue eyes. A flurry of softly uttered endearments and tender embraces startled and confused her. Alice hugged and kissed the surprised children, and, before saying anything else, asked if they remembered her. Wary about showing his emotions in front of Aunty Rosa, Rudyard responded coolly. Trix quickly followed his lead. With no advance notice of her arrival and no idea of her intentions, the children were unsure how they should act. Alice was disappointed and puzzled by their odd behaviour, baffled by their well-learned, self-protective strategies for avoiding Aunty's temper. 'She did not know that well-trained animals watch their tamer's eye, and the familiar danger-signals of 'Aunty's' rising temper had set both [children] fawning upon her'.[28]

Alice remained for a constrained and awkward dinner with Aunty Rosa and the children. When it was Trix's bedtime, she tucked the little girl in with hugs and kisses. When Rudyard rose to leave the table, Aunty offered her withered cheek for a kiss. Ruddy defiantly refused to give what had never been requested of him before. After Ruddy had retired to his room, Alice went alone upstairs to say good night to him in the attic room he shared with Harry. Groping her way in the dark, she located him lying in bed. As she bent down to embrace him, he instinctively thrust out his arm to ward off a blow. This dramatic demonstration convinced Alice of the dangers she had exposed the children to. When she saw that her son was accustomed to defend himself against nightly attacks, she begged him for his forgiveness. Fairly quickly, she forgave herself.

She also soon discovered that Rudyard was half-blind.

Alice was distressed to find that Trix had become a plump little prig, devoted to Aunty and quick to spout her pious words. Trix had been schooled in Mrs Holloway's religion and, despite some doubts, had taken on her teacher's evangelical fervour. Alice and Lockwood, both children of Methodist ministers, had left their religion behind when they had removed to India. Alice, with her usual wishful thinking, had assumed that her own rejection of religion had somehow been imparted to Trix and was dismayed to find that, on the contrary, Mrs Holloway's stern teachings had been fully absorbed by the impressionable child.

After recognizing on her first visit that the children were deeply unhappy, Mrs Kipling resolved to end their misery. Arriving back the next day at Lorne Lodge, she announced that she was taking the children away. Mrs Holloway protested, asserting her devotion to her young charges. Trix, fearing that her mother might find Mrs Holloway's false assurances convincing, was struck with nervous dread. She could not control her darting eyes and twitching fingers, and these signs of

---

28   Alice M. Fleming, 'Some Childhood Memories of Rudyard Kipling'.

alarm were clear even to Mrs Kipling, who was eager to minimize the children's misery. Forced to recognize Trix's terror, she resolved to remove the children immediately and reward them with a vacation in the country.

The mother believed she could quickly return the children to their original love for her, as if she had never abandoned them. Trix, who had no memory of her, had no original love she could be returned to. Rudyard, who remembered and loved her, could never return to his original love for her nor to his original innocence.

When Rudyard wrote about his childhood in the autobiographical story, 'Baa Baa, Black Sheep', he called the boy Punch and the little sister Judy. When Trix wrote about this period in her memoir, 'Through Judy's Eyes', she adopted the same names.[29] Punch and Judy seemed appropriate names to both Rud and Trix for the poor beaten and embattled children they had been at Lorne Lodge. The narrator of Rudyard's story, reflecting on what he had lost from the harsh experience of his childhood, wrote, 'When young lips have drunk deep of the bitter waters of Hate, Suspicion and Despair, all the Love in the world will not wholly take away that knowledge; though it may turn darkened eyes for a while to the light and teach Faith where no Faith was'.[30] (These lines appear above the drawing on page 16 from 'Baa Baa, Blacksheep'.)

Rudyard recognized that his mother wanted what had been most convenient for her to have been most comfortable for the children. On the contrary, what had been most convenient for her had been decidedly uncomfortable for them. When Trix wrote about her childhood, she attempted to be understanding and to accept her mother's rationalizations for deserting the children. But her attempts are not altogether convincing. Here is how Trix imagined her mother's careless thoughts about the effects of abandoning her children. 'Besides they [the children] would be quite happy in their new surroundings after a bit, children always were. They'd forget, children always did. Unluckily Punch [Rudyard] never forgot, acute nostalgia made the new

---

29   Rudyard Kipling, 'Baa Baa, Black Sheep', in *Something of Myself*, ed. by Thomas Pinney (Cambridge: Cambridge University Press, 2008) and Trix Kipling, 'Through Judy's Eyes'.
30   Rudyard Kipling, 'Baa Baa, Black Sheep'.

life difficult to him, and though Judy [Trix] could and did forget details in the past, the 'mother want' in her world was never supplied'.[31]

Rudyard remembered the actual terrors of the place—how he was humiliated, shamed, and beaten. Trix focused on her imagined losses—what she missed, what she was denied, what she never had. She recognized how her character was distorted and damaged by the experience. Her most insightful conclusion about her childhood deprivation was that she suffered from 'mother want', which was never supplied. 'Mother want', borrowed from Elizabeth Barrett's Browning's *Aurora Leigh*, is a beautiful and plaintive phrase, which poignantly captures what Trix had been denied.[32] Much of her later life—her speechless sorrow and mad rages—was spent tragically and vainly trying, in one way or another, to satisfy this want. But, as Trix was sadly to learn, mother want must be satisfied in childhood; no adult experience can ever make up for its loss.[33]

---

31 Trix Kipling, 'Through Judy's Eyes', p. 356.
32 Trix frequently quoted memorable lines and phrases from her favorite authors, most often from Shakespeare. This phrase from Elizabeth Barrett Browning's *Aurora Leigh* is quite appropriate. The line refers to the author's loss of her mother at age four. Like David Copperfield, Aurora Lee grows up to be a famous author. There are multiple not-quite-parallels between Trix's early life and Book 1 of this long novel-poem. Aurora, an actual orphan, survives her desolation by secretly reading verse, which rouses in her a passion to create her own poetry. Eventually, Aurora goes to London to earn her living as a writer and succeeds in creating her masterpiece. With the phrase 'mother want' Trix evokes her chief childhood loss, but also evokes another later loss—her failure to become an independent woman who successfully follows her vocation as a writer. The half-buried reference to Aurora Leigh suggests both the orphaned and displaced child Trix was, and the powerful writer Trix might have become.
33 Trix knew she had been hurt by the inexplicable separation from her parents. She wrote in both of her novels about the hurt inflicted on children by having been deserted by their parents for their entire childhoods.

2. Macdonalds and Kiplings

The obvious villain of this childhood story is Aunty Rosa. The less obvious, although hardly hidden villain, is the mother, Alice Kipling. It was her decision to reject the offers of her many relatives and to leave the children with strangers. To send children, whose parents were living in India, back to England was standard practice. The climate of India was not good for European children, and the dangers of disease were real. For these reasons English parents were accustomed to send their very young children back to England to be raised and educated. The Kiplings were especially sensitive to the health hazards of the subcontinent, as they had lost their third child, John at birth in April 1870. With their class consciousness and snobbery, they were also aware of the social advantages of sending children back to England. Like most of the English living abroad, they believed it was next to impossible to bring up English children in India. Close contact with native servants—the pampering care of a bearer or ayah—was a bad influence on children. They would not learn self-reliance and self-discipline. The greatest danger was the *chi chi* accent—the term used for English contaminated by a native tongue. The fear was that once acquired, the accent would be hard to erase, even after years of later life in England. Pure speech was essential for an Englishman or woman. Schools for English children existed in India, but they were frequented by undesirable types, including lower-class English and foreigners. Anyone who could afford to send children away did so.

If relatives or friends back in England were asked to take children in, they usually obliged. But the Kiplings chose to board the children with strangers located from a newspaper advertisement. Family members on both sides were able and willing, if not enthusiastic, to take Rudyard and Trix. The little Kiplings could have been left with either of their grandmothers, the Kipling grandmother in Skipton or the Macdonald grandmother at Bewdley. Alice had the choice of her several sisters. Her three younger married Macdonald sisters all offered suitable homes for the children. Her sister Georgiana was married to pre-Raphaelite painter, Edward Burne-Jones; Agnes was married to Edward Poynter, a fashionable painter and member of the Royal Academy; and Louisa was married to Alfred Baldwin, a wealthy iron manufacturer. The fourth sister, Edith, remained unmarried. At the time Trix and Rudyard were left with the Holloways, the three married sisters all had children who would have been appropriate playmates for Ruddy and Trix. The Burne-Joneses had two children, Philip and Margaret, aged ten and five. The Poynters' son, Ambrose, and the Baldwins' son, Stanley, were both four.

On a previous visit, when Alice had come to England in 1868 for Trix's birth, the three-year-old Rudyard had earned the reputation of being a troublesome little boy. Alice's sisters, Louisa and Edith, thought he had turned the house into a bear-garden. His screaming temper tantrums made Grandfather Macdonald, already old and ill, far worse and perhaps hastened his death. He died only days after the departure of the Kiplings. The sisters were thankful to see the ill-ordered child on his way.

When Alice brought the two children to England before leaving them at Southsea, the aunts and uncles were enchanted by Trix, already a beauty at three. But Ruddy was a problem who upset the households he visited. When the children stayed with the Baldwins at Wilden House, Alfred was especially charmed by Trix and tried to persuade Alice and Lockwood to leave her with him. She would have made a great companion for the Baldwins' son Stanley, who was just nine months older. Trix was sharp enough to share Stanley's lessons. She would have had a lovely life with a garden and a pony and aunts and uncles who cherished her. Ruddy was to have been shared between Uncle Fred Macdonald, his godfather, and his uncle and aunt the Burne-Joneses until he would be old enough for a day school. Brother and sister were always to spend holidays together.

Alice rejected this sensible plan, because it included separating the children from each other for periods of time. She was opposed to any plan that kept brother and sister apart. It was bad enough that they were to be parted from their parents; they shouldn't have to be parted from each other. Alice also claimed to be concerned about the stability of the

Burne-Jones' marriage, which several years earlier had been threatened by Edward's love affair with one of his models. Alice remained hurt by her sisters' criticisms of Ruddy's behaviour on his earlier visit and was offended that they had not been more enthusiastic to take him in.

Alice told loyal family friend, Edith Plowden that she thought the plan of leaving the children with strangers was 'a good arrangement'. 'She had never thought of leaving her children with her own family, it led to complications: the children were quite happy—much she knew!—and she was able to be with John and help him with his work'.[1]

'It led to complications' was Alice's vague explanation. The complication she feared most was that her children would come to love their aunts more than herself. Alice often expressed her concern that someone might take her place in her children's affections. The chance that someone might be one of her own sisters was not a pleasant possibility. To safeguard her own position as her children's best beloved, Alice chose not to send them to live with her sisters. But why she also chose to reject her sisters' well-informed recommendations of another suitable place for the children is harder to understand. She simply could not tolerate her sisters' participation in the raising of her children. Stubborn and self-centred, Alice sent her babes to their hideous fate.

Earlier, competition among the sisters had, not surprisingly, focused on prospective husbands. Alice, the oldest, had been expected to make the most spectacular match, but surprisingly had made the least brilliant. In the 1870s, the husbands of Alice's three married sisters were rising in prominence and wealth far more rapidly than Lockwood, who advanced slowly in his undistinguished job in a distant outpost of the empire. To Alice, the least well situated of the four married Macdonald sisters, her sisters' kindness and generosity felt like condescension, even charity. It wounded Alice's pride to feel financially or emotionally beholden to her sisters. Although the expense of boarding Rudyard and Trix abroad strained the slender Kipling finances, Alice insisted that they take it on.

A further consequence of having rejected familial help was the aunts' subsequent careless appraisal of how the children were being treated. When Grandmother Hannah Macdonald and aunts Georgie (Lady Burne-Jones), Aggie (Mrs Edward Poynter) with her five-year-old son

---

1   Arthur W. Baldwin, *The Macdonald Sisters* (London: Peter Davies, 1960) p. 115.

Ambrose, and Louie (Mrs Alfred Baldwin) travelled to Lorne Lodge in late August and early September 1872, one year into the children's captivity, they found nothing amiss. They had several visits with Rud and Trix, including a jolly outing to the beach. They thought the children very well and happy, improved in every way. Mr Holloway seemed kind and Mrs Holloway seemed a very nice woman. After this one trip, they never visited Lorne Lodge again. They saw nothing worrisome in Rudyard's behaviour when he visited on holidays, until, after more than five years, he started furiously striking out at the trees with a stick. His eyesight, which steadily deteriorated over the years, did not attract their attention until it was almost completely ruined.

The aunts did recognize that the Holloway house was bare and gloomy compared to their own homes, which were ablaze with decoration and design, but they chose not to focus on this. The aunts wanted the situation to be good for the children, and they were prepared to find it so. It would have been simply unkind to recognize and report an unhappy situation that could not be easily remedied. The sisters may also have been (unconsciously) punishing Alice for choosing to send the children to the Holloways rather than to them. They and other family members had offered; she had demurred. Let her and her unfortunate children suffer the consequences. The children never complained and, being good actors, may have misled their relatives. Certainly, Mrs Holloway was practiced at disguising her true disposition and character. The aunts never visited after Mr Holloway's death, when the situation for the children worsened. They had no reason to believe that the later years at Lorne Lodge were different from the first.

While the children never blamed their mother directly for their unhappy childhoods, they made it clear in many ways that they felt her to have been responsible. However much they tried to justify and excuse her actions to themselves and to others, they knew she was the one who had consigned them to their fate and left them to it. The children couldn't be angry with their parents, who wrote to them often and always said how much they loved and missed their little boy and girl. 'A fat lot of good that does us',[2] was Rudyard's later bitter response to these reassurances.

---

2   Trix Kipling, 'Through Judy's Eyes', p. 362.

Both Rudyard and Trix, when writing of their unhappy childhood experience, gave their mother a large and confused role. As Rudyard tells the story in 'Baa Baa, Black Sheep', the two children, Punch and Judy, are five and three years old. When their parents in India discuss sending them away to England, the mother prays, 'Let strangers love my children and be as good to them as I should be, but let **me** preserve their love and their confidence for ever and ever. Amen'.[3] (The selfish emphasis on **me** is in the story.) The mother's final and most passionate appeal to Punch, as he and his infant sister are sent away, is to never let Judy forget Mamma. Judy promises to 'bemember Mamma,' Ruddy assures her. Aside from remarking that this prayer is 'slightly illogical', Punch makes no comment. Without explicitly remarking on the selfishness and short-sightedness of the prayer, he makes certain that a reader will mark it.

What sort of woman would do this to her children? Alice Macdonald was, by all accounts, a remarkable woman. She was one of seven surviving children of George and Hannah Macdonald. George, a Methodist minister, travelled the circuit, preaching in different cities, including Manchester and Birmingham, for three-year stints while his family grew. In 1853, he settled into a good living in Chelsea, London. The Macdonalds ran an unconventional and artistic household where they welcomed their children's unusual friends. There, the lively sisters met their brothers' classmates. Alice, the oldest (born in 1837) was beautiful, brilliant, witty, rebellious, and fascinating to men. Still a teenager, she became engaged to William Fulford, a schoolboy friend of her brother Harry's, studying divinity at Oxford. She broke off this engagement while her younger sister Georgiana became engaged to another friend of her brother's, the artist Edward Burne-Jones. This engagement led eventually to marriage in 1860 and to close ties with the Pre-Raphaelite circle, including William Morris, Dante Gabriel Rossetti, John Ruskin, Ford Maddox Brown, and William Holman Hunt. Alice attended parties with this group of intellectual young men, hoping to meet men of literary, artistic, and romantic interest. She met and enthralled several, including Anglo-Irish poet William Allingham, to whom she was engaged for a month.

---

3   Rudyard Kipling, 'Baa Baa, Black Sheep', p. 162.

Fig. 4 Photograph of Alice Macdonald by J. Craddock.

In 1862, George Macdonald was transferred to Wolverhampton, while Harry, having failed to take a degree at Oxford, moved to New York in the hope of making his fortune. Alice's younger and more sober brother Frederick was beginning his duties in the Methodist ministry in Staffordshire. When he invited Alice to visit him in Burslem, she readily accepted. There, she was introduced to Frederick's new friend, John Lockwood Kipling. They met at a picnic at Rudyard Lake in the summer of 1863 and immediately fell in love. Although engaged almost at once, they waited until March of 1865 to marry, when Lockwood was appointed as an artist craftsman at the Sir Jamsetjee Jejeebhoy School of Art in Bombay. Alice had turned down many suitors and broken several engagements before happily settling on John Lockwood Kipling.

Petite and attractive with blue eyes and fair hair, Alice played music and sang, composed songs, and wrote verses of a better-than-amateur standard. She possessed the nimblest mind and quickest wits of all her family. She delighted all her sisters and especially her brother Frederick, who said of her,

> Her wit [...] on occasion was a weapon of whose keenness of point there could be no doubt, and foolish or mischievous people were made to feel it [...] She saw things in a moment, and did not so much reason as pounce upon her conclusions. Accuracy in detail was not so much her forte as swift insight, and the kind of vision that is afforded by flashes

of lightning. Her power of speech was unsurpassed—I might almost say unsurpassable—her chief difficulty being that she found language a slow-moving medium of expression that failed to keep up with her thought.[4]

Of the five Macdonald sisters, four made exceptional marriages. Georgiana married Edward Burne-Jones, later to be one the most famous painters of the time, a leading member of the pre-Raphaelites. Agnes married Edward Poynter, an artist well-respected in his day and a President of the Royal Academy. Louisa became the wife of Alfred Baldwin, a wealthy ironmaster, and the mother of Stanley Baldwin, a British Prime Minister. Edith, the fifth sister, never married, remaining the loyal maiden aunt to her many nieces and nephews. As for their two brothers, Harry, the elder, was a brilliant failure, while Frederick became a solid success in the Wesleyan Church.

To her sisters, Alice represented everything that was daring and unexpected. They never tired of discussing her exploits, admiring her poems and songs, and blushing over her flirtatious overtures. Although she was considered the most desirable of the sisters, Alice made the least striking match, going off with her artist husband, a few weeks her junior in age, to a minor position at an obscure Bombay art school. When she made her late and less than brilliant marriage, she disappointed the high expectations placed on her by her sisters and perhaps by herself. From the start and through her long and happy marriage, she suffered from the feeling that she had been bettered in the marital competition by her three less gifted sisters.

Like most Victorian wives, Alice considered her own needs and desires as secondary to her husband's. She followed Lockwood where his work took him. She fulfilled her roles as his wife, mother of his children, manager of his household, and mistress of his table. But she was a strong personality who demanded attention and worked to win favour, especially from men. On two occasions, Alice asserted her needs forcefully. She insisted on returning to England for the birth of Trix. And, of course, it was she who rejected the offers of family and arranged to board the children with the Holloways when it was time to send the children back home.

---

4   Frederick Macdonald. University of Sussex.

John Lockwood Kipling—born in 1837, referred to in the family as the 'Pater'—deferred to his talented and charming wife on most social and domestic matters, including arrangements for the children. While he was aware and sensitive to his children's thoughts and feelings, he allowed Alice to make decisions for them, which often appear to have been influenced more by social ambition, sisterly competition, and financial considerations than by maternal sympathy.

Fig. 5 Photograph of John Lockwood Kipling by J. Craddock.

He came from a less distinguished but similarly devout Wesleyan family in North Yorkshire. Schooled by severe Wesleyan ministers at The Woodhouse Grove School and later by encouraging teachers at the Stoke and Fenton School of Art, he early determined to become an artist. He claimed that his choice of profession of artist, sculptor, and architectural designer was influenced by a boyhood visit to the Great Exhibition of 1851, held at London's Crystal Palace. While working as an architectural designer at the Department of Science and Art at South Kensington, he travelled between London and the potteries in Staffordshire and there met Frederick Macdonald, who was just beginning his career as a Methodist minister at Burslem.

A less sparkling personality than his wife, John Lockwood Kipling was known for his patience, his deliberate judgment, gentle wisdom, wide-ranging interests and abilities, and exactness of taste. While

Alice worked to inspire admiration and excite envy, he cultivated and sustained long-lasting friendships. He was not only a talented teacher and able administrator but a brilliant artist in many mediums—oil, water, and mural painting, illustration, sculpture, architecture, sculptural decoration, stone carving, tapestry, and textile design. He was an early and influential champion of the revival of ancient Indian arts, crafts, and design.[5] His beautiful and evocative drawings adorned many of his son's books as well as his own. He was a writer with a graceful prose style. In India, he carved out a distinguished career, and, after ten years at the Bombay School of Art, was appointed Curator of the Central Museum and Head of the School of Industrial Arts at Lahore. His sober worth was reflected in his serious demeanour—short, bearded, and balding, even in his early twenties.

Although less successful than the husbands of the other Macdonald sisters, Lockwood eventually earned the recognition and esteem of the family. And Alice adored him.

Fig. 6 Photograph of Alice and Lockwood together.

---

5   Julian Bryant, Susan Weber et al. (eds.), *John Lockwood Kipling: Arts & Crafts in the Punjab and in London*, 14 January 2017–2 April 2017, Victoria and Albert Museum, London; September 15 2017–January 7 2018, Bard Graduate Center Gallery, New York (New Haven, CT and London: Yale University Press, 2017). This is the catalogue of a show of Lockwood's work and influence.

3. Rescue

After rescuing the children from the horrors of Lorne Lodge, Alice was determined to erase the experience from their minds and hearts, a process she believed could be easily accomplished by a few months in the fresh country air. It was clear that Rudyard's eyes needed a rest. It wasn't clear what else was needed, what had been damaged and what needed to be repaired.

Alice dismissed Mrs Holloway as caretaker of the children, organized their things, and speedily removed her babes from the wood where she had abandoned them. She took them on a train trip, first to Staffordshire, then on to Essex. Everything was new for Trix, who had hardly been anywhere or seen anything aside from the dull landscape of Southsea. During the short train trip north from Southsea, Trix watched in wonder as the green and gold countryside flew by.

When they arrived at the Golding's Farm on Clays Lane, on the edge of ancient Epping Forest, they were formally introduced to Mr Dally, a kind and gentle farmer who had been hired to provide a vacation for the children. He treated the children with respectful attention, showing them around the farm, touring them through the various out-buildings and describing their many purposes. Although everything about country life was new to Trix and Ruddy, they found it easy to adapt to its simple pleasures, quickly learning to run wild out of doors.

On the first morning at the farm, Mr Dally told the children the farm's few prohibitions: NO 'leaving open gates, throwing stones at the animals, breaking down the orchard trees'. Trix and Ruddy, used to the many restrictions of Lorne Lodge, 'promised faithfully to do none of these things [...] and entered into Paradise'.[1] They easily obliged their

---

1   Trix Kipling, 'Some Childhood Memories', p. 172.

mother, whose one command was not to come in to meals with the blood and dirt of the stables and woods on their boots.

During the warm summer months, Trix and Rud learned to ride plough-horses, climb trees, milk cows, drive the pigs out of the fields, and collect mosses, ferns, and acorns. They found the cows good-natured and responsive, and considered the lady pigs elegant with well-turned ankles and long eyelashes. Their teacher was Jarge, a farm boy who was about Harry's age, but who resembled him in no other way. He never teased or made fun of the children's ignorance, answering their questions seriously and thoughtfully. He let them ride with him in the farm wagon to the mill, where there was an actual windmill, a sight right out of a fairy tale.

For the whole summer, Rud and Trix played together outside in the fields and among the animals, birds, trees, and flowers. After accompanying the children to the farm, Alice left them largely to themselves. Trix was still wary, but knowing that Alice was nearby assured and calmed her.

Lessons had been completely suspended due to Rudyard's poor vision. He had been prescribed strong glasses and banned from using his eyes for reading or studying. Thus, books were banished from the farm for Trix as well as Rudyard. Used to reading and hearing stories, Trix longed for her books. When she wanted to hear a story, she begged Rudyard to tell her one, and he happily obliged, making them up especially for her. Trix loved his stories, which 'never began in Fairyland, or in a country so far away that it had a moon and stars of its own, as my attempts at romance did, but started from an old log in the duck-pond, or a ruined cottage half seen in the Forest, and then became wildly exciting. He had the gift, even then, of "hanging with jewels a cabbage-stump."'[2]

In the autumn, when an outbreak of scarlet fever threatened the Baldwin home, Cousin Stanley was packed off to the farm to avoid possible infection. Rudyard, who had spent time with Stanley during his holidays, welcomed him to the farm and introduced him to the daily routines. Trix had never met her cousin. She liked him at once because Ruddy liked him. But she was not happy to have to share her brother. She and Rud had been a jolly twosome for the summer months and

---

2   Ibid., from a poem by Thomas Hood, 'Miss Kilmansegg and Her Precious Leg: A Golden Legend' (1869).

had been all in all to each other for as long as Trix could remember. Trix had to adjust to her cousin, a natural playmate for Rudyard—a boy who was slightly older than Trix, slightly younger than Rud. Stanley, a sweet and sensitive boy, made it easy for Trix to like him. He made sure to include her as part of a threesome when the older boys became great pals. Stanley tried to introduce Ruddy and Trix to cricket, but the rules of the game were too complicated and restrictive for them. They were in no mood for rules of any kind. Instead, they initiated Stanley into their riotous play, which he entered into with enthusiasm, quickly becoming the wildest of the three.

Trix had only one complaint—against the special rules that applied to her as a girl. When they visited the mill, the boys were allowed to jump around in 'lovely, rumbling floury places',[3] while Trix was directed to stay still and keep herself neat and clean. She was not allowed to participate in rough and tumble activities with Ruddy and Stanley and was often reminded by Alice to behave properly, to comport herself like a young lady. She had no choice but to accept these restrictions, but she chafed under them. On Guy Fawkes Night, when there was great bonfire, Trix had to sit still and watch the flames, while Ruddy and Stanley pranced and capered through them. She was taught to ride properly on donkey-back, while the boys were allowed to sit face to tail in their shirt-sleeves. Trix wished for the freedom allowed to the boys and longed to have short-cropped hair and wear boy's clothes like Ruddy and Stan.

When the winter weather arrived, the country idyll necessarily came to an end. Stanley was sent home, and the original Rud and Trix twosome was restored. In November, Alice became ill with shingles, and her sister Georgie came to the farm to look after her, while Rudyard and Trix were sent on ahead to London. Alice had taken lodgings for them in the city with an ex-butler and his wife in a tiny lodging-house in the Brompton Road, at number 227. When Alice recovered in a few weeks, she rejoined the children in London. This was Trix's first visit to a big city, and she was not terribly impressed. She hardly noticed the grand buildings and broad boulevards, although she could not help but be awed by the huge red brick expanse of the old South Kensington Museum, just across the street from their lodging house. Trix, who was always ready to find

---

3   Ibid.

romance in her new surroundings, invented a history for their unusual city home, imagining that the small, cozy house was a little country cottage that had been picked up and set down in a London street.

In the city, as in the early days in the country, Rudyard and Trix were thrown together. Mischievous Rudyard invented adventures and created stories to occupy their time. The city house provided the background for a whole new set of games. Using odd bits of paper and string, Trix and Rud created little packets which they filled with worthless scraps. From the low windows at the front of the house, which looked directly on to the street, they dropped the little packets on to the paving stones. Breathlessly, they waited and watched to see who would pick up the mysterious bundles. The fun of the game was seeing the reactions of the people who stooped down to retrieve the packets quickly transform from eager expectation to disappointment. From the back of the house, the children looked out over slate roofs and small gardens, where stray cats prowled. Rudyard bought food from the 'Cats'—Meat Man' on the street and then, with Trix's help, dangled the meat from strings for the hungry cats below to jump up for. Brother and sister were both entertained by the nimble leaps and harmless spills, as the cats tried to devour the tid-bits. Both games seem somewhat taunting and mean, reflecting the children's need to be the teasers instead of the teased.

There was a delicious, sweet smell, which seemed to hang about the neighbourhood, and tantalized the children. Rud and Trix were convinced there must be a bakery nearby, which, despite several scouting expeditions, they could not find. One day, they begged their mother to locate the bakery and take them to it. She obliged and walked the excited children around the corner to the bakery. Once inside, surrounded by a variety of treats, they had trouble deciding what looked best. After much indecision, they chose to buy savoury meat pies, which, when tasted, were sadly disappointing. After sampling the pie, Ruddy lamented to Trix, 'In fact, it is another lost illusion'. When they were alone on the walk home, Trix asked Ruddy 'if the illusion had ever been in the pie; if so, had it been lost in the baking; and finally, what was it?' Without any condescension, Ruddy explained the nature of an illusion, and how it was quite apart from meat and pastry. Trix was grateful for his words, which she said, 'as usual let a flood of light in on my stupidity'.[4]

---

4   Ibid., p. 507.

Trix was always grateful for Rudyard's help in explaining the hidden secrets of the world. He and Cousin Stanley were her favourite teachers. She was especially grateful to Stanley for explaining one of the stubborn mysteries of life to her—how to tell the time. She could not learn, although she had struggled long and helplessly with the clock. One day, playing with Stanley at Wilden and still trying to hide her ignorance, she had inadvertently revealed that she could not tell the time. Stanley, less than a year older than herself, in three minutes of simple instruction in front of a clock, explained everything she needed to know.

Unlike Aunty, Ruddy and Stanley understood what it was that puzzled her and knew how to unravel mysteries. From her own experience, she concluded that young children would be best taught by children only a few years older than themselves. Young teachers, who had not lost touch with their students' minds, would be able to explain difficulties and correct errors that had only recently puzzled themselves.

One day as a special treat, Alice took Trix on an outing along Brompton Road. Trix followed her mother along the crowded street, admiring the colourful shop window displays, until they arrived at the Lowther Arcade, which was a paradise of toys. Hoping to please Trix, Alice took her into a toy store to choose a doll, but Trix wasn't interested in dolls. She didn't care about glass eyes, curly wigs, and gaudy frocks. As they walked farther along Brompton Road, they came to a shop called Lorberg's whose window displayed objects that fascinated Trix—'all steel and iron treasures, knives, scissors, some of them gold-chased and shaped like storks, chains, padlocks, revolvers, tools of every kind, and many of them small and glittering. It was better than any toy-shop, for everything was real'.[5] Here was where Trix wished to choose a toy. Trix's imaginary play featured adventure, violence, torture, and death, where revolvers, knives, scissors, and padlocks played their parts. Dolls had no part to play.

Directly across the street from the house on Brompton Road was the huge old South Kensington Museum (now the Victoria and Albert Museum). The children were given special student tickets, good for the whole season. Every day, Trix and Rudyard crossed the wide street and passed through the decorated entrance into the vast museum, where they roamed at will through the enormous halls, filled with the treasures

---

5   Ibid., p. 509.

of the world. Trix returned again and again to gaze up at a replica of Michelangelo's David and to visit a large black and white marble Newfoundland dog, resting on a red marble cushion, embellished by fruits made of semi-precious stones.

Trix was fascinated and half-afraid of a watch in the shape of a skull made from ivory, enamel, and gems. After staring at the skull during the day, she was troubled by visions of it at night, where it appeared to be floating in the dark, growing large and menacing. Although she did not confess that the skull terrified her, Rudyard guessed there was something frightening her and told their mother about it. Alice responded sympathetically and had a night-light installed in Trix's room.

The museum was crammed with wonders—animals, skeletons, minerals, costumes, fabrics, weapons, paintings, books, and more—all inspiration for new stories and games. When Trix and Rud discovered a statue of Buddha, big enough to enter through a little door in its back, they included it in a fantasy jewel heist they planned to pull off. The Buddha would be the hiding place for the stolen goods at the heart of the elaborate robbery plot, which also included disguises—soft shoes, dark clothes, plaited hair, and caps. Sandwiches were to be packed, forged telegrams were to be sent, a special parcel for the swag (a word they loved) was to be provided. The museum was their playground until January 1878 when the holiday ended, as Trix knew it would, and new accommodations had to be found for the children.

At the recommendation of the Macdonald sisters, Rudyard was enrolled at The United Services College, known as Westward Ho! The headmaster of the school, Cormell Price, was an old friend of the family.[6] When Rudyard went off to school, Trix divided her time between lodgings in London with her mother and a return to Lorne Lodge.

Sending Trix back to Lorne Lodge seems at first both inexplicable and cruel, but Trix was not unhappy to return to Mrs Holloway and Southsea. While Rudyard wholeheartedly hated the place and its mistress, Trix did not utterly despise the house or the woman. Mrs Holloway had been her close and constant companion for six years, her teacher, and, in some ways, her protector. She had been the only mother Trix had ever known,

---

6   The school serves as the setting for Rudyard's 'Stalky and Co.' stories.

and she had loved Trix. What troubled Trix the most during her years at Lorne Lodge was helplessly witnessing her brother's mistreatment and misery. What had also caused her hurt, shame, and confusion was the taunting and touching of the loathsome Harry. But now, with Rudyard far off at Westward Ho!, Trix was freed from having to watch as he was bullied and beaten. With Harry working at a bank and no longer living at Lorne Lodge, she was clear of his unwanted attentions. Thus, the most unbearable aspects of Lorne Lodge were removed, while the familiar presence of Aunty Rosa remained.

The extreme loneliness Trix had suffered at Lorne Lodge was relieved on this second stay by the presence of two other boarders. Trix now had companions, two sisters—Florence (always known as Flo) and Maud Garrard. Although Florence was four years older than Trix, she welcomed Trix's friendship and appreciated her wider knowledge, learning from her how to read properly, recite verse, and compose letters. Trix thought Florence both simple and sophisticated, with odd areas of wisdom and ignorance. One day when Rudyard came to collect Trix from Southsea in June of 1880, he met Flo and was immediately smitten. He remained enslaved by Flo for eleven painful years,[7] while Trix grew apart from her after a year.

Alice chose to enrol Trix in the Notting Hill High School for Girls, an academic girls day school, which Trix's cousin, Margaret Burne-Jones, as well as Jenny May Morris (daughter of William) had also attended. This time, Alice accepted the suggestions of her sisters for the board and education of her children. The United Services College, where Rudyard spent his school days, and Notting Hill both came highly recommended by family members. Trix entered Notting Hill as an untutored little girl and remained there from the beginning of the summer term 1878 until July 1883. When Trix first entered school at age ten, she was found to be not only poorly educated but oddly ignorant of the world. Her teachers were surprised that she had read a great chunk of eighteenth- and nineteenth-century fiction and poetry and astonished to hear that seemed to know all of Shakespeare's plays and could quote at length from them. Although she was behind in most of her studies when she

---

7   Rudyard was obsessed by Flo Garrard for years despite her discouragement. His novel *The Light that Failed* is based on his long infatuation with and eventual disappointment by her.

arrived at the school, she quickly excelled in French, history, geography, dancing, music, and sewing, advancing properly from grade to grade. With encouragement, she became an excellent student.

During the first two years of Trix's second stay at Lorne Lodge, Alice remained in England. She led her own life, staying with her sisters, visiting her friends, and occasionally looking in on Trix. Although Trix was comforted to know that Alice was nearby, she never had the expectation that she would live with her mother. When Alice could prolong her stays in England, she did, never feeling completely at ease in India. Lockwood, who had remained behind in India, visited Paris in 1878 in charge of the Indian Exhibits of the Paris Exhibition of 1878. He arranged for Rudyard to meet him there for a memorable five-week vacation, during which Rud had free run not only of the exhibition but of the entire city. Eleven-year-old Trix was not invited to join in this Parisian adventure. In 1879, Lockwood joined Alice in London, but at the end of the year, he sailed alone back to India, while Alice remained. Alice did not return to India until November of 1880, having spent three years in and near London. Before leaving for India, Alice arranged a new situation for Trix, close to the home of the Burne-Joneses.

Alice chose to board Trix with a female trio, the Misses Mary and Georgiana Craik and Miss Hannah Winnard at 26 Warwick Gardens in London. The three old maids had distinguished connections in academic, publishing, and literary circles. Georgiana was herself a prolific writer of children's books and romances. The ladies ran a salon, attended by many cultured people, including poets Jean Ingelow and Christina Rossetti. The house was filled with lively literary talk, which Trix was encouraged to participate in. She was allowed to borrow freely from the large library and did. The ladies fed her rich food as well as good books. Rudyard frequently called on Trix at Warwick Gardens and spent most of his school holidays there. Initially, he enjoyed the ladies' kind and decorous company, but eventually he found the ladies tiresome and boring. The ladies were solemn and serious, but Trix, who had an old-fashioned streak in her nature, enjoyed their society. Most of the time, Trix behaved as she had been taught, but at times she felt restless and weepy, acted like a baby, and demanded attention. The ladies indulged her. They encouraged her tendency to show off and appreciated her ability to recite and act.

Alice, back in India with Lockwood at the end of 1880, kept track of Trix's progress through Rudyard, through the aunts who invited her to their homes, and through faithful family friend Edith Plowden, who visited Trix often.

While Trix's aunts and uncles had neglected her when she was growing up at Lorne Lodge, they were generous and welcoming to her during this period. They invited her to dinner parties and to spend holidays with them. Finally, Trix got a taste of the intellectual and artistic richness of her aunt and uncles' homes. She tested her experience against the many stories of almost unbelievable opulence and grandeur she had heard from Rudyard over their childhood years.

While spending the half-term holidays at the Grange in March of 1882 with her aunt and uncle, the Burne-Joneses, she was included in a dinner party where the celebrated Oscar Wilde was the guest of honour.

Excited to attend a party with adults, Trix dressed with care, spending extra time on her unruly hair. Her fringe (bangs), which refused to lie flat, was a life-long torment to her. Although by now she knew the Burne-Jones's home well, she had rarely seen it displayed with such splendour. The dining room was bright with crystal and silver; white damask covered the heavily laden table. A menu card announced the many courses of fish, meat, game, pudding, pies, and jellies. To her surprise, she was seated opposite the famous wit and, from across the table, she observed him closely. She was not impressed. She thought he looked 'like a bad copy of a bust of a very decadent Roman Emperor, roughly modelled in suet pudding'. His lips reminded her of the 'big brown slugs we used to hate so in the garden at Forlorn Lodge'. She thought his pleasant voice was spoiled by his affected manner, and his floppy black bow better suited to her waist than to his neck. Throughout the meal, he talked incessantly, and, at any pause Phil [Philip Burne-Jones], who sat next to him, gasped, 'Oscar, tell us so and so', and set him off again. 'He hardly seemed to look at Margaret who was as white and beautiful as a fairy tale, and took very little notice of Aunt Georgie. Uncle Ned [Edward Burne-Jones] was unusually silent, and winced, I think, when Oscar addressed him as 'Master.'"[8]

---

8 Lord Birkenhead, pp. 106–07.

Fourteen-year-old Trix was a keen observer and a clever reporter. She had strong feelings about unconventional and outrageous behaviour. Trix paid close attention not only to Wilde but also to the others' reactions to him. She recognized that while both Phil and Ned admired Wilde, only Phil flattered and fawned over him. Wilde completely ignored the ladies, whom Trix found worthy of admiration. Trix's remark about Wilde's neglect of the ladies may have been a completely innocent observation or may have expressed her understanding or suspicion of his sexual nature.

Trix's criticisms of Wilde, his demeanour, dress, and conversation were her own direct observations, but they were typical of the Kiplings' view of eccentric behaviour. Alice Kipling and her Macdonald sisters socialized with bohemian artists, writers, and poets, yet cared deeply about appearances and propriety. On her own, Trix possessed and exercised the family's ability to observe and report with acuity, even acerbity, while sharing the family's bourgeois social values. Attracted to bohemian experiences while burdened with bourgeois values, three of the Macdonald sisters had married artists, but artists of a very respectable kind. At fourteen, Trix shared with her family this contradiction between artistic and intellectual interests on the one hand and social expectations and aspirations on the other. Inviting Oscar Wilde to dinner and then disapproving of his dress, demeanour, and conversation is a perfect expression of the Macdonald/Kipling attitude—intrigued and admiring but also distanced and disparaging.

By fourteen, Trix knew how to read a novel and how to interpret a poem. Living with the artistic ladies at Warwick Gardens, Trix was invited to compare her reactions to their more learned opinions. Shortly after the Oscar Wilde dinner party, Rudyard sent Trix one of his poems. It described a caged bird that had flown away and then been found dead. Mrs Winnard, Miss Georgie Craik, and Trix read the poem over several times and talked about how to interpret it. The older ladies found fault with the poem, considering the emotion expressed over the bird's death to be disproportionate to the event. Trix explained with precocious certainty that the poem was an allegory about the death of love. The ladies dismissed Trix's allegorical interpretation, and Mrs Winnard remonstrated, 'Really Trixie I hoped we had eradicated your unfortunate tendency to think yourself wiser than your elders, but I fear we have only repressed it. Do you seriously think a little girl of your age [14] can understand somewhat abstruse verse better than two educated and mature ladies?' Trix attempted to placate the ladies by responding, 'Oh no—of course not. Only I know Ruddy so well, and the way he thinks and writes, that I feel I can understand him better than anyone'. Unconvinced, Georgie wrote to Rudyard expressing her doubts about Trix's critical abilities. Rudyard replied that Trix's interpretation was absolutely correct and vindicated her as an excellent reader of poetry and of himself. Trix felt triumphant. She understood her brother better than anyone else, and she understood how to read poetry, at the age of fourteen, better than many people of any age.[9] At fourteen, Trix was already confident about her literary interpretations and unafraid to express them.

Rudyard visited Trix frequently while she boarded at Warwick Gardens and reported back to their parents about her progress. Although his reports were positive, Alice fretted over Trix's state of mind and health and missed her sweet and bright company. She was concerned about the child she knew to be fragile. She beseeched Edith Plowden to take an interest in her, gain her confidence, and help her in whatever ways she could. She did not make these appeals of her sisters, who she felt were too occupied with their own lives to be bothered about Trix. As in the past, she did not encourage her sisters to become overly engaged with Trix, protecting her own place in her child's affections. Nonetheless, Trix did visit with her aunts during this period and enjoyed the company of her cousins. Edith Plowden fulfilled her role as good friend, frequent visitor, and trusted reporter.

At the age of fourteen, when she began to menstruate, Trix became strangely sad. She was suddenly troubled by morbid religious thoughts. She recalled Mrs Holloway's strict evangelical teachings and the violent, gruesome, and terrifying images they brought to her mind. When she saw menstrual blood and felt pain in her belly, she imagined these were expressions of her own guilt and sinfulness and was tormented about her own bad behaviour and worse thoughts. She was especially fearful that she would disappoint her parents in some way. When Rudyard visited her, he recognized that something was amiss. He believed his

---

9   Ibid., pp. 53–54.

sister was delicate and shy and in need of careful handling, but he didn't understand what was troubling her and could do nothing to help her. Then, as suddenly as these fears appeared, they vanished. Trix healed herself, banishing her melancholy or disguising its obvious signs for the time.

When Trix was at her most depressed, Rudyard was alarmed enough to write to their parents. Although Alice was concerned by Rudyard's report, she did not consider returning to England to check up on Trix, nor did she consider removing Trix from England and bringing her back to Lahore. She had established a schedule by which she would return home with Ruddy and Trix in the cool weather in the early spring of 1883. Upsetting Alice's plan, Rudyard returned home on his own six months earlier in November of 1882.

Trix remained in school in England, where, in her final year of studies, she performed so well that she was encouraged by her school mistress to apply to university. Trix was pleased to be recognized and recommended to go on with her education, but she knew this plan would never go forward. She knew that there was not enough money to support a university education for either child. If there were, it would have been used for Rudyard, who had also been encouraged to continue at university. Lockwood did not seriously consider sending Rudyard to Oxford and reassured himself that Rudyard's bent towards literature was sufficient to carry him forward. Only Stanley, son of the wealthy Baldwins, attended university.

When Alice went to fetch Trix, as planned, in the spring of 1883, she found her in glowing health. Trix, who had been well cared for and well fed, was a blooming, buxom girl. Alice did not approve of her daughter's extra pounds and immediately set out to eliminate Trix's new curves.

At the end of the year, Trix and Alice set sail towards home, towards India. On the voyage home, Alice was charged with looking after Maud Marshall, a girl of Trix's age who had also been at school in England. Her family, stationed in Malaysia, had followed the usual course and had sent her home to be educated. Trix and Maud quickly discovered that they had much in common, especially a love of novels and an ambition to write them. They talked and read together over the long trip, becoming inseparable and promising to continue the friendship once they were settled back with their families. Trix was troubled by sea sickness on the long and often difficult voyage, but this important new friendship eased her queasy stomach. This was the beginning of life-long friendship.

Returning to India with her mother at fifteen, Trix was neither a child, nor a woman. She understood little of life and little of herself. She had suffered much as a child with unkind strangers, recovered in her adolescence with helpful friends, and was now returning to the family she had never really known. She had little idea what to expect or what was to be expected of her. Most of all, she wanted to please her family and make them proud.

4. The Family Square

At the end of the year 1883, Alice and Trix disembarked from The S.S. Ancona at Bombay. They had made the arduous, three-week journey through the straits of Gibraltar to Marseilles, to Port Said, through the Suez Canal to the Red Sea to Aden, finally arriving at their destination. After the long sea voyage, Trix was anticipating the soothing solidity of land. Instead, she was met by the overwhelming clamour and squalor of the port of Bombay. Faces darker than she had ever seen before appeared all around her. Almost naked men, children covered with flies, stray dogs, goats, and cows crowded everywhere. Acrid fumes from burning cow dung burned her eyes, while the sweet noxious odours of spices filled her nostrils. The incomprehensible shouting and chatter that accompanied the violent arm-waving of the men confused and alarmed her, while the brilliant colours of the women's saris—cherry red, emerald green, orange, yellow, blue, and mauve—dazzled her. Although she had been told about the noise and filth of India, nothing had prepared her for the teeming chaos of the port of Bombay.

Trix and Alice were met by bearers—dark men in strange, ragged clothes, who led them through the riotous crowd along the palm-fringed, curving coast to their hotel. In the distance, Trix could see clock turrets, church steeples, and the oddly shaped domes and spires of strange tall buildings.

But mother and daughter did not stay to explore the city. After resting and recovering from the long voyage, they set out on the onerous four-day train journey north to Lahore. Riding for days through the dun-coloured plains, unaccustomed to the oppressive heat, the incomprehensible noise, and the unfamiliar smells, Trix just wished to arrive at Lahore in time for Christmas. The Lahore train station, which Trix looked forward to as an end of the ordeal, was a vast echoing stone hall filled with the clamour of vendors, the shouts of policemen, and the shuffling of women gathering up their children and their baskets. Making their way through the dusty crowds, Trix and Alice secured a carriage to drive them past the old walled city to the newly built British expatriate area, called 'Donald Town' after Donald McLeod, the lieutenant governor of the Punjab from 1865–70. As she rode down the centre of town on a broad boulevard known as the Mall, Trix could see on either side grand imposing buildings—brick and stone, multi-domed Anglo-Saracen extravaganzas as well as imposing and fanciful colonial and neo-classical buildings. In the distance, extensive leafy gardens and pleasure parks were barely visible. Out of sight was the British military command where infantry and artillery battalions were always in residence.

As Trix rode along the Mozang Road, she could see the Kipling house from afar. It stood alone in a wide open plain. The large, low house was surrounded on all four sides by a wide veranda of graceful arcades. No trees or shrubs surrounded the house, as Lockwood believed they spread disease. Thus, the dry and dusty house was named Bikanir House, after the great golden Indian desert of that name. Inside, Trix found many large square rooms with high, white-washed walls, wooden floors, and furnishings in the current Anglo-Oriental style—heavy English furniture, Persian carpets, and old master engravings. Family photographs decorated the walls, vases of brilliant flowers and feathers stood on the many small tables. Heavy draperies covered the windows to protect the interior from the heat and dust of the day. The windows faced the pointed arches of the arcade, from which there were unobstructed views in every direction. Most wonderful of all for Trix was her own bedroom, her childhood wish at last fulfilled. Lockwood had decorated the room just for her with lacquered furniture patterned in graffito, a high dado of Indian cotton, and a painted fireplace where her initials were so twined among Persian flowers and arabesques that they seemed part of the design. Trix had never had a room decorated just for her before, and she was thrilled to have this beautiful space, all for herself.

Once settled in her own room, Trix tried to make herself feel at home in the exotic land she had only fantasized about. At first, she dared only to go from Bikanir House down to the Mall, where the Lahore Museum was housed in an extravagant, red-brick, multi-level, multi-domed building. Here Lockwood served as director of the museum and keeper of its wonders. Close to the museum were the offices the of *The Civil and Military Gazette*, where Rudyard had been toiling as sub-editor for more than a year. Trix soon felt comfortable in the imposing, irregular pile which housed the museum and in the two low, wooden sheds, which held the modest offices of the *Gazette*.

Like most young people, Trix accepted the world she had been deposited in, engrossed as she was in her new impressions and old worries. Soon, guided by her mother, Trix learned how to move around in this world. She was taught to model her behaviour on the customs, rules, and beliefs of the community of which she was a part. She learned that she was a member of a small ruling elite—the British Raj. To understand the Raj, she was required to learn something of the larger history of the country in which she lived.

She was taught that the British had been in India as traders, mostly under the direction of the East India Company since the sixteenth century. When she arrived in the 1880s, she was taught and she could feel that the British were secure in their position as conquerors and rulers. They were confident in their belief that they were on a great civilizing mission, bringing British laws and culture to a primitive society. But she also could sense anxiety. Just beneath these national certainties was the terrifying memory of the Mutiny of 1857, which, while not fresh in mind, was uneasily and frequently recalled. The memory of this violent revolt was subtly but surely conveyed to Trix, although the rebellion itself had been firmly and finally suppressed a decade before her birth. Stories of the rebellion included details of extreme cruelty on both sides—a cycle of brutal acts by the Indians and horrific reprisals by the British. After the rebellion was contained, the East India Company was dissolved, and the British reorganized the army, the financial system, and the entire administration in India. From 1858 onward, India was administered directly by the British government under the new British Raj. This new administration provided a tiny band of British civil servants, who ruled over the vast sub-continent and its huge population with apparent confidence and ease.

From fear, discomfort, and ignorance, the British distanced themselves from Indian culture, shielding themselves from contact with Indians, except as servants. They laid out their own closed communities with parallel streets on a regular grid. They built spacious bungalows and planted shady English gardens. In their attempt to reproduce the feel of home, they decorated with chintz fabrics, cooked with imported tinned food, and dressed in heavy British woollens and tweeds. They entertained with pomp and pageantry—dinners, balls, teas, and picnics. They practiced British sports—riding, badminton, and tennis. All of this was supported by a host of Indians servants, who cooked, cleaned, tended the garden, served at parties, and watched over children.

To the British, the Indians were useful only as servants. To understand the many complicated differences among Indians was simply too difficult and confusing for most of the British to attempt. Indians looked different—some tall, some short, some dark-skinned, some yellow-skinned, some with light skin and pale eyes. They dressed differently—some women wore bright silk saris, some pants, some were completely covered in long veils. Men wore trousers, skirts, as well as unusual wrappings and bindings of white muslin. Many appeared shirtless, bare-legged, or practically naked. Some wore large, coloured turbans, some skull caps, some were bareheaded. They spoke more than a hundred different languages, the most common being Hindi. Indians were divided into many religions—Muslims and Hindus primarily, but also Buddhists, Jews, Christians, Parsees, Zoroastrians, Sikhs, and Jains. Within these religions were many subdivisions. There was also a powerful caste system, which established and maintained strict and distinct rules and provided harsh punishments for transgressing those rules. The caste into which one was born controlled what jobs one could do, how one could dress, where one could live, and with whom one could associate. The British learned as much of this system as was necessary for them to keep their households running smoothly, recognizing, for example, that a member of the lowest caste, an 'untouchable', could serve as a sweeper but only as a sweeper.

Trix adapted to the ways of her family and her class, fitting herself into the society that surrounded her. When she learned, with help from her mother, how to behave properly, she was rewarded with approval and praise.

Thus, at the age of fifteen, Trix entered into the happiest period of her life. At last she was a cherished member of a warm, loving, and cultured household. Safe in the embrace of 'The Family Square'—a pet name invented by Alice Kipling to describe the four Kiplings together as a group—Trix was content, doted on by her parents and at ease with her brother. At the home she had dreamed of for years, she felt accepted and loved. With the longed-for attention of Alice, she attempted at last to satisfy her 'mother want'.

With her family, Trix followed the seasonal patterns of the British, spending the winter months at Birkanir House in Lahore and, during the hot months, travelling with her mother, first to Dalhousie and later to Simla. In the heat, Rudyard and Lockwood remained in Lahore for their work, joining the women at intervals. In Dalhousie, Trix was thrilled by the many compliments she received. Everyone said how fresh and pretty she was, how lively and pleasant. Unself-conscious about her weight and her manners when she first arrived, she responded to Alice's reminders and remonstrances by quickly slimming down and smartening up. She wore her fair hair in a smooth chignon, with what she referred to as her fringe (bangs) curling over her brow. Keeping her unmanageable fringe, which became frizzy in the humid weather, under control drove her almost mad. She had deep-set blue eyes, a small, delicate mouth, and luminous white skin. She showed off her small waist and ample bosom in the tight bodices of her fashionable dresses. When she was in costume for amateur theatricals or dressed for the evening, she exposed her graceful neck and shoulders. She quickly became an acknowledged beauty, an expert dancer, and soon a heartbreaker.

Alice and Lockwood did what they could to please their daughter, spoiling her with presents and pets. They bought her a Persian cat and a fox terrier puppy. When she began to improve her skill on horseback, they provided her with her own pony, named Brownie. Lockwood, 'the Pater', had pet ravens, named Jack and Jill; Ruddy a bull terrier named Buzz. Alice did not take kindly to pets, but was fond of Trix's cat and, as a great concession, allowed it to sit on her lap.

Living with the family at Bikanir House, Trix seemed untroubled. As her mother had wished, she seemed to have erased all the possible ill-effects of her difficult childhood. If she suffered from doubts and depression, she hid them well. Rudyard from time to time complained that he was beset by 'blue devils'.[1] He suffered from insomnia, night-time wanderings, and hallucinations. But Trix never complained of unhappiness or melancholy either to Rudyard or her parents. Her parents wanted her to be happy, and she wanted to please them by being what they wanted. She was practiced in dissembling and could without much difficulty produce the look and sound of happiness when needed. But this was a time when she was truly happy.

Used to the routine of school, Trix was surprised by the relaxed requirements of her new home. She could do whatever she wished. In the morning, she rode; in the afternoon, she paid visits; in the evening, she attended dinners and dances. When she was at home, she played with the household pets, read novels, and wrote letters. She had no domestic duties, few intellectual pastimes, and no religious observances to attend. She was told to simply enjoy herself, and she did her best to follow this gentle order. But after a short while, she wanted to be useful. She pestered Alice to give her something to do, and Alice reluctantly allowed her to arrange some meals, order a few things at shops, and keep some household accounts.

The members of the Family Square formed a tight group who encouraged, appreciated, and supported each other. When Trix arrived, the three older Kiplings were all busy writing essays, stories, poems, and reviews. There were pens and ink in every room of the house. Lockwood served as special correspondent for the *Bombay Pioneer* and was a brilliant artist. Rudyard was a talented amateur caricaturist and illustrator. Both Rudyard and Alice served as reporters on the local social scene for the weekly papers. Alice, who had been publishing poems and stories, had an ear for a false rhythm or a false sentiment and worked with Rudyard to develop his writing style, correcting his poems and prose. Trix naturally and easily picked up a pen herself and joined in with her family on their various projects.

The parents were proud of their two obviously gifted and clever children and were pleased having them at home and showing them off abroad. Rudyard laboured hard and long at *The Civil and Military Gazette*, leaving himself little time to enjoy a social life. Still devoted to

---

[1] Rudyard Kipling, letters to Edith Macdonald, 10–14 July 1884. Library of Congress.

Flo Garrard, he avoided other romantic encounters. Trix, the youngest, was not expected to produce anything, although her scribbles were met with approval. She was praised simply for being pretty and polite.

Trix and Rud, who had played word games and invented stories when they were children, were often together now with pen in hand. In Trix's first year at Lahore and Dalhousie, she and Rud played what they called pencil and paper games, scribbling together through the long evenings. Collaborating or more often competing with each other, Trix and Ruddy wrote clever imitations of the poets they both knew, from Tennyson to Whitman. Parody was easy for Trix. She was a facile imitator of other poets' styles, and despite her age (she was only sixteen), she wasn't shy about mocking the verses of older, famous writers. For their own amusement, Trix and Rudyard lolled around the table together, reciting lines aloud, breaking in on each other to approve or correct the words, tone, and rhythm of each other's poetic attempts.

What they considered just playing around was recognized by the parents as accomplished verse and resulted in a little book called *Echoes, by Two Writers*—a collection of thirty-nine imitations and parodies in verse. Eight of the poems were composed by Trix. 'Hope Deferred' was Trix's imitation of 'Hope' or 'De Profundis' by Christina Rossetti, and 'Jane Smith' was her smart parody of Wordsworth's 'Alice Fell'. The book appeared in 1884, published by *The Civil and Military Gazette*.[2] It made a modest but favourable impression on the local British community. The poems were published without individual attribution, and it was impossible for readers to know which had been written by Rudyard and which by Trix. All the poems were considered astonishingly clever for the two teenaged authors. Rudyard was nineteen and Trix sixteen when the book was published. Rudyard later said he found it difficult to disentangle her work from his own during this period because, working together in the same room at the same table, they not only tried to influence each other but, without trying, shared a sensibility for points of reference, rhythms, and language.

---

2 Rudyard Kipling and Trix Kipling, *Echoes, by Two Writers* (Lahore: Civil and Military Gazette, 1884).

Fig. 7 The front cover of *Echoes*.

Both Rudyard and Trix considered imitation a fair way to learn from older poets, a clever way to show off, and a pleasant way to pass the time. Trix found it easier to imitate other poets than to attempt to write from personal experience or feeling. At sixteen, she had had little experience to write from. Elizabeth Barrett Browning's poem *Aurora Leigh* was important for Trix in identifying 'mother want'. But Aurora, the heroine of the poem, disdains imitation and struggles to write true art. Trix seems never to have tormented herself with the desire to write serious art. Writing was a game, a frivolous and fun pursuit. Aurora Leigh scorned imitation.

> And so, like most young poets, in a flush
> Of individual life, I poured myself
> Along the veins of others, and achieved
> Mere lifeless imitations of live verse,
> And made the living answer for the dead,
> Profaning nature.[3]

---

3 Elizabeth Barrett Browning, *Aurora Leigh* (London: J. Miller, 1864), First Book.

One wonders what Trix made of the whole poem, how she responded to Aurora's passionate plea to become a true artist. Trix, at this time, did not imagine herself to be or to become an artist. Writing was a happy pastime. One wonders further how Trix understood Aurora's assertion that she would be not only a true artist but an independent woman. Independence was beyond imagination.

For the six cool months of the year, from November to April, the Kiplings lived in their large, dusty house at Lahore. In the hot season of 1884, the women left the parched plains of Lahore for the drenched greenery of the hills of Dalhousie. Alice chose the serene and beautiful Dalhousie, which Trix later referred to as 'Dullhouses'[4], rather than risk exposing Trix to Simla with its somewhat raffish reputation. In Dalhousie, where Trix was still allowed to be a child, she was at ease and comfortable. The only thing that made her uncomfortable was Alice, whose continued criticism, meant to eliminate what remained of her schoolgirl clumsiness, was a constant reproach.

When Rudyard came up to Dalhousie to visit, he and Trix played like babies, behaving disgracefully together, sharing jokes and a private language, giggling, teasing, and crumpling up with laughter. Having been denied the chance before, they took whatever opportunities there were now to behave like naughty children together.

Nearly every morning, Rud took Trix out riding, determined to teach her how to trot. She loved the lessons, walking out slowly in the dawn, then trotting back as hard as she dared. She bumped a good deal, as was natural for a beginner, but she didn't mind. With the colour in her cheeks, her hair down and blowing about in the wind, and her hat jammed at the back of the head, she seemed to Rudyard as lovely as any girl could be. He rewarded her progress on horseback by buying her a side saddle. In exchange for having taught her to ride, Trix taught Rudyard to dance.

Riding out in the morning, the two roamed about on the slopes of the Himalaya Mountains, stopping to gaze thousands of feet below where rivulets cut across the valleys. Exploring on foot, they danced on stepping stones, ran up and down boulders, picked wild flowers, splashed in streams, and sailed bark boats and bread crumbs down the currents. On one outing, they came across a mother lizard who had laid five crimson eggs on the ground at the edge of a cliff. After exhausting

---

4   Lorna Lee, p. 16.

themselves climbing and running, they went home singing at the top of their voices, simply for the pleasure of hearing how far the sound carried. They gloried in the wild freedom of the place, where they could sing as loudly as they liked and play as madly as they dared in their oldest clothes, unobserved and unafraid.

In her first summer at Dalhousie, Trix met up with her ship-board friend Maud Marshall, the clever bookish girl she had met on her crossing to India. Trix was thrilled to meet Maud again, a girl smart enough to appreciate the Family Square and its literary pursuits. Soon, Trix and Maud became constant companions—recommending, exchanging, and discussing books. Like most teenage girls, they also gossiped about other girls, handsome boys, and party clothes. Trix allowed Maud's sister Violet to become a friend and confidante as well. In Dalhousie, the pretty and innocent Trix earned the name 'Rose in June',[5] pleasing herself and her mother.

The following year, Alice concluded that her daughter was sufficiently sophisticated to tolerate the excitements of Simla and took her there in the hot weather. The arduous journey from Lahore to Simla began with the train to Umballa, followed by over 100 miles from Umballa to Simla over rough terrain in a 'tonga'—a two-wheeled cart pulled by ponies. If the weather was poor or the fatigued travellers needed to rest, the trip could take three, four, or more days.

Simla, the most prestigious and the most disreputable of the Indian hill stations, had been carved out of the slopes of the Himalayas, whose snowy peaks rose up stupendously behind it. The remote village was tightly compressed along a high ridge in the cool mountains, where a strange collection of structures clung to the sides of the hills. Along the central upper Mall stood a Gothic church, mock-Tudor public buildings, an English hotel with wicker chairs and striped awnings, an imposing stone town hall, and Swiss-style chalets. Lower down, a hodgepodge of small shacks comprised the Bazaar. Still lower down the ridge were an open-air market and a park for waiting rickshaws and tonga taxis. Planted terraces and plains spread out in the foothills below. The entire place looked unusually, even defiantly, confused and incoherent; the buildings were at odds with one another architecturally and unrelated to the landscape, the native people, or their culture.

---

5   Ibid.

4. The Family Square

Fig. 8 *The Play's the Thing*. Simla, 1884.

Fig. 9 A watercolour painting of Trix by Lockwood.

During the season, the jostle of the bazaar, the eager crowds strolling on the Mall, and the clatter of mountain ponies created a bustling confusion. Simla offered incessant entertainment to the frivolous, fashionable, pleasure-seeking grass widows and the holiday-making military men on leave. There were balls, races, polo matches, picnics, sketching parties, and amateur theatrics. Behind all the gaiety, there existed serious strivings for social supremacy and professional advancement. Petty intrigue and gossip flourished in this atmosphere.

Psychic enquiry was a fashionable past-time in many circles. Silly school girls as well as the most genteel Anglo-Indian ladies and gentlemen dabbled in psychic experiments and attended seances in darkened rooms. Theosophy was especially popular, as two local residents—Alfred Sinnett, editor of the *Pioneer*, and Allan Octavio (A.O.) Hume—were patrons of Madame Blavatsky's newly founded religion. Even sober Lockwood Kipling attended a séance conducted by Madame Blavatsky. He concluded that she was an interesting and shrewd fake. Here in Simla, Trix was introduced to informal spiritual experimentation and entertainment. Alice, the eldest of seven sisters and a Macdonald of Skye, and her younger sisters all claimed to be receptive to occult experiences and gifted with second sight. Thus, Trix was following in an established female family tradition when she became interested in conjuring visions in a crystal and writing verse while in a trance.

Simla was also the summer seat of the government. The presence of the viceroy gave the place its exalted social standing. Among all the cool and moist hill stations, Simla held the supreme social status. When the Kiplings first arrived in Simla in 1885, the socially ambitious Alice was eager to enter into viceregal society. This was not easy to accomplish, as Lockwood, the curator of a museum, held a position at the low end of the Anglo-Indian hierarchy. Artists and intellectuals were not accorded precedence, and precedence was all important in Anglo-Indian social life. But when the Kiplings came to Simla, a new Viceroy had been in place for less than a year. The new Viceroy, Lord Dufferin—a sophisticated traveller, scholar, and wit—did not allow precedence to govern his choice of guests. He appreciated sharp and intelligent conversation more than social position. His wife, Lady Dufferin, was a celebrated beauty and fitting consort for her exceptional husband. The Dufferins discovered the Kiplings through their daughter Lady Helen, who studied drawing with Lockwood. They were immediately won over by the clever and charming Kiplings and welcomed them into viceregal society. Lord Dufferin was especially enchanted by the vivacious and loquacious Alice.

Staying at a cottage named 'The Tendrils' (later cottages were named 'Violet Hill', 'Victoria Cottage', and 'North Bank'), Alice worked at advancing in Simla society. As the gossip columnist for the *Bombay Gazette* and *The Civil and Military Gazette*, she was obliged to know what was going on in Simla, and, as a mother, she used that knowledge to introduce her daughter into the respectable parts of Simla social life.

Trix succeeded without really trying. She was naturally beautiful and had become, with her mother's constant criticism, graceful and slender. She astonished her many suitors with her knowledge of English poetry. One admirer claimed she could recite all of Shakespeare. When her talents became known to the theatrical society, she was invited to use her natural gifts on stage. She proudly displayed her talent for memorizing and reciting in the society's plays. Rudyard somewhat reluctantly wrote witty prologues for the dramas, and, on several occasions, Trix had the special treat of reciting prologues written by her brother. On stage and off, Trix loved dressing in pretty clothes, favouring bright colours and floating draperies. When preparing for parties and balls, she fussed and fretted over her dress, her jewels, her gloves, her fan, and, of course, her fringe. She felt her best in black for the evening with coral jewellery, red shoes, and a red fan. When she tired of this dramatic combination, she decorated her dress with a gold bow, gloves, and a fan along with topaz jewellery. For the Simla Fancy Dress Ball of 1885, Trix wore a simple Caldecott Olivia Primrose dress designed by her father, and the next year, for 'The Calico Ball', another viceregal costume extravaganza, she represented Mooltan pottery in a dress designed by Lockwood in shades of blue. She was a great success in both dresses. She never passed a glass without giving herself an appraising glance. And most people agreed she was well worth looking at.

Fig. 10 Photograph of Trix in Simla.

Fig. 11 Trix in a Grecian costume, in 1887.

At first, Trix innocently and happily displayed herself, unaware of the dangers she was exposing herself to. But soon, she became aware that male admiration easily led to serious courting and even marriage proposals. She was not prepared for this at all. She had never been as content as she was living in the Family Square, and she did not want anything to interfere with this, her first truly happy time. She ceased encouraging suitors. She kept her eyes down when walking on the Mall and ignored the many bold glances and remarks aimed at her. At parties, she spent her time talking gaily to older colonels, majors, and captains, while paying no attention to young subaltern admirers who hovered hopefully around her.

Rudyard, who knew his sister well, became aware of this situation and became concerned that Trix, whom he referred to as the 'Maiden', was attracting more attention than she desired. Rudyard understood that she was unprepared for romance and worked to protect her from being rushed out of her childhood. He approved of her strategies to avoid serious advances and proposals and encouraged her to stay at home and concentrate on her writing, beseeching her to cling to the inkpot. Trix happily complied, writing poems and stories for Rudyard's approval. Rudyard not only encouraged her to write, but also pestered her to submit her stories for publication. Trix was reluctant to publish but eventually allowed Rudyard to consider a ghost story she had recently completed. He was thrilled when she agreed to let him print it.

The ghost story was a form Trix knew well and found easy to imitate. The story she offered Rudyard was titled 'The Haunted Cabin'.[6] Within the conventional form, Trix expressed some of her most unacceptable and angry thoughts. 'The Haunted Cabin' has, at its centre, a merry ghost—a little girl named May Rodney. (May is the name Trix used later for the autobiographical heroine of her first novel, *The Heart of a Maid*.) The story is narrated by a young mother, sailing from England back to India with her three-year-old son, Robbie. She discovers that her cabin is haunted by a blue-eyed, yellow-haired, round-faced child of four. Dressed in only a nightgown and with bare feet, the child roams the ship. The child appears only to the young mother and her son. When they see her at a distance and try to approach her, she capriciously disappears. After repeatedly tempting them to follow her and then withdrawing, they conclude that she is a difficult and tiresome creature. But at the end of the voyage, the

---

6   Trix Kipling, 'The Haunted Cabin', *Quartette* (Lahore: Civil and Military Gazette, 1885).

little ghost appears perched on the sill of the stateroom porthole when the young mother comes in to take a nap. As the mother enters the cabin, she startles the little creature into losing her balance. Unable to move, the mother watches helplessly as the child's tiny hands vainly clutch at the air and the little golden head disappears with a 'short stifled cry which was more like a sob than a shriek'. The young mother screams, and a stewardess comes to calm her, explaining that the little girl is a ghost, not a real child. The woman insists, 'I tell you a child has fallen overboard and is dying—drowning! She must be dead by now, and it is your fault. They might have saved her if you had called at once! God forgive you for being so wicked!' The stewardess explains, 'you've seen little May Rodney. She fell out of this very port six years ago [...] She had been sitting on the sill of the port leaning out, and her mother came in and spoke to her suddenly, and she was startled and fell [...] I didn't hear her scream. It must have been a very soft, stifled little cry'.

It is difficult not to read the story as describing a piece of Trix's own early history. At three, golden-haired, blue-eyed Trix had sailed to England and had been abandoned without warning at Southsea. Her cries, soft and stifled, were never heard at all. Her bright young life slipped away, unvalued, unheard. In the ghost story, there are two mothers, the mother of Robbie who narrates the story and the mother of ghostly May Rodney. Both mothers prove themselves helpless to ward off catastrophe. The ghostly child roams about the deck improperly dressed and unattended in dangerous situations. Her capricious comings and goings vex the narrating mother rather than alarm her. Annoyed by finding the child sitting perilously on the sill of the porthole, she speaks sharply and precipitates the same catastrophe that had occurred before.

At the age of seventeen, Trix was not prepared to write directly about the misery of her childhood in fiction or memoir, nor was she prepared to cast blame for that misery. Instead, she worked within a well-known and highly stylized genre—the ghost story—to express her feelings about a crucial piece of her own history. Here, a young mother is haunted by a lost child. The mother is doomed to watch as the child slips helplessly away with a muffled cry. Trix believed herself to be a child who had been thrown away, and here she created a mother who recognizes what she has done to her innocent child. The central act of the story, maternal carelessness, and its result, the death of a child, lead to the somewhat crude moral of the tale. If you neglect your child, she will die and you will suffer endless remorse. Trix's first published story can easily be read as a thinly disguised accusation against her mother and a fitting punishment for her.

The story was published along with a group of stories and poems by the three other members of the Kipling family in *Quartette* in 1885. The volume had only one contribution by Trix, this seemingly inoffensive ghost story.

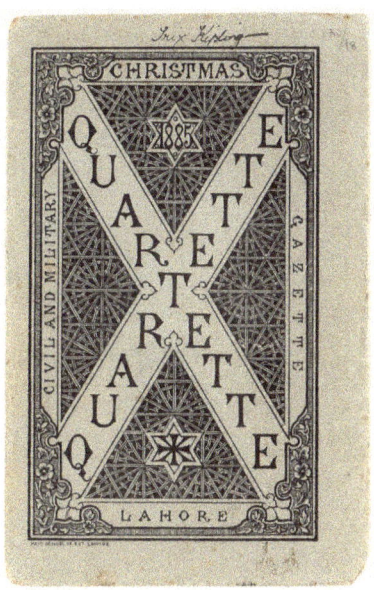

Fig. 12 The front cover of *Quartette*.

In all of her social activities, Trix was accompanied by her accomplished and confident mother. During her first seasons, Trix struggled to overcome her shyness. She wanted to become composed and calm, like her mother. She knew that Alice was recognized as a beauty and a flirt, while she was seen as little more than a pretty child. When Trix eventually conquered her nervousness and began to be noticed, Alice seemed pleased. But when Trix began to shine, Alice was not altogether pleased to be thrown into the shade by her brilliance. In 1885, Rudyard published a poem titled 'My Rival', in *Departmental Ditties*.[7] The subject of the poem is a rivalry between a forty-nine-year-old mother and her seventeen-year-old daughter, the ages of Alice and Trix at the time. The

---

7   'My Rival', *Departmental Ditties* (Lahore: Civil and Military Gazette, 1886).

poem is usually attributed to Rudyard alone, although some give the sole credit to Trix. Trix herself described it as a spontaneous collaboration between the brother and sister, arising from a passing remark. One morning, when she and Ruddy were walking together along the Mall in Simla, a rickshaw passed by with a stout painted matron inside, accompanied by a smiling youth. The night before, Trix had had a dull time at a dance. She had actually sat out two or three dances. As the rickshaw passed, the older lady called out, 'Hullo Darling, walking with your Brother, wonders will never cease'. Trix turned to Rudyard and said bitterly, 'there goes my rival! She never sits out'. Rudyard laughed and said, 'Jove! There's a verse in that'.[8]

MY RIVAL

I go to concert; party, ball–
    What profit is in these?
I sit alone against the wall
    And strive to look at ease.
The incense that is mine by right
    They burn before Her shrine;
And that's because I'm seventeen
    And She is forty-nine.

I cannot check my girlish blush,
    My color comes and goes;
I redden to my finger-tips,
I'm very gauche and very shy,
    Her jokes aren't in my line'
And, worst of all, I'm seventeen
    While She is forty-nine.

The young men come, the young men go
    Each pink and white and neat,
She's older than their mother, but
    They grovel at Her feet.
They walk beside her 'rickshaw wheels–
    None ever walks by mine;
And that's because I'm seventeen
    And She is forty-nine.

She rides with half a dozen men
    (She calls them 'boys' and 'mashers')

---

8   Trix Kipling, letter to Edith Plowden, 7 October 1936. University of Sussex.

> I trot along the Mall alone;
>   My prettiest frocks and sashes
> Don't help to fill my programme-card,
>   And vainly I repine
> From ten to two A.M. Ah me!
>   Would I were forty-nine.
>
> She calls me 'darling', 'pet', and 'dear',
>   And 'sweet retiring maid'.
> I'm always at the back, I know,
>   She puts me in the shade.
> She introduces me to men,
>   'Cast' lovers, I opine,
> For sixty takes to seventeen,
>   Nineteen to forty-nine.
>
> But even She must older grow
>   And end her dancing days,
> She can't go on forever so
>   At concerts, balls, and plays.
> One ray of priceless hope I see
>   Before my footsteps shine;
> Just think, that She'll by eighty-one
>   When I am forty-nine.[9]

Whether written by Trix or Rudyard or as a collaboration between the two, the poem clearly expressed Trix's annoyance at her mother. Trix wrote directly to her friend Violet Marshall (Maud's sister) about her competitive feelings for her mother. She recalled her early shyness and lamented that she had earlier sat 'as dumb as a fish while men talked to Mother. Now it sometimes happens that if there are not two men Mother goes on alone & the man rides by my rickshaw & talks to me. I like that'.[10] While she was pleased with these small triumphs, Trix continued to be worried about their larger consequences—unintentionally encouraging serious suitors.

As she entered into her second season at Simla, Trix well understood that continuing to flirt was a dangerous game. She retreated into herself, causing her pet name to change radically from 'Rose in June'[11] to the

---

9 'My Rival'.
10 Trix Kipling, letter to Violet Marshall, 28 August 1885.
11 Lorna Lee, p. 16.

'Ice Maiden'.[12] In order to remain in childhood, a stage she had not been allowed to enjoy before and was happy in now, Trix cooled herself down. This chill did little to deter suitors. She resolutely turned down all offers, including several from Irishmen. In her first year at Simla, she had four proposals, in her second year, three. She assumed that, by the law of averages, there would be more in the next year.

Trix may not have been aware, but Alice certainly was aware that Trix was judged not only by her talents and beauty but by her social standing and financial status. And she had neither position nor provision. Many ambitious young men, eager to make an advantageous match, avoided her. But many other men appreciated her for her beauty, poise, and wit and were untroubled by her lack of status and money. Trix found that even a brief conversation on the Mall or a single dance at a ball too often led to a proposal she did not want to entertain but felt uncomfortable having to refuse. She found herself repeatedly caught in distressing situations that forced her to be rude or seem insensitive.

Alice, on the other hand, was pleased that Trix had so many suitors. Husband hunting was her job. She understood Trix's discomfort and sympathized with her, but she could also make light of the situation Trix often found herself in. Together they teased each other. Trix often vexed her mother by sighing dramatically, 'Oh horrible fate! He's going to adore me!' when she was encouraged by Alice to ride or dance with someone she didn't care for. Once Alice asked her if she was getting to be like Miss Barbara Baxter; it was Miss Baxter who 'refused all the men before they axed her'.[13] When an unexpected offer surprised and pained Trix, Alice tried to console by saying, 'Poor dear—you never have any lovers only men who want to marry you at once'.[14] The pleasures of the chase did not attract Trix.

The Pater was more sympathetic, but hardly helpful. While Alice often encouraged unwanted suitors, the Pater discouraged all comers. He often lamented that he did not have enough money to make Trix independent, begging her to study hard so she could be a governess after his death. Trix, with unusual sharpness, pointed out that he should then have left her at school instead of taking her out at fifteen. She reminded

---

12   Ibid., p. 18.
13   Trix Kipling, letter to Edith Plowden, 7 October 1936.
14   Ibid.

him that her Head Mistress had encouraged her to stay for at least two more years and perhaps go on to Girton College. This had never been considered as a real possibility. Independence was not a choice for a pretty and popular girl.

During her second season at Simla, Trix attracted the attention of the Viceroy's son, Lord Clandeboye. Trix was flattered by the flurry of praise and wonder that attended this aristocratic notice, but she was not interested in the young lord. Alice was thrilled, but the Dufferins were not delighted by the possibility of a match between their noble son and a poor girl. Lady Dufferin suggested to Alice that Trix be sent to another hill station. Feisty Alice suggested that it should be Lord Clandeboye who be sent away. And it was the young lord who went home. The Kiplings were pleased that they were so highly valued by the Dufferins that this difficult situation was resolved without any loss of love between themselves and the ruling family. Trix understood that a penniless wife was the last thing Lord and Lady Dufferin wished for their son.[15] She was untroubled by the whole situation, which excited other members of the family and the community far more than it did her. She was relieved when it was all over.

Another of Trix's suitors was Rudyard's fellow journalist and best friend in India, Kay Robinson. He met Trix when she was just eighteen. Robinson was immediately beguiled by her, impressed by her literary memory and her witty conversation. He admired her statuesque beauty and was especially charmed by the loveliness of her face in repose, and her face was rarely in repose. When he expressed his feelings to Rudyard, Rudyard heartily discouraged him, vowing to declare war on him if he were to write to their parents. Rudyard was appalled at Robinson's audacity in approaching Trix. Although Robinson, a literary and cultured man, would have made a suitable husband for Trix, he did not dare to approach her.

When another suitor continued to pursue Trix, she complained to Rudyard and asked him, 'What am I to do?' He responded, 'Shoot the

---

15   This is one of the few stories that older members of the Kipling Society (founded in 1927 for the advancement and appreciation of the life and works of Rudyard Kipling) know about Trix. When I have mentioned to members of the Kipling Society that I am working on Trix, many say, 'Ah, yes, the one who captivated the viceroy's son'. The story is flattering to Trix and to the entire Kipling family.

brute!' 'That was all the help I got from him,' Trix concluded.[16] Rudyard was certain that Trix didn't care for the man and would laugh at him. Rudyard was furious that someone might dare to smash the Family Square. He was intensely, even violently, interested in keeping Trix at home and with him for a while longer. Rudyard admitted that he had his own selfish motives in holding Trix back. He wrote to Margaret Burne-Jones about his 'intense anxiety about the Maiden' and his 'jealous care lest she should show signs of being "touched in the heart." [...] Of course we can't hope to stave off the Inevitable [marriage] but I promise that unless he is a most superior man, I'll make it desperately uncomfortable for the coming man—*when* he comes. I want two years more of her if I can get it'.[17] Rudyard, who knew his sister well, was conscious of Trix's lack of feeling for any of the men who approached her. While his interference in Trix's love life was for his own peace of mind, it also served Trix. She was grateful for Rudyard's possessive interference. While Alice pushed Trix forward, Rudyard tried to hold her back. Trix knew the inevitable was coming and tried to enjoy the time she had with her family.

Trix may have been in love with one of her many suitors, or more likely wished herself to be in love. One bold young soldier, after dancing with Trix at a ball, pledged himself to her forever. She was doubtful of his intentions when he went off to Burma, where he was killed in an attack on a fort. The doomed soldier may have touched her heart, but it seems unlikely. It is more likely that Trix found it easier to bemoan the loss of a gallant lover than to account for her reluctance to consider the proposals of her many suitors. The story of the tragically lost lover was one she liked to tell (and much later told in a short story), but it is hard to believe.

In the fall of 1885 after the busy season in Simla, Trix settled back into the joys of the Family Square once again reunited in Lahore. As the weather cooled, Alice suffered from an unusual bout of rheumatism in her left shoulder. Dr Elizabeth Bielby, the Punjab's first woman doctor and Professor of Midwifery at Lahore Medical School, was called in to attend her. Trix had met this woman before at Bikanir House, which

---

16   Trix Kipling, letter to Maud Diver, 24 May 1944. Edinburgh.
17   Rudyard Kipling, letter to Margaret Burne-Jones, 27 September 1885. *Letters*, ed. by Thomas Pinney, 2 vols. (Iowa: University of Iowa, 1990), vol. I, p. 94.

had become Lahore's nearest equivalent to an intellectual salon. Of the smart and influential people who visited, seeking Lockwood's advice and enjoying Alice's hospitality, Dr Bielby was the one who most impressed Trix. When the doctor came to examine Alice's shoulder, Trix used the occasion to exhibit her nursing abilities. She carefully looked after the patient as well as the house, showing off for the new woman doctor. She was anxious to win permission to attend Dr Bielby's lectures. In recognition of her obvious interest, the parents allowed Trix in early 1886 to attend the doctor's lectures and, for a short spell, she was ambitious to become a nurse. From attending the lectures, she proudly received ambulance certificates. She was not encouraged to continue with this interest by Rudyard or the rest of the family. She was positively discouraged by Alice, who considered such a life to be beneath her beautiful and talented daughter. Trix's charms were meant to secure a brilliant husband.

Fig. 13 Rudyard in Lahore in the 1880s.

When not attending parties or imagining herself a nurse, Trix remained attached to the ink pot. After the publication of *Echoes* and *Quartette*, Rudyard and Trix went on with their literary games—writing poems, stories, parodies, and pastiches together.

In 1886, Kay Robinson took over the editorship of *The Civil and Military Gazette* (*CMG*), where Rudyard's reputation as an editor and contributor was growing. Hoping to put a little sparkle into the dull publication, Robinson instituted 'turnovers'—light 2,000-word pieces of local interest that began on page two or three and continued on the next inside page. Titled 'Plain Tales from the Hills', they were published anonymously. Robinson assigned the pieces to Rudyard, who, in turn, passed some of them over to his sister. Thirty-nine of the brief stories appeared between November 1886 and June 1887. Of the thirty-nine, Rudyard disowned seven (including the first two). Kipling's bibliographer and most Kipling scholars agree that the tales not written by Rudyard were by his sister, Trix.[18] While Rudyard sometimes attributed the creation of the clever punning title of the series to a family council and sometimes to Alice

---

18 *Plain Tales from the Hills* (Lahore: The Civil and Military Gazette, 1886–1887).
David Richards, *Rudyard Kipling: A Bibliography* (Delaware: Oak Knoll Press, 2010). Richards cites Rudyard's repudiation of 'Love-in-a-Mist' 'How It Happened, 'Love: A Miss', 'A Straight Flush', 'A Pinchbeck Goddess', 'On Theatricals', and 'A Little Learning'. Richards concludes, 'Indeed, it is likely that the series was envisioned as a joint effort, like *Echoes* and *Quartette*. Certainly the overall title of Plain Tales From the Hills was decided in family council'.
Harry Ricketts in *Rudyard Kipling: A Life* (New York: Carroll & Graf, 2000), p. 95, writes, 'Again the idea [of Plain Tales] originated in the Kiplings' penchant for literary games. Although in his autobiography Rud referred only to a family council over the overall title, his sister was certainly a contributor, and it seems like that the series was initially envisaged as another joint effort, like *Echoes*.
Of the thirty-nine "Plain Tales" printed in the CMG, Rud later repudiated seven (including the opening two) and an eighth, 'A Scrap of Letter', has never been accepted as his. These stories – though the evidence is not conclusive – were probably Trix's work. One, "A Pinchebeck Goddess", was definitely hers, and it is hard to imagine who else could have written the others'. Lord Birkenhead in *Rudyard Kipling*, p. 87, writes, 'It is probable that Trix also had her fingers in this particular pie [Plain Tales], and it was even suggested that she wrote several of the stories that appeared in the *Civil and Military Gazette*, but were not republished. Trix knew Simla better than her brother, and was able to give him a great deal of information about personalities'. Hilton Brown, in *Rudyard Kipling: A New Appreciation* wrote, 'In the early Indian days, Ruddy and Trix worked closely together. It would be interesting to know how much of *Departmental Ditties* was first strung together by Trix, or how much of the recondite femininity of *Plain Tales* sprung from that shrewd judgement and delicate observation...'
Many of the 'Plain Tales from the Hills', while attributed to Rudyard alone show Trix's helping hand, including 'Lispeth' (CMG, 2 November 1886), published as the opening story in most collections, and always attributed to Rudyard alone. The story is about a girl from the Hills, a savage who is taken in by a Chaplain's wife, a good Christian woman. The good Christian woman deceives the poor girl as does her lover, who abandons her to return to England. Broken-hearted, the girl weeps over the map of the world and the unimaginable distance between herself

alone, he id not attribute any of the stories to Trix, either as hers alone or as hers in part. When *Plain Tales from the Hills* was published under his name as a single volume in 1888, Trix's stories were properly omitted. But, upon their initial publication in the *CMG*, all the tales, his and hers, were unsigned and assumed to come from the same hand.

Trix, now more confident in her skills as social satirist, wittily and often witheringly described the Anglo-Indian social scene she had been participating in for a while. The first tale of the series, 'Love-in-a-Mist' (2 November 1886), tells the sorry story of newlyweds who, when left alone with only each other, become miserably bored after one day of marriage. Tale number two, 'How It Happened' (11 November 1886), describes a chance meeting between a young man and woman, who find themselves inadvertently and unfortunately engaged after one brief conversation. In story number thirteen, 'A Pinchbeck Goddess' (10 December 1886), a woman disguises her plain self to attract a husband and succeeds. (Ten years later, Trix expanded this story into her second novel, giving it the same title.)

Number eighteen, 'A Little Learning' (14 February 1887), tells of a young woman who, having attended nursing lectures, believes herself competent to act as a doctor to her ailing aunt. In her overconfidence and self-importance, she does more harm (although not lasting) than

---

and her lover. The innocent and ignorant girl seems likely to be a creation of Trix's. Rudyard created few such girls as central characters.

'Three and—an Extra' (DMG, 17 November 1886), is told from the point of view of a young wife grieving excessively over the death of her baby. When her husband starts paying attention to another woman, the wife, recognizes the danger and plots successfully to win her husband back. "Take my word for it, the silliest woman can manage a clever man; but it needs a very clever woman to manage a fool." (CMG, 17 November 1886)

'Miss Youghal's Sais' (sais is a groom) (CMG, 25 April 1887), has at its center, an Indian policeman who disguises himself as a groom and courts his beloved on horseback. The happy romance plot is more feminine than most of Rudyard's fiction. 'Bitters Neat' features a young man who is blind to the affection of a girl, who loves him dearly. When he finally discovers her love, it is too late. 'Yoked to an Unbeliever' focuses on a young woman who loves a man who goes off to Darjeeling and leaves her. She marries another, and when he dies, she returns to find her first love. He has in the meantime married a hill girl who is 'making a decent man of him'. In 'False Dawn' a man proposes to the wrong sister while riding at night in a fog. In 'The Other Man' a woman is forced to marry a man she doesn't love. The one she does love comes to visit her, but when his rickshaw arrives, he is seated in it stiff and dead. 'Cupid's Arrow' tells the story of a young girl who is pressured by her ambitious mother to marry a rich, older man she does not love. She cleverly defeats her mother's plan by intentionally losing an archery contest.

good. In the end, she is scolded and humbled for her presumption and punished cruelly for it. This story is the most autobiographical of the group and describes Trix's feelings about wishing to have a useful career as a nurse or doctor. Betty, the young nursing student, is 'an enthusiastic girl, with strong ideas concerning Woman's Mission and Work in the World and their Duty'. She believed that 'Every one should have a Vocation, a Purpose in Life; and she had tried hard to find hers. She had been forced to realize that she could not be an artist, author, actress or musician; but no matter, she would be useful and practical, doing actual good [...] she would be a nurse. No—a lady doctor [...] Unfortunately for her high resolves, she had a prejudiced and narrow-minded father and mother, who imagined that their daughter would be better and happier living with them in India, than studying medicine in London'.[19]

Trix may have had the same high resolve as her character, Betty, but, like her, she had been convinced by her 'prejudiced and narrow-minded' parents that she ought not to aim for anything but marriage.

These four stories ('Love-in-a-Mist', 'How It Happened', 'A Pinchbeck Goddess', and 'A Little Learning') are, without question, by Trix. Other stories most likely by Trix are number fifteen 'Our Theatricals', and number seven, 'Love: A 'Miss.'' All six of these stories, which originally appeared in the *CMG* under the title 'Plain Tales from the Hills', were omitted when Rudyard published the stories as a collection, indicating that they were not by him. All six of Trix's stories were good enough to appear with Rudyard's and were assumed to be by the same author. Rudyard had been praised for his precocity, writing these stories when he was only twenty-one. Trix was only eighteen when she wrote hers. Several other stories, especially those with a female point of view or central female presence suggest Trix's active participation. Rudyard never acknowledged that he collaborated with Trix on the stories, and she never claimed her share in them. Thus, it is difficult to assert absolutely that they were a shared effort, but much internal evidence supports her guidance in feminine matters.

By the time Trix was nineteen, she had come into full recognition that, like most girls, she would marry. It was clearly her mother's wish that she marry, her society's expectation that she marry, and her own scant knowledge of other possibilities that recommended marriage to

---

19 Trix Kipling, 'A Little Learning', *The Civil and Military Gazette*, 14 February (1887).

her as her only possible path. Trix had been taught that duty, not love or happiness, ruled a woman's existence, and her duty was to marry.

Rudyard, now twenty-one and promoted to special correspondent on *The Pioneer* in Allahabad, had moved up to the more senior position at the more important paper. He was therefore away from home much of the time, leaving The Family Square an unbalanced triangle with Trix perched between her parents.

Although Trix was still comfortable at home, she felt some tension between herself and her mother. She believed that Alice was becoming impatient to have her off her hands once again. Always prepared to think of herself as excess baggage, Trix began to feel that it was time for her to unburden her parents of her care. It was time for her to end her time as a dependent daughter and to take her place in society as a wife.

In itself, this is disturbing, but it is doubly so given Alice's own premarital history. She too came from an impecunious family, with many daughters to marry off, not just one. From the age of fifteen to twenty-seven, she had amused herself with a series of romantic interludes and broken engagements—twice to William Fulford and once to William Allingham—and hung on the family tree until the ripe age of twenty-eight. Although she and her sisters were in competition over finding the best husbands, the parents brought little pressure on the girls, confident that they could choose well for themselves. When Alice at last decided on John Lockwood, to whom she remained engaged for almost two years, the parents waited patiently for the marriage to take place. Without similar compassion, Alice prepared to hustle her sensitive child into marriage, believing that Trix's fragile and clinging nature required a strong male protector.

Alice fretted not only about Trix but also about Rudyard and encouraged both to accept or at least entertain romantic prospects she found promising. Both brother and sister were openly disdainful of Alice's marital projects. While Rudyard could dismiss Alice's interference, Trix could not ignore it.

One of Alice's more inappropriate choices for Rudyard was a young woman named (Augusta) Gussie Tweddell. Gussie had met Rudyard at a dinner party and had confided to him that she wrote verse. Alice thought that Ruddy ought to fall head over ears in love with the poetry-writing girl, and she pressured Trix to ask her in for tea. When Gussie sent some of her poems over in advance of her proposed visit, brother and sister were appalled. The packet of poems arrived as the two lounged about on the softly cushioned sofa in the large, bright drawing room. Rudyard declaimed the poems aloud for Trix's entertainment. Then she, snatching the pages, read aloud to him. Together, they mocked the poor girl's execrable poetry and excruciating sentiments. Trix, who had no patience for girls who moaned over silly affairs in vile verse, was especially unkind. Alice thought them both 'hard hearted cynics' when she walked in on them shrieking and howling with delight at the recitation. 'How did I ever bring you two into the world?' asked Alice, as Trix pranced about the room spouting poor Gussie's rhymes and vowing in between the lines that such an idiot should never come to her girls' teas. All the while, Rudyard sprawled on the sofa, grinning and bellowing from time to time.[20]

While Trix was flattered by the many proposals she received, she was unmoved by all of them. Her many marital prospects were indistinguishable to her—all equally possible and impossible, likely and unlikely. Neither Kay Robinson nor the Viceroy's son had excited her. Yet, she realized as she approached twenty that she would have to make a choice, that marriage was inevitable. From the several suitors who were available to her at the time, she chose one. Their first meeting was 'dull and average' compared to the often told fairy tale story of Alice and Lockwood's first meeting at Rudyard Lake. In her diary, Trix wrote: 'Danced with two new men—both fairly pleasant—Capt Taylor and M. Fleming—the former I never saw again—the latter called next day'.[21]

Tall and handsome John Murchison Fleming was a soldier from a soldiering family. His father had been a respected Army doctor. John, always called Jack, had served with the King's Own Scottish Borderers during the Afghan War of 1880-81 and had taken part in expeditions north of the Khyber Pass and east across the border into the Laghman Valley. He was an excellent draughtsman and painted in watercolours, skills that were useful when he was seconded to the Survey of India in July 1885. The Survey, which served as the mapping unit of the government, provided topographical information about the frontiers of the Raj, and often gathered military and political intelligence. Members of the survey were thought to be engaged in espionage in addition to

---

20 Rudyard Kipling, letter to Edmonia Hill, 9–10 July 1888. *Letters*, ed. by Pinney, vol. I, p. 242.
21 Trix Kipling, letter to Edith Plowden, 7 October 1936.

their other duties. Jack was ten years Trix's senior, a stiff Scotsman of no remarkable achievement, from a family of some minor distinction. Tall and dashing in his military uniform, he was most remarkable for his good looks. He was not intellectual or artistic and had little natural sympathy for Trix's story-writing or poetry-reciting. He and Trix 'scarcely shared one thought or pleasure. He was Army to the toe-tips and looked on all writing or painting as rather riff-raff stuff'.[22] He was an odd choice for a girl who might well have been able, despite her lack of position, to find a more appropriate, more sympathetic partner. But he was her choice. After a brief courtship and a dramatic proposal on horseback, Trix became engaged to Jack Fleming at nineteen.

While Alice pushed Trix forward, Lockwood made a weak attempt to hold her back. It was Rudyard who recognized and sympathized with Trix's reticence. Rudyard understood that Trix was ambivalent not about marrying Jack Fleming but about marrying at all. He wanted to help her, but she did not make it easy for him to either comfort or advise her, unaware herself of exactly what was troubling her. If anyone would have been able to help her, it would have been Rudyard, who understood her better than anyone else in the family. But she did not know how to ask for help.

Alice was relieved that Trix had managed to make a choice. She was neither pleased nor displeased by the choice itself, but Rudyard disliked Fleming and thought him a poor match for his sister. 'He's an unresponsive sort of animal but appears an honest man,' Rudyard wrote to his cousin, Margaret Machail.[23] Lockwood liked him no more than Rudyard did and predicted that Trix would grow weary of him soon. While Lockwood had some knowledge of his daughter and her needs, he had very keen knowledge of his wife and her views about Trix's future. He was in the habit of acquiescing to Alice on most domestic subjects, and, on this particular matter he was not going to contradict her views nor countermand her plans. Although Rudyard had objections, he too bowed to his mother's determination.

Trix, who had her own doubts, strengthened by Lockwood and Rudyard's lack of enthusiasm for the match, soon broke off the engagement. She had not been compelled to accept Jack, had given

---

22 Katherine Crossley, 'Letter to Gwladys Cox', in Lorna Lee, p. 95.
23 Rudyard Kipling, letter to Margaret Mackail, 11–14 February 1889. *Letters*, ed. by Pinney, vol. I, p. 289.

herself time to make the choice, but then, after only three months, found herself so unhappy and uncertain that she could not continue.

Alice was distressed by her daughter's capricious change of plans. Rudyard was sympathetic, but he had little understanding of his sister's initial choice of Fleming or of her subsequent rejection of him. Lockwood, recalled to England on business matters, was unavailable to voice his objections. When Trix told Rudyard that she was allowing Jack to continue to write to her after calling off the engagement, Rudyard recalled how Flo Garrard had prolonged his agony, like a worm on a hook, by permitting him to hope. Identifying with Fleming in this one instance, he counselled Trix to make a complete break for the young man's sake. Trix, attempting to follow Rudyard's advice, was firm in her refusal to see Fleming, but she was confused by her own unhappiness and indecision.

Five months later, while Lockwood remained in England attending to his affairs, Alice, Trix, and Rudyard were invited to stay outside of Simla at 'The Retreat'—the country house of Sir Edward Buck, the Secretary to the Government of India. They happily accepted the invitation to stay at this splendid English-style house, with its extensive gardens of rare flowering plants, imported fruit trees, and large vegetable beds. Sir Edward grew rhubarb, mushrooms, English pears, and strawberries. One bright and blustery afternoon, Trix asked Ruddy to walk with her over a hillside blooming with wild raspberries and strawberries. She needed advice and hoped that, in private, among the vines and berries, Ruddy would help her. Alone on the hill, she sank down on the ground and poured out her troubles. Haltingly, she told Rudyard that Jack had insisted on another last-despairing interview with her the morning before, and, while she had persisted in her refusals, she had been shaken by his appeals and protestations. She had told Jack that she was indifferent to him, but he had persisted with unreasonable and unfounded self-confidence. When she had told him directly that she did not love him, he had been unfazed. He had relentlessly pressed his suit. He had accepted her lack of feeling and in turn had told her with perfect self-assurance that she would learn to love him. She did not know what to believe.

Trix had not tried to hide her true nature from Jack. She felt comfortable enough with him to admit her lack of romantic feelings and trusted that, by telling him the truth from the start, she would have an explanation and excuse for any later coolness. She was confused and sad that she didn't have romantic fantasies and feelings and was candid in confessing their absence to a man who had proposed marriage.

She told Ruddy all she could, and then, shivering with cold and confusion, she burst into tears. Sitting among the pine-needles, she shook and sobbed, hoping Ruddy would have words to comfort her. He had only a few, and they hardly helped. Recognizing that she would get little help from Ruddy, she pulled herself together and, half crying and half laughing, stood up and brushed herself off. To end the awkward conversation, Trix started some silly chatter, concluding that never, since the world began, had there been a sorrow like her sorrow. Back on their feet, they returned to hunting for raspberries until Trix's tears were dried and their fingers were blue-red. Trying to recapture their earlier playful days and happier moods, they began to steal from each other's vines and throw pine-cones at each other's heads. But somehow, the foolishness was not amusing, and, when Trix collapsed on a rock and said, 'Oh how miserable I am!' it was clear that they could not play at being babies any more. Thus, they came home solemnly to tea and announced to their mother that they had had a riotously jovial afternoon.[24]

Trix's tearful explanations only confused Rudyard. They failed to account for what he could see was her very real misery. Rudyard was not sure if Trix was uncomfortable because Fleming's relentless pursuit caused her to reject him over and over again, because she cared for him too much, or because she didn't care for him enough. She seemed overwhelmed by her inability to know her own heart and, at the same time, she despaired to find herself acquiescing to another's will. Rudyard said that she told him 'as much about it as a woman would ever tell a man'.[25] This was her modest excuse for ending their conversation. Trix's feminine modesty may have inhibited her, but simple emotional fatigue may have worn her down. Fleming's stolid insistence moved her towards his point of view, as did her mother's warm approval of Fleming's suit. Pushing her in the opposite direction was Rudyard's disregard for the man. Her own point of view was a muddle. Behind the muddle was Trix's knowledge that she would soon have to marry someone, and Fleming had seemed as likely a choice as any other. Now he seemed

---

24 Rudyard Kipling, letter to Edmonia Hill, 28 June 28–1 July 1888. *Letters*, ed. by Pinney, vol. I, p. 223.
25 Ibid.

more likely than any other. But she was also aware that she did not love him. She was bewildered and genuinely miserable.

Two days after this tearful conversation, Trix and Rud awoke to find their mother in bed, past her usual hour, and complaining of feeling ill. Rudyard called the doctor, who, with some reservations, reassured the children that the illness was not serious. Trix spent the day at her mother's bedside, relieved to have her mother's health to worry about rather than her own romantic dilemma. After a day of waiting and watching at twilight, just as Alice's fever was at its height, Jack turned up in the front garden of The Retreat. He was off his head completely and begged Trix for a quarter of an hour, a few minutes, any time at all. Weary from nursing Alice and worn out from having to repeat herself over and over to Jack, Trix promised Rudyard she would get rid of him with dispatch. Reluctantly, she went downstairs, intent on dealing with him in the space of fifteen minutes. After more than the allotted time, Jack finally went away, leaving Trix on the verge of tears. She restrained her tears but complained bitterly to Rudyard about having to repeatedly reject Jack's unwanted pleas. Expressing these thoughts made her feel more at ease, as she dragged herself back upstairs to check on her feverish mother. When, after a while, Alice seemed to be resting comfortably, Trix left her mother's side and returned downstairs.

There, she found Rudyard looking haggard and complaining of hunger. Putting their worries aside, they sat down and had a sad little dinner together. Trix, trying to display good humour and good cheer, said amidst her tears, 'It's not nice to have to make poultices with one hand and stave off an importunate lover with the other. Now if I could clap the poultice on his mouth…'[26] Trix was pleased to see a slight smile appear on Rudyard's face. Then she and Ruddy fell to laughing and joking, thinking up fresh torments—Trix falling off a horse, Kay Robinson collapsing in Lahore, and so on until they convinced themselves that they were cheerful again.

Trix concentrated on caring for Alice, distracting herself from fretting over Jack by exercising her nursing skills, but she was annoyed at them both. And she missed Jack. She attempted to be cheerful, hiding her confused feelings from Rudyard, but he recognized that something was not right. Ten days after the last meeting with Jack, when Trix was

---

26 Rudyard Kipling, letter to Edmonia Hill, 4–6 July 1888. *Letters*, ed. by Pinney, vol. I, p. 232.

having trouble hiding her feelings, Rudyard appealed to her for some explanation. She was wandering aimlessly in the garden, when Rudyard found her, shook her gently but firmly, and demanded that she tell him what was the matter. Finally, she confessed that she had changed her mind again and wished to see Jack once more. When Rudyard absorbed what Trix was trying to tell him, he felt that he had been 'keeping two loving souls apart [...] and unconsciously acting the stern parent'. After hearing Trix describe her attachment, he softened towards Fleming, 'the poor, humble brute' who had been banned from the house. Trix convinced him that the two only wanted to know each other better. She reassured him that there was to be no engagement; she only wanted to meet with him again. 'Only let him see me,' Trix pleaded, 'and try not to hate him so and then—if there is another quarrel it will be all over—indeed it will'.[27] Alice persuaded Rudyard to be lenient, reassuring him that letting them see each other and get to understand each other might as easily lead them apart as together.

When Jack next came to call, Rudyard rushed outside, caught him before he entered the house, and explained that, while he was as much annoyed with him as ever, he desired his sister's peace of mind. Consequently, Jack wasn't to stay at the Club making a 'gibbering baboon' of himself but was to come down to see Trix now and again with the assurance that he would not be regarded as a burglar and an assassin. Jack gratefully shook hands with Rudyard, highly pleased with the concession of resumed visits.

Without Lockwood's dislike of Fleming to back up his own, and with mounting pressure from both Trix and Alice, Rudyard dropped his objections. He concluded, 'Isn't the heart of a maid a curious thing. I always thought that the maid was so wise and sensible. But she said to me, 'in these things I'm no wiser than anyone else—and I care for him ever so much.'"[28] In fact, she was less wise and less caring than most, having no strong feelings to help her make this crucial decision. Unhappy, confused, and bullied, she agreed to renew the engagement.

Thus, the engagement was reinstated, and wedding plans put into motion. When Rudyard learned of this final development, he said, 'I ain't one little bit pleased, but console myself with Mrs Kipling's practical

---

27 Rudyard Kipling, letter to Edmonia Hill, 15 July 1888, *Letters*, ed. by Pinney, vol. I, p. 254.
28 Ibid.

philosophy. Here it is. "The older I get the less inclined I am to bother about the future until it becomes the present. The future generally arranges itself." So far good but how about the futures of other people—sisters par example—which are arranged it would appear by detestable irrepressible subalterns'.[29] Rudyard was uncharacteristically forthright in his disgust with his mother's carelessness. He sarcastically 'consoled' himself with her 'practical philosophy', the same philosophy that had allowed her to cast off her children with strangers, and that allowed her now to cast Trix adrift with an unsuitable husband.

Lockwood, away in England, on hearing the news of Trix's re-engagement, feared that Trix might 'one day when it is too late find her Fleming but a thin pasture, and sigh for other fields'. He found Jack 'a model young man; Scotch and possessing all the virtues; but somewhat austere, not caring for books nor for many things for which Trix cares intensely'.[30] After accepting Jack's second proposal on horseback in the hills above Simla, Trix felt calmer. Once the decision was made, the situation secured, and the engagement announced, Trix relaxed. No longer pressured by her mother or by Jack, she felt excited and happy about the immediate prospect of the wedding. Between the engagement and the marriage, Jack had to return to England. Trix bore the separation bravely. While waiting patiently in Lahore for Jack's return, she was happily occupied with mastering new house-keeping jobs. Alice, assured of her daughter's future, was easier on her. Rudyard, finding Trix more carefree and light-hearted, felt at ease making fun of her rudimentary new skills, especially her attempts at cooking something she claimed was a cheesecake. He teased her about constantly writing letters to Jack and mooning over her photo-books, filled with the many photos they had taken of each other. Trix proudly jangled about the house ornamented with the jewels Jack had presented to her—pearl necklaces, curb-chain bangles, and three different engagement rings.

The decision to marry Jack—not the decision to marry at all, which had been made for her by her society and her mother—had been the first important decision Trix had made on her own. Up until this point, everything had been decided for her, but the choice of Jack Fleming was

---

29   Rudyard Kipling, letter to Alexander and Edmonia Hill, 6 October 1888. *Letters*, ed. by Pinney, vol. I, p. 258.
30   John Lockwood Kipling in Arthur Baldwin, *The Macdonald Sisters*.

hers. Naively, she hoped that Jack's ardour would compensate for her coolness, and that her mother's firm direction would serve to replace her own weak will. She had little else to guide her. She felt little for Jack Fleming, but she was aware that she also felt nothing for anyone else and never had. She had had girlish fantasies of herself in love, had written romantic verses and love-sick letters, but she knew her own nature. If she had to choose a husband, she could do worse than Jack Fleming. He was tall and handsome and wore his uniform with distinction. Ten years older, with a position on the Survey of India, he seemed to offer security and protection. He had assured her that she would learn to love him, and in her hopeful innocence, she believed him. She wanted to love someone.

Rudyard was traveling in America at the time of the wedding. He was not present at the ceremony in Simla, when Alice Macdonald Kipling married John Murchison Fleming—an officer of the King's Own Scottish Borderers, seconded to the Survey of India. The date was 11 June 1889, Trix's birthday. She had just turned twenty-one.

Fig. 14 Framed photographs of Trix and Jack early in their marriage.

5. The Heart of a Maid

Trix's first novel, *The Heart of a Maid*, written only months after her marriage, begins with this scene.

Two riders rein in their horses. They are tiny figures against the backdrop of the towering mountains of the Himalayas. They make a striking pair perched on horseback high above Simla, queen of the North Indian hill stations. The man, tall and commanding in the saddle, turns eagerly towards the girl. She pretends at first not to understand that he wishes to speak, then reluctantly agrees to hear him out. Despite the manly posture of the man, the shy beauty of the girl, and the romantic elevation of the scene, a strikingly unromantic conversation takes place.

May Trent, twenty years old, an acknowledged belle of Simla society—beautiful, intelligent, and talented—rides with her handsome suitor, Percy Anstruther. May is not happy to hear a second proposal from her importunate suitor. Here is May's response to Percy's renewed unwelcome proposal.

> 'What can I say that will be different from the last time?' she said, her eyes filling with tears. 'It is cruel of you to make me give you and myself all this pain again! You know that I don't love you!' Then, noticing the change in his face, she added quickly, 'Oh! Don't look like that! Please don't, I can't bear it. You force me to hurt you! I don't love anybody in the way you want; I don't think I ever shall. I must be a stone—I'm not worth caring for.'
>
> 'Only give me a chance. Let me try and teach you to love me, darling,' said Anstruther hopefully [...] May unconsciously drew her reins tighter [...]
>
> 'Tell me what I should say. You know me better than anyone does. I am not happy at home; you have seen that. My parents think that they have been good to me long enough, that it is my bounden duty to get married [...] That's about the bitterest feeling a girl can have [...] that her

father and mother would gladly give her to any man who would take the trouble to support her [...]

'I shall regret having said this tomorrow, and be very much ashamed of it, but I will speak plainly for once. My mother was angry with me for refusing you last year, and said, that, as I cared for no one else, I should end by caring for you. Now I know you better than I did, but my feelings for you are unchanged. How can you ask me to marry you?'

'It sounds hopeless, but I am not easily frightened [...] Oh! Can't you trust me, May? I am some ten years older than you, and I do not speak thoughtlessly [...]'

'I may look on you merely as a means of escape, then?'

'As you will. I trust very much to time [...]'

May had unwittingly worked herself into a state of revolt against her father and mother, and the life she had led for the last two years; sooner or later most girls feel, for a time at least, that anything is better than what they have [...]

'Yes, I will marry you,' she said quietly; then, to her great surprise, she felt his arm round her, and as he kissed her, she realized what she had done.[1]

While it is simplistic to read fiction as a direct representation of the author's life, as barely disguised autobiography, it is difficult not to read this scene as taken from Trix's recent experience. Trix, like May, had received an unwanted second proposal from her suitor while spending the hot season in Simla. While she never reported the dialogue that preceded her acceptance of this second proposal, here in fiction she recreated the conversation that may well have passed between herself and her soon-to-be husband.

May agrees to marry Percy after he kisses her and then brutally crushes her hand. She knows that she does not have romantic feelings for him. She tells Percy that she has never loved a man as a husband wishes to be loved and believes that she never will. She asserts these beliefs with great certainty. She gives no explanation for her lack of feeling. This is simply how she is made. The narrator supplies these bits

---

1   Beatrice Grange, *The Heart of a Maid* (Prayagraj: A. H. Wheeler & Co., 1891), Number 8 of the Indian Railway Library, published in New York by Beatrice Kipling, *The Heart of a Maid* (New York: John W. Lovell, 1891).

of explanation. May Trent and her mother had little sympathy for each other. They had not lived together, except for a few baby years, until May returned home at eighteen. The narrator comments, 'This is one of the many evils of Anglo-Indian life [...] for the enforced separation of parent and child, the alienation of years, cannot be done away with in a few months, and half the hasty, ill-assorted marriages that take place have for a cause the fact that the girl was not happy at home'.

Trix accepted Jack's first proposal because she felt pressured to marry someone, and he seemed at first as good a choice as any other. After a few months, feeling uncertain and anxious, she reneged. After breaking off the engagement, she was aware that she had disappointed Jack, had irritated her mother, and was still faced with the same predicament—having to marry someone. When Jack proposed again, she accepted.

In the novel, May explains herself to Percy with stunning candour. She does not try to mislead him or misrepresent herself. And she seems to understand herself very clearly. Although she understands precisely how she feels, she does not at all understand why she feels this way.

Trix married Jack in Simla in June 1889 in a torrent of rain (an omen no one seemed to notice) with only a few family members in attendance. The newly married couple went off together on a tour of northern India. Just weeks into the honeymoon, Jack was ordered to interrupt the tour and leave for Burma to continue his work on the Great Survey of India. Trix did not accompany her husband to his new posting. Having been married for only a matter of weeks, Trix found herself deposited, like an unwanted parcel, back with her parents in Lahore. She had looked forward to a new role and a new life. Instead, she had been dispatched back to her family and was unexpectedly and unhappily reprising her old role as a daughter.

Alice and Lockwood took Trix in. Back with her parents, Trix had no wifely duties or family chores to take up her time, and she needed some occupation. Always comfortable with a pen in her hand, Trix picked hers up and started to write. Perhaps she had had the plot of this novel in mind for a while, perhaps she had only envisioned the dramatic proposal on horseback, perhaps she knew only the character of her heroine. The opening is surely and confidently written. The early years of the unhappy marriage ring true. The large cast of minor characters is clearly and competently introduced, and the scene in Simla is vividly set.

Although she had never written anything longer than a short story, Trix worked at a rapid pace on a complicated plot.

The novel continues: As May prepares for her wedding, she felt 'that she was entering a dungeon, worn by the steps of those who had passed before'. Her prediction proves to be correct. Three months after the wedding, May knows that there is no sympathy or comfort in her marriage to Percy. Then, she has a baby. Suddenly and wonderfully, she discovers intense feelings of love for the baby. When her baby dies suddenly, she goes mad with grief, furiously and madly accusing her husband and her mother of murder. Eventually, she calms and apathetically agrees to voyage to England to meet her husband's family. All places and people are the same to her.

Trix had reached this point in her novel when, in January of 1890, she was required once again to move. After less than six months of lodging with her parents, Trix learned that Jack, while in Burma on the Survey, had become ill with sunstroke and fever, possibly malaria, and was required to leave his post. He was on his way back to Lahore and to her. The comfortable routine that Trix had established was at an end. She was needed to care for her ailing husband. It was her duty to tend to Jack who, when she saw him, appeared to be a ghost. She was amazed at the sudden transformation of the strong soldier she had married into the pale patient who was now in her care.

Trix had been working steadily on her novel when Jack unexpectedly and, from a writer's point of view, inconveniently arrived home. She had set her several sub-plots going forward and knew where they were to end. What she had not resolved was the central conflict of the novel—the uncertain outcome of the marriage between May and Percy. Would this shaky marriage survive? Jack's poor health required not just abandoning his post, but prolonged home leave. This leave was soon granted and plans for the voyage home were set in motion. Trix needed to pack up all her things, bid farewell to her parents, and head home with her weak and defeated husband. Her novel was almost complete. She had a difficult sea voyage ahead of her, an unknown place to establish with Jack's family, and an uncertain marital future to work out with her very compromised husband. She could have postponed finishing her novel. She could have put it aside indefinitely. With so many unpredictable events in front of her, she decided to hastily conclude her novel. Passage for the voyage back to England was booked just as Trix began to write the final scenes. She set those scenes on shipboard. The end of the novel takes place at sea.

The plot continues:

Feeling dull and despairing, May sails to England. On shipboard, she reflects on her own feelings and behaviour towards Percy. She blames herself for having been meanly unforgiving and spiteful. She did too little and expected too much. She was selfish and took pleasure in being miserable.

While at sea, she considers the histories of the other girls she knows and the one new girl she meets at sea and compares their feelings with hers. She recognizes that each of them had found some happiness, even as she had made compromises and had committed errors. The frivolous young woman who marries for money and position enjoys the real benefits she attains. May's sister, although she does something shameful—being engaged while her fiancé's mad wife still lives—will eventually marry him properly and joyfully. The girl who is advised to marry for wealth and position but chooses to follow her heart's desire easily accepts the poverty that her choice includes. The new bride May meets on shipboard manages to find pleasure in what she has. May concludes that the lack of joy in her life is her own fault. Filled with regret and remorse, she vows to be a better wife. She recognizes in herself 'a kind of disdain in her mind, which now grieved her as the commission of an actual sin might have done. Life had not given her its best, so she had refused to see any good in what she had, feeling even a kind of perverted pleasure in mourning over the ruins of her happiness, though she had not given a finger-touch to try and save it from ruin'.

Just as she reaches this self-critical and possibly life-changing conclusion, her story suddenly ends. The final line of the novel comes as an unexpected blow. 'May never saw her husband again'.

The abrupt ending feels rushed and incomplete, as if the author could not imagine the heroine's softened spirit and reformed heart, did not want to make the effort to imagine it, or, having struggled to imagine it, did not sufficiently believe in it. Allowing the heroine to remain angry, accusatory, and alone was another narrative possibility Trix could not fully imagine. A reader can almost picture the author throwing up her hands, putting down her pen, and walking away in defeat.

Before marrying, May confesses that she does not think herself capable of love, calls herself a stone, and warns Percy that she is not worth caring for. After marriage, she glories in her own unhappiness and refuses to work at love. She openly acknowledges her lack of sympathy and, in fact, utter disdain for her husband. She blames herself for her shortcomings. She does not pretend that her feelings are other than what they are, although they are inconvenient and unattractive in almost every way.

She knows she could be different, she wants to be different, and the novel briefly holds out the possibility of reformation. But change is denied to her. After dangling the happy ending of reconciliation and marital concord before the reader, the author suddenly and ruthlessly cuts the possibility off. This ending seems at first to be a punishment. May repents, but too late. But it is also a reprieve. She will not have to try to make this marriage work. She is free.

In 1890, when Trix wrote *The Heart of a Maid*, it was unusual for a novel to begin with a marriage proposal. Traditionally, the marriage proposal arrived as the happy conclusion of the novel. More exceptional is the heroine herself, who accepts the proposal with stunningly bad grace and continues to struggle unsuccessfully with feelings of coldness, indifference, and repulsion. Beginning with an uncomfortable marriage proposal, the novel continues to describe a marriage as it turns sour. The unhappy heroine places the blame for the collapse of her marriage not on society or on the institution of marriage but on herself. She does not doubt the rules of society nor her role in it. She is not a rebel. May insists that it is her own unfortunate temperament that is the problem.

May is an unusual heroine in her refusal to pretend. She is remarkable for her insight into herself and for truthfully expressing her unpleasant and unusual feelings of coldness, remoteness, and rage. May's truth-telling feels, at first, like a breath of fresh air. But, as the novel progresses, her forth-rightness seems excessive and, at the death of her baby, it seems crazy. It feels good to May to be true to herself, but it also makes others feel bad. She wounds her mother and Percy. A truth-teller is simply who she is, who she must be. And she has terrible personal truths to tell.

Trix had no trouble describing this heroine and her prickly nature. She persuasively dramatized her discontent with her husband. Her passionate love for her baby and her extreme grief at the loss of the baby are less well developed. But most troubling of all was finding an appropriate and satisfying conclusion for such a heroine. Freed from her husband, and unburdened by other societal demands, she has nowhere to go. Finding no place for her to rest comfortably and feeling rushed to complete her story, Trix abruptly ended her novel inconclusively and inadequately.

The minor stories in the novel, variations on the traditional 'Marriage Plot', end well. Romantic desire drives the stories forward. The heroines are rewarded with marriage as the ultimate goal for achieving personal fulfilment and social integration. Courtship, romance, and marriage structure their stories and move inevitably to their happy endings. But May's story is left suspended and untethered.

As Trix sailed home to England with her ailing husband, perhaps she pondered the many disappointments and few joys of her short marriage. Perhaps she vowed, after some initial failure, to be a better wife, a more loving partner. Perhaps she despaired, gave up hope of finding happiness with Jack, and wished never to see him again. Perhaps, as the ending of the novel intimates, less than a year into the marriage, Trix wished her husband gone or even dead.

Fig. 15 The front cover of *The Heart of a Maid*.

In 1891, slightly more than one year into the marriage, Trix's novel, *The Heart of a Maid,* appeared under the name Beatrice Grange.² The first name of Trix's pseudonym derives from her nickname Trix, which seems to, but does not, have its origin in Beatrice. The Grange, her pen surname, was the home of her uncle and aunt, the Burne-Joneses, where she was born and spent happy school holidays. Publishing anonymously or using a pseudonym was common practice for women authors who felt the need to conform to Victorian modestly and decorum. Trix's novel, bearing so close a resemblance to recent parts of her own life, demanded disguise.

Trix did not have to trouble herself to find a publisher for her first long fictional effort. Rudyard arranged for the novel to be published by A.H. Wheeler & Co., Allahabad, India, and issued in a paper cover as Number 8 of the Indian Railway Library. The first six volumes of this series consisted entirely of short stories by Rudyard Kipling, 'Soldiers Three', 'The Gadbys', 'In Black and White', 'Under the Deodars', 'The Phantom Rickshaw' and 'Wee Willie Winkie'. These thin, cheap booklets were sold at bookstalls at Indian railway stations and had a wide circulation.

Fig. 16 The front cover of *Under the Deodars,* by Lockwood Kipling.

---

2   Ibid.

5. The Heart of a Maid

Fig. 17 The back cover of *Under the Deodars*, by *Lockwood Kipling.* This illustration is a portrait of Trix.

Trix's novel was good enough to be published on its own merits, but it was especially attractive coming with a recommendation from Rudyard, the firm's newest and most promising author. Thus, at twenty-two, Trix was the author of a published novel.

Publishing a novel at this age was a quite a feat for a young woman. Even Trix's precocious brother had not yet published a novel. Trix seemed poised for literary success.

6. Wife of Jack

I can see Trix, dressed in her most modest but still softly pretty clothes, sitting in the dimly lit Fleming drawing room. As the cold Edinburgh rain falls steadily outside, she tries to make herself comfortable on her hard chair. This is her first introduction to the Fleming family. She had been warned that the Flemings were serious and severe, but she hoped to charm them. Despite the Flemings' cool greetings and prim postures, Trix chatters on about her recent rough voyage from India. Her descriptions of the roiling seas, the rocking ship, and the retching passengers are met with discouraging silences and barely polite nods. The dour and stiff Flemings in their dull tweeds and sensible brogues assess Trix's brightly coloured clothes and her many necklaces and are confirmed in their earlier long-distance judgment of her as a vain, silly Bohemian. They know she has the habit of scribbling stuff and publishing it, and they find no delight in her clever remarks, sprinkled, as usual, with quotations. To the stolid and unsmiling Flemings, Trix seems frivolous and flighty, interested in poetry, drama, and other useless things, for which they have only disdain. Trix is surprised and hurt by this cool reception. She is used to being liked, even admired, and feels that she is failing with her in-laws. Even worse, she begins to recognize that she will always fail, that the Flemings will always judge her harshly. Jack offers her little comfort or reassurance.

Fig. 18 Trix (far right) and Jack (far left) early in their marriage.

When Trix and Jack had arrived in England four days earlier, on 10 February 1890, their marriage, just eight months old, was already tense and troubled. Jack was ill, uncomfortable, and full of complaint. Trix was vexed that the fever he had developed in Burma hung on so persistently. She knew it was her job to get Jack speedily to Edinburgh where he could be looked after by his family, but she longed to stay in London to spend a little time with Rudyard, who was now living there.

The day after she arrived in London, Trix insisted that she pay a visit to Rudyard at his Embankment chambers. When she arrived at his modest apartment, she was shocked to find him miserably depressed. He was suffering from the gloom of the London winter but also from the end of his short-lived engagement to Carrie Taylor. He poured out his sorrows to Trix, but she kept her troubles to herself. Had his spirits been better, she might have shared her sorrows, but Rudyard seemed barely able to carry his own load of grief. Trix begged Jack to allow her to remain with

Rudyard in London a few days longer, but Jack was determined to reach Scotland as soon as possible. After just four days in London, Jack and Trix proceeded to his family's home in Edinburgh. There, on 14 February, Trix had her first encounter with the Fleming family.

Two days after her initial appearance in the Fleming drawing room, on another damp, raw, drizzling Edinburgh day, Trix walked to church with the family. As she sat in the dim, high-vaulted space, surrounded by unsympathetic and uncongenial Flemings, she considered how foreign this family was, how different they were from her own eccentric, artistic, and dramatic people. At the end of the service, as she tried to rise, she felt light-headed and dizzy. Suddenly, her strength gave way, and she fell to the ground. Faint and frightened, she was helped to her feet, led from the church, and carried home. Two days with the Flemings had literally brought her to her knees.

Fig. 19 Photograph of Trix early in her marriage to Jack.

Fig. 20 Photograph of Trix early in her marriage to Jack.

After her collapse in church, she rallied. She was determined to carry on as was required. She attended dinner parties, viewed the International Exhibition of Science, Art and Industry in Edinburgh, travelled to Aberdeen, and accompanied Jack on his many golfing trips. While in Edinburgh, which she soon likened to 'a beautiful woman with a bad temper',[1] she made a few more attempts to impress the dull Flemings. Staying with Jack's family, she longed to be with her own extraordinary relatives—the Macdonald sisters, Burne-Joneses, Poynters, and Baldwins—in Southern England, or with Rudyard in London. When she was given leave to visit her family, she worried she was neglecting and possibly offending Jack's people. Pulled in opposite directions, she was comfortable nowhere. Struggling just to stay on her feet, she had no time or space to write, or even to think about writing.

---

1   Lorna Lee, p. 78.

Fig. 21 Photograph of Trix early in her marriage to Jack.

Fig. 22 Photograph of Trix early in her marriage to Jack.

Despite Jack's discouragement and displeasure, Trix travelled alone to London in May to be with her unhappy brother. He had been so depressed that he had asked his parents for help, and they had made the long trip from Lahore to London in response to his extraordinary call. With Trix's arrival, the Family Square was briefly reunited. Rudyard's fame, newly but firmly established, had worn him down. Having recovered from his broken engagement, he had been flirting again with his first love, Flo Garrard, who had, by chance, appeared on the scene. The affair with Flo, like the engagement to Caroline Taylor, had ended badly. With so many disappointments, Rudyard was grateful to have his family around him. Although anxious about herself, Trix was happy to be with her family and to be, even for a few weeks, a part of the old Family Square.

She continued to keep her own worries to herself. She did not want to burden her parents, already concerned about Rudyard, with her own distress. Embarrassed and ashamed, she did not want to tell them of her growing discontent with Jack. She was grateful to be mercifully removed from her husband, who was irritating her more and more. She and Jack were already quarrelling and having frequent 'royal rows'.[2]

After less than a month in London, Trix returned to Scotland to be with Jack on their first anniversary, her twenty-second birthday, 11 June. While Jack pursued his passion for golf at St. Andrew's and other courses, Trix tagged along. Despite bad weather, he often played two rounds a day. And despite all the exercise and fresh air, he slept badly and was often ill. Trix did not feel well either and had a second dramatic fainting spell in church. Both frequently took to their beds with colds, flu, and other complaints. When Jack and Trix made a trip to York, they fought so bitterly that they visited the York Minster separately. By this time, their fighting had become a habit. Trix reported that they were 'fighting as usual',[3] as if it were a regular part of the marriage, just one year on.

In the spring of 1891, hoping to find some relief from their continuing health problems, Trix and Jack travelled to Europe, to spas in Nuremberg and Carlsbad. They consulted doctors, took the waters, and went for long walks, but they improved little. In the end, they concluded that the waters were useless. In the autumn of 1891, Trix returned to London and had some time to be with her parents, uncles, aunts, and cousins, followed by a few days' visit with the Baldwins at Wilden. But soon she was required to go to Scotland and spent the new year 1892 visiting Jack's sister Moona Richardson at Gattonside House in Melrose, a small town in the Scottish Borders. Moving from the intellectual excitement of her own family in London to the dull world of the Flemings in

---

2   Trix Kipling, letter to Maud Diver, 16 March 1898.
3   Ibid.

small-town Scotland, Trix once again measured the vast gulf between her family and his.

After one year with Jack, Trix had few illusions about her marriage. She and Jack had incompatible and unalterable temperaments. Jack was naturally self-contained, undemonstrative, often dour, while Trix was extroverted and effusive. Trix, who spoke with speed and verve, became more and more annoyed by her husband's slow, monotonous voice, which often made her clasp her hands together in silent, intense irritation. Trix had married Jack to make him happy, and she wanted assurances from him that his happiness was now complete. But it seemed to her that marriage had made very little difference to him. In fact, he had been ill and ailing almost from the start. And her feelings, which had always been cool, had not grown warmer, as Jack had promised they would. She had initially been attracted to Jack's reassuring solidity and certainty, but she now recognized his strength as rigidity and withdrawal. Similarly, Jack, who had married Trix to bring spirit and sparkle into his life, soon recognized that his wife's constant chatter and nervous energy annoyed and agitated him. They had both discovered that the traits that had initially attracted them to each other were exactly the traits that now most irritated and repelled them. The marriage, which was meant to provide support, if not love or passion, failed even at that.

In 1892, Rudyard married Caroline Balestier, a wife displeasing to Trix as well as the Kipling parents. Caroline, always called Carrie, was, in the most negative assessment, hard, bossy, interfering, and opinionated. From a more positive point of view, she appeared forceful, intense, and courageous. Rudyard had been an extremely close companion and collaborator with her charming brother Wolcott, who had come from America to London with bold literary ambitions. Rudyard's friendship with Wolcott lasted only a few years. Wolcott died suddenly of typhoid at the age of thirty. At Wolcott's death, Rudyard was impressed by Carrie, who competently took charge of his affairs. Although Rudyard was uncertain about Carrie and unready for marriage, he proposed to her very shortly after Wolcott's untimely death.

Soon after meeting Carrie, Alice recognized her forceful character and her decided intentions towards Rudyard. She immediately and unhappily sensed that Carrie was going to hustle Rudyard into marriage and that the Balastiers were going to replace the Family Square and become Rudyard's chosen intimates. She was fully justified in her fears, as Rudyard precipitously married Carrie and moved with her to the Balastier family home in Brattleboro, Vermont.

The first two years of Trix's marriage were not ideal—a rushed honeymoon followed by an unexpected separation and darkened by Jack's steep and sudden decline from good health to illness. Traveling to meet the Flemings in Scotland, then to spas on the continent to regain their health, they were almost constantly on the move.[4] Trix had had no chance to be a proper wife, run a household, or establish a routine. She also had had no privacy or leisure to write.

Then, in early 1892, after almost two years of home leave in England, Scotland, and on the continent, Trix and Jack returned to India to begin their married life together. Trix was ready to start again as the new bride of an officer under the Raj. She knew the requirements and restrictions of this position. She had been brought up to respect the rules of class, caste, precedence, and power and to love, cherish, and obey her husband.

Home was Calcutta, the capital as well as the commercial and industrial centre of India.

Jack was stationed here in his position with the Great Survey. The sprawling, busy city was crammed with an endless, ceaseless stream of people, causing a constant bustle and din. Warehouses, factories, and offices lined the docks on one side of the Hooghly River, while, on the banks of the other side, the wide lawns of grand mansions sloped down to the river's edge. Monumental buildings of various designs—Grecian, Indo-Gothic, Italian, Egyptian, Turkish—with columns, cupolas, and domes sprang up in unlikely profusion in the sky above the city. The centre of the city was a jumble of wide avenues, dingy lanes, rows of dark shops and offices, stalls selling garlands of flowers, woven baskets, pottery images of the gods, small gated temples, open pumps with crowds washing, and always beggars clambering and pleading.

Used to the relative calm of Lahore, Trix was unprepared for the noise, stench, heat, dust, and squalor of the city. But she was rarely required to visit the poorest, shabbiest, and dingiest parts of the city, as she and Jack

---

4   Trix's fan reproduced in Lorna Lee, pp. 118–19. The fan, now in the Kipling Collection at Yale University, shows Trix traveling constantly in the fall of 1891 back and forth between Edinburgh, London, St. Andrew's, Wilden, and Blanefield before returning to India.

lived in the well-ordered 'White Town', where the streets were set out on a regular grid. Here, the spacious bungalows of the British were set apart from the dilapidated shacks and huts of the Indians. The British lived in large houses surrounded by expansive lawns and elaborate gardens, decorated with potted plants, and perfumed with jasmine. Nearby were the beautiful, lushly planted Eden Gardens, where Trix walked in the leafy shade to avoid the mid-day heat. In the evening, she and Jack strolled on the Strand beside the beautiful Hooghly River, where brass bands often played.

Trix was familiar with the Indian climate and the British seasonal changes of residence. In April, following the usual pattern, Trix often visited Lahore. From May to November, she retreated from the heat to the hill stations of Mussoorie or Simla. In the cool weather she resided in Calcutta, her primary residence.

After two years of marriage, Trix finally had the responsibility of setting up and running a household. She had wanted to take on these wifely duties for a long time and undertook them with enthusiasm—choosing furniture, fabrics, and paint colours. Although she was not responsible for cooking or cleaning, she busied herself with minor household chores—mending, tidying, and folding and airing the clothes, cushions, and napkins. She wanted to show Jack that she could make things neat and comfortable. Jack was very particular about his surroundings and had an eagle eye for the details of both décor and dress. Trix was pleased that Jack took an interest in the order of the house and the smartness of her dress, but it took time and trouble to keep up to his mark.

Although Trix understood the complicated caste system, she had never before had to operate in it as a memsahib, literally 'the master's woman'. The Indian caste system, more complicated even than the British class system, organized her interactions with Indians—mistress to servants. The simple household machinery was run by a multitude of servants—to cook, to clean, to wait at table, to attend to ladies' dress, hair, and toilette. Like most of the English memsahibs, Trix expected her servants to understand and adjust to English ways without herself adjusting to Indian manners and habits. She learned to speak some small bits of their language in order to have her household run smoothly.

Occasionally, Trix ventured into the bustling open markets, where she shopped among a profusion of stalls selling an eccentric assortment goods—cotton, silks, jewels, slippers, necklaces, and spices. Shop after shop displayed brightly coloured saris, hanging like banners. Trix was never comfortable among the running porters, pushing crowds, and beggars with crutches, bandages, and missing limbs and eyes. Scrawny dogs with open sores, chickens, goats, and buffaloes made it dangerous to walk from stall to stall. She feared losing her way among the jumble of bicycles, rickshaws, oxcarts, and carriages. Filthy piles of bundles and baskets impeded her steps. On most days, Trix stayed home and sent her servants to the closed Hogg Market to buy supplies for the house. She became a clever hostess, improvising meals and entertainments for the unexpected guests Jack often brought home. When she was not obliged to host parties, she attended with good grace and good cheer an endless round of garden, tea, tennis, and dinner parties.

This domestic routine was interrupted by long trips to the jungle, where Jack was required to go for his work on the Survey. Trix accompanied him and stayed in several jungle camps for months at a time. Sleeping under a canvas tent, she found camp life mostly delightful. The conditions were hardly primitive. There were cane chairs, tables with starched cloths, silver and china, makeshift chests and dressing tables, and always an abundance of servants to cook, clean, set up, and replenish stores of food. In camp, Trix was happy to be excused from attending social events and from maintaining the house up to Jack's standards. In the early mornings, she took horseback rides through the lush green mango groves. She relaxed under the stars in the beautiful cool of the evenings. During the many idle hours of the day, when Jack was occupied with his surveying duties, Trix had uninterrupted leisure. At last, Trix was able to resume her writing. She had the time, the privacy, and the energy. She did not attempt another novel but returned with spirit and verve to short, mostly satiric pieces.

During one long period in camp, Trix produced a series of dialogues, which were published anonymously in *The Pioneer*, the Allahabad-based sister paper to *The Civil and Military Gazette*. These brief sketches, which ran from April to December 1892, while never attributed to Trix, unmistakably bear her mark.[5] Trix's collected unpublished writings

---

5 'Wife in Office', *The Pioneer*, 2 January 1892; 'My Sister-in-Law's Alarms', *The Pioneer*, 28 April 1892; 'Mrs John Brown Protests', *The Pioneer*, 7 May 1892; 'Hunter on Marriage', *The Pioneer*, 12 May 1892; 'My Aunt-in-Law's House', *The Pioneer*, 19 May 1892; 'Casual Love', *The Pioneer*, 22 June 1892; 'The Judge's Whist', *The Pioneer*,

include a series of strikingly similar dialogues (written years later) featuring a married couple named George and Mabel.⁶ That unpublished series and these sketches for *The Pioneer* present marriage as a comedy of miscommunication between a mismatched husband and wife. *The Pioneer* pieces are signed alternately John Brown and Mrs John Brown, obvious pen names.

In the first piece, titled 'Wife in Office' and published on 28 April 1892, a husband complains of his wife having invaded his office. She defends herself with stubborn self-righteousness. They are an evenly matched pair of selfish whiners.

In the second, titled 'My Sister-in-law's Alarms' and published on 12 May 1892, signed by John Brown, the put-upon husband complains again—this time about a visit from his sister-in-law, who is a nervous, selfish, disagreeable guest. John's wife naturally defends her sister. (Mrs Brown is named Winnie, the name Trix used later for the heroine of her novel *A Pinchbeck Goddess*.)

The third in the series, published on 19 May 1892, is signed by Mrs John Brown and is titled 'Mrs John Brown Protests'. The title accurately describes the intention, but the effect is self-serving carping and complaining. Mrs Brown reveals herself to be as silly as her husband has portrayed her.

The fourth, 'Hunter on Marriage', published on 22 June 1892, contains more marital friction and fault-finding. In the fifth, 'My Aunt-in-Law's House', published on 7 September 1892, John dutifully agrees with every foolish thing Aunt Hetty says about her house. The sixth, 'Casual Leave', published on 27 October 1892, describes a shopping spree where a long-suffering husband accompanies his wife as she buys a dress, gloves, and hat. The seventh, 'The Judge's Whist', published on 24 November 1892, ends with the teaser 'but that, as Kipling says, is another story'. It catalogues the annoying habits of a card player. The last of the series, published on 1 December 1892, 'In Shadowy Thoroughfares of Thought', is a dialogue in which Mrs Brown continually interrupts her husband. He is, as usual, long-suffering and silent. She is insufferable and unstoppable.

---

7 September 1892; 'In Shadowy Thoroughfares of Thought', *The Pioneer*, 27 October 1892; 'Our Own Correspondent', *The Pioneer*, 24 November 1892; 'In the Blues', *The Pioneer*, 1 December 1892.

6   'Prose of Trix Kipling', in Lorna Lee, pp. 170–266.

All of the dialogues begin with a literary quotation, and most are dotted throughout with many more—from Shakespeare, Samuel Johnson, and Rabelais. Constant quotation was Trix's hallmark, in writing and speech.

Also signed by John Brown is 'Our Own Correspondent', published on 2 January 1892. In this essay, Mr Brown gives a lesson in how to write boring clichés. He recommends reporting at length on the weather and on the most trivial local doings. He remarks that only the author bothers to read the 'turn-overs'. These short pieces were the continuation of a story begun at the front of the paper. 'Plain Tales from the Hills', written by Rudyard and Trix five years earlier, were the most popular and best known turn-overs published and read by the British in India. Thus, this is a reverse compliment and an inside joke from Trix to Rudyard.

John Brown also signed a piece titled 'In the Blues' (published on 7 May 1892), where he, as an undersecretary, describes in tedious detail the need for systematically colour-coding files.

These pieces, like many in *The Pioneer*, appeared anonymously. They have never been positively attributed to Trix, but the Winnie and John Brown exchanges sound very much like Trix's later George and Mabel dialogues, and they bear Trix's signature use—perhaps overuse—of quotation. In all of them, the speaker or writer damns him or herself with his or her own words. Trix was especially adept in the use of this narrative device.

The Flemings had been married three years when these pieces appeared, enough time for Trix to know well the shape and sound of marital discord. She had also had enough time and enough art to transform spousal disagreement, dissatisfaction, and resignation into a brilliant comic routine. She easily mimicked both parts—the silly jabbering wife and the silent suffering husband. With great exuberance and confidence, Trix turned her possibly tragic marriage into delicious, dark comedy.

Trix did publish one story under her own name, a short and slight tragic love story titled 'At a Christmas Ball', in the Christmas edition of *Black and White* in December 1892.[7] At a club ball, a handsome artillery

---

7   Alice M. Kipling, 'At a Christmas Ball', *Black and White*, December (1892). This is a ghostly version of the story Trix liked to tell of a handsome officer who pledged himself to her and then died in battle six months later. See page 64.

officer promises a fair, pretty girl that he will return in a year to claim three dances from her. She waits longingly for his return but learns, after six months, that he has died of cholera. When she sadly attends the next annual club ball, she sees his ghost... perhaps.

Although Trix was productive and content in camp for a while, after months of living in tents at Purunpur, she longed to return to Calcutta to get her house put to rights. She dreamed of curtains and cushions and all the little details of framing pictures, hemming napkins, and shining silver. Returning to Calcutta meant returning to social life with Jack's fellow officers and their often new, young wives. Trix, by now, had accepted her role as social hostess and guest, and had learned to accommodate herself to the company of silly, simpering women.

Trix was not like these women who became the wives of army officers under the Raj. The young women who went to India to seek or meet a husband, in what were called 'fishing fleets', were not the best-educated or best-connected girls. If they could have, they would have married men back home in England. Conventional behaviour was expected of them. They had been educated to be proper wives of the most desirable men they could attract. They practiced on the piano, rode, and played golf and tennis. They could make up a fourth hand at bridge. Sewing and sketching were their preferred hobbies. Drawing or flower arranging were acceptable enthusiasms. They could dance and make superficial conversation at parties. They were educated but decidedly not overeducated.

They were taught to remain British, not to let down the race, the Raj, or the British Empire. The worst bad form was 'going native', knowing or caring too much about India.

Encouraged to ignore India, cling to the ideas of home, and establish a community that reminded them of what was familiar, British women found Indian ways uncivilized, Indian music unpleasant, and Indian paintings garish. Indians were considered useful only as servants, and as servants were constantly found to be inadequate. Few English women learned the language apart from a few words of kitchen Hindustani or knew anything about the culture.

These women were expected to support their husbands, to further their husbands' careers, and be useful to their husbands' advancement. Anglo-Indian society was especially backward in granting women any other role. There were few opportunities in India to take nursing classes, attend lectures, or visit hospitals and bring flowers or relief to the old or the sick. Volunteering or performing good works was viewed with suspicion, and young women, who needed to defer to their elders, could not undertake a service if the older memsahib in their area had no interest in the project.

Most of the young women who came out to India met the challenges of life in India—boredom, loneliness, homesickness, dirt, disease, and dangers of various kinds—with courage and good humour, but many others grew depressed and were sooner or later defeated.

Trix was obviously more intelligent, more cultured, and more broad-minded than most of these women, who accepted without question the prevailing culture, which discouraged curiosity, individuality, or originality. But she was not completely unlike them. She was not overly intellectual, had no excessive enthusiasms, was not careless or faithless, did not get too involved in Indian culture, or go native. Like them, Trix had little curiosity about the strange people among whom she was living—Sikhs, Moslems, Hindus, Parsees, as well as the many castes within these groups.

Trix was obliged to socialize with these women when she was with Jack and his fellow officers. But, on her own, Trix found a small group of like-minded women friends who met regularly for tea and talk. These women, including Nettie Webb, an old school fellow from Notting Hill, Sibyl Healey, and Violet Marshall, appreciated Trix's lively conversation and were curious about the stories she wrote for publication. They approved of her ambitions to succeed as a novelist. Trix confined her conversations about novels and poetry to this chosen group.

Maud Marshall—sister of Violet, and Trix's friend from her first voyage home and from her teenage years in Dalhousie and Simla—was initially a central part of this literary group. Like Trix, she dreamed of becoming a novelist. Soon after her marriage to Thomas Diver in 1890, Maud moved to Ceylon, abandoning India and her group of friends there. Trix felt her loss deeply. From a distance, Maud remained Trix's dearest friend and the strongest supporter of her literary hopes.

Maud and Trix were constant correspondents, sharing personal and literary news. They recommended books to each other, quoted favourite lines of poetry, explained their narrative likes and dislikes, and, most importantly, exchanged and edited each other's manuscripts. Maud was disciplined and productive, sending Trix many pages to approve or amend. Trix envied and admired Maud's industry, while always chastising herself for laziness. Over the years, Trix and Maud suggested plots and characters for each other, sent their stories to the same magazines, dealt with the same editors, and complained of the same publishing problems and payment delays. Maud was crucial to Trix's self-confidence and development as a writer during the early years of her marriage in Calcutta.

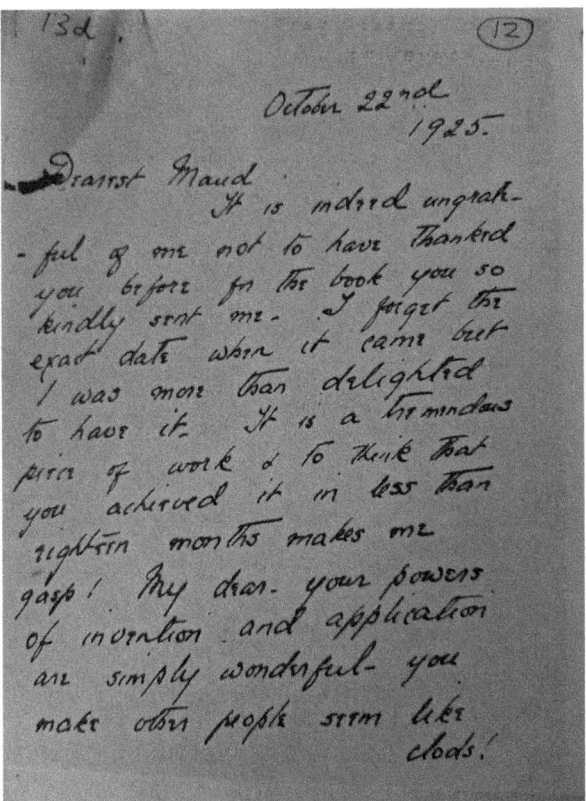

Fig. 23 A letter from 1925 from Trix to Maud Diver (part 1).

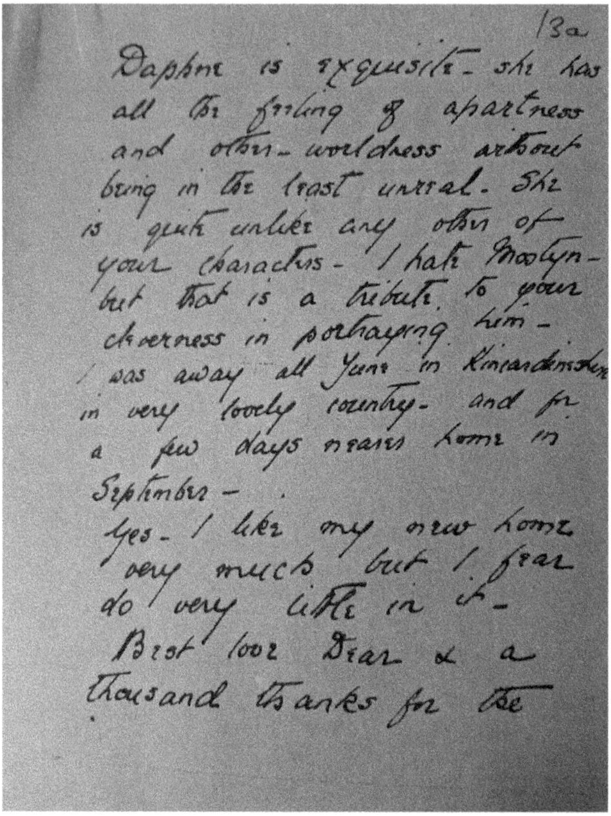

13a

Daphne is exquisite – she has all the feeling of apartness and other-worldliness without being in the least unreal. She is quite unlike any other of your characters – I hate Mostyn – but that is a tribute to your cleverness in portraying him – I was away all June in Kincardineshire in very lovely country – and for a few days nearer home in September – .

Yes – I like my new home very much but I fear do very little in it –

Best love Dear & a thousand thanks for the

Fig. 24 A letter from 1925 from Trix to Maud Diver (part 2).

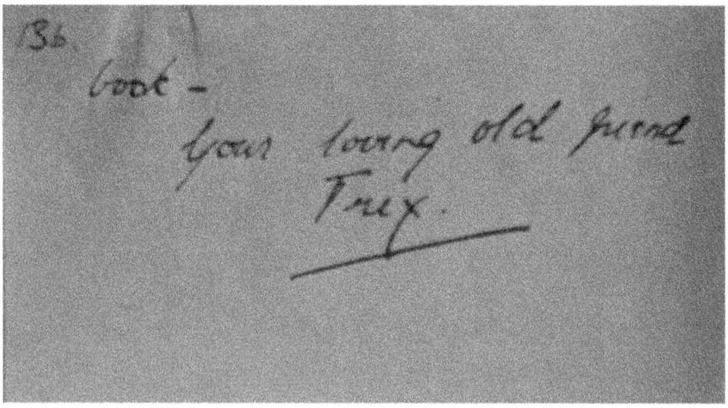

13b

book –

Your loving old friend
Trix.

Fig. 25 A letter from 1925 from Trix to Maud Diver (part 3).

Two years after marrying Thomas Diver, Maud gave birth to her first and only child, Cyril. Maud and Trix had married at about the same time. Maud quickly fulfilled her wifely duty by producing a son and heir. Trix did not have a child early in her marriage as was the norm, and this was a great personal sadness as well as a great failing in the eyes of her society. Motherhood was expected of British wives everywhere but especially in India, where children represented a stake in the community and a consciousness that the ruling caste would endure. A childless wife was considered not simply unfortunate, but unpatriotic. In the first year of her marriage, instead of producing a child, Trix wrote and published a novel. While her childlessness was painful to her, she never explained it and rarely referred to it. Trix's early experiences—abandonment by her parents, possible abuse by Harry, lack of privacy, and invasion of her personal space by Mrs Holloway—may all have contributed to making sexual life problematic for her. Her childlessness was a continual sadness to her, although she never revealed how deep the sadness nor its source. She was devoted to the children of her friends and to her nieces and nephews. She entertained them with stories and magic tricks, sent them presents of books and pictures, and proudly displayed their photographs. In her fiction, Trix imagined children making a great difference in the fate of a marriage, but, having none herself, she could not know how they might have affected her own marriage. Nor could she know how motherhood might have changed her.

If she could not produce a child, she could be a proper wife, a competent hostess, a charming guest, and a published author.

7. A Pinchbeck Goddess

Moving about as the seasons changed from Calcutta to Mussoorie and to jungle camps, Trix dutifully looked after her house and her husband, but she also made time for herself to write. Unable to work with interruptions, she rose early before the rest of the household awoke and took her pen and paper out in the cool morning air. Resisting what she thought of as her own slothful nature, she produced story after story. Despite publishers' excuses, delays, and rejections, she gamely persisted in sending her stories out to many of the leading literary magazines of the day—*Temple Bar, Argosy, The Queen, The Gentlewoman,* and others.

Her greatest support came from her continued correspondence with her friend Maud Diver, who wrote with constancy from Ceylon. Corresponding with her parents, now in Southern England, also provided some comfort. In 1893, Lockwood had retired from his position in Lahore, and he and Alice had returned to England. Rudyard, married to Carrie, living in Vermont and moving farther and farther away from the family, had little time for Trix. Already famous and traveling the world, he never returned to live in India after the age of twenty-three. Great distances separated Trix from the members of the Family Square.

Most of Trix's stories were not unlike the 'Plain Tales from the Hills' she had written years earlier. They were longer but still light and clever. In April 1894, *The Pall Mall Magazine* accepted 'The Little Pink House', although to Trix's annoyance, they did not publish it until August. This unusually dark story is a stark cautionary tale about an innocent English girl who comes to India to marry but refuses, with fatal consequences, to alter her way of life. With no curiosity or interest in the East, 'she lived in India, save for the wide difference of heat, discomfort, and loneliness, exactly as she would have lived in England'.[1] In March 1895, the editor of *The Pall Mall Gazette* published 'A Woman of Seasons'[2], after having expressed reservations about its length. The story has a sophisticated and suspenseful structure. The narrator of the story (and the reader) is intrigued and mystified by a woman she meets at a party, who, on every subsequent meeting, seems to be a different person. At first, she is self-centred and frivolous, later she is charitable and self-sacrificing, later still she is dreamy and debauched. Eventually, the baffled narrator learns that the woman is a series of poses, lies, and make-believe.

Although the narrator solves the riddle of the woman's personality variations, she never understands why the woman chooses to present herself in these poses, nor how these false selves serve her for good or ill. A woman with no true self, who invents a false self or a series of false selves is a character who appears repeatedly in Trix's fiction. Trix was quick to hear a false note or notice a fake attitude and was particularly scornful of attitudinizing, especially over children. She took wicked pleasure in reprising the 'come-and-be-kissed-my-precious' scenes that featured reluctant children and gushing adults that had been performed before her. The woman of seasons is a series of attitudes and has no true self.

Trix well understood the necessity and the utility of pretence. Imposture was a strategy many women used to land a desirable husband, without even acknowledging or understanding what they were doing. Many ordinary, clever women, not imposters or outlaws, practiced being what they thought men wanted them to be. They did not consider themselves to be liars or deceivers, but simply alert and aware of the values of the society in which they lived. Most women had internalized their society's preferred feminine roles and felt these roles as internal assumptions, not as external controls. Pretence, sometimes as inconsequential as professing an interest in sport or orchids or as crucial as declaring love or swearing fidelity, was not viewed as unnatural or untruthful. Trix, having to disguise her true feelings from Mrs Holloway as a child, was especially sensitive to pretence and especially keen in spotting and describing it. Although she understood the initial pain

---

1   Beatrice Kipling, 'The Little Pink House', *The Pall Mall Magazine* (1894); reprinted in Lorna Lee, pp. 297–304.
2   Beatrice Kipling, 'A Woman of Seasons', *The Pall Mall Gazette, March* (1895).

and the eventual peril of disguising and denying one's true self, she was reluctant to expose these consequences too fiercely or explore them too deeply. Her society approved and rewarded pretence when it was applied gracefully, gently, or, best of all, invisibly.

It is likely that Trix completed, although she did not publish, a short story titled 'Ricochet or Boomerang's Return'[3] during this time. The story focuses on a young and attractive unmarried woman, who, as a caprice, weaves a complicated web of malice and deceit. After making mischief for a husband and wife and sowing discord between them, she transfers her affection from the husband to his elder brother. The brother flirts and toys with her, as she chatters and giggles. While her feelings actually grow deeper, his remain shallow. He interprets her malicious and flirtatious behaviours as part of her light and silly nature and never takes her seriously. And thus, her own spite and hatred spoil her chances to capture a man she cares for. The story ends, 'She at the one time of her life when straightness mattered most, was deliberately crooked'.[4]

The story is flawed, as many of Trix's stories are, by the young woman's lack of motivation. She is unaccountably malicious and spiteful. She hardly cares for the husband she tries to seduce and has no reason at all to hate the wife. Yet she manoeuvres and manipulates with great energy and some invention to win the husband's favour and deride and diminish the wife. Why she bothers to do this is never explained. When she transfers her attentions onto the brother and is rejected, she suffers appropriately. But her punishment is hardly the ingenious retaliation the title of the story promises. Like May in *The Heart of a Maid*, this young woman seems insufficiently motivated in her bad nature and her bad behaviour. She, at least, is properly punished for her malice.

Trix also completed the only short love story she ever wrote but was afraid her parents would think she had not handled the subject delicately enough. 'Waiting for Cargo' was the simple name of this story, which did not survive her parents' scrutiny or her own reservations.

---

3   Alice Fleming, 'Ricochet or Boomerang's Return', dated 30.12.36 but probably from the mid-1890s. Never published, the manuscript is written in a very neat, even hand, as if copied from another earlier and messier manuscript, probably dating from this earlier period, mid-1890s. Trix definitely did not write this in 1936.

4   Ibid. In manuscript form.

Having competently managed her household and cared for her often ailing and complaining husband, Trix gained permission to return alone for a visit to England. She had been separated from her parents for two years. In the spring of 1895, Trix set sail for England without Jack. On the way, she stopped in Ceylon for a three-day visit with Maud. This was a rare treat, a chance to spend a little time with Maud's husband Thomas and her toddler son Cyril, but most importantly a time to talk at length with Maud. Although Maud was thin and pale-cheeked, she talked energetically and enthusiastically about her work, detailing her short story ideas and encouraging Trix's plan for her second novel. This brief visit strengthened Trix's resolve to begin the new novel she had been mulling over for many years. The two old friends spent their time together in what Trix called an 'orgie of talk'.[5] The all-night conversations so exhausted Trix that she slept the whole day after her visit, but she enjoyed every minute of her time with Maud.

From Ceylon, she sailed for England on the S.S. Simla and, by July, arrived in London. Most of this visit was spent with the Kipling parents in Tisbury. Lockwood and Alice had settled in a modest pleasant house, The Gables, in Tisbury, Wiltshire—about a dozen miles from Salisbury. They had considered settling in Rottingdean, near the Burne-Joneses, but Alice did not wish to be too close to her sister. Tisbury was sufficiently distant from all her relatives.

From the summer of 1895 until the spring of 1896, Trix remained in Tisbury with her parents. She took one break in the fall of 1895 to dutifully visit her in-laws in Scotland. As before, she was hurt by the small-minded prudery of her mother-in-law, who made little effort to hide her low opinion of her son's shallow and childless bride.

Without the distractions of caring for Jack, running a household, and maintaining a social schedule, Trix had time to focus on her own work. During this relaxed and calm year in Tisbury, Trix worked steadily on her second novel, *A Pinchbeck Goddess*. As a new bride almost a decade earlier, Trix had written her first novel, *The Heart of a Maid*, also while staying with her parents when Jack was in Burma on the Survey. Then, as now, Lockwood and Alice provided a peaceful and private space for Trix. This time, Trix showed them the manuscript in progress and welcomed their comments and suggestions. With Lockwood and Alice,

---

5   Trix Kipling, letter to Maud Diver, 20 June 1897.

both writers, immediately involved in the work, Trix completed a draft of her second novel.

In the summer of 1896, just as Trix was leaving for the return to India, she missed the chance to meet with Rudyard and Carrie, who were to return from their disastrous American experiment just a few months later in September. Rudyard and Carrie had tried to live near Carrie's family in Brattleboro, Vermont, building a house, 'Naulahka', there. This experiment had ended badly with accusations, law suits, and estrangements.

On her return to India, Trix joined Jack at Mussoorie, one of the less fashionable hill stations. During this hot season, she allowed herself to ignore many of the usual entertainments and spent much of her time writing—correcting and refining *Pinchbeck*. She wrote other small pieces, including verses titled 'The Cry of the Mother', which caused a stir. The poem, about the sorrows of young mothers whose children return to England, excited passionate public argument in *The Pioneer*.[6] The poem prompted a heated exchange of letters, including, on the one hand, complaint that the poem was morbid, dreary, and sentimental and, on the other hand, praise for its true deep feeling. Trix was thrilled to have caused a controversy in print.

Although Trix always claimed that her writing wasn't serious, referring to her short pieces published in *The Pioneer* as 'Pi scribbles'[7], her private thoughts and hopes may have been very different. To Maud, she wrote that her stories were just for her own amusement. It was her household duties that demanded and deserved her serious attention. If she neglected the house in order to write, she felt as much to blame as if her 'diversion took the form of larking about with silly boys'.[8] At the same time, she was pleased and perhaps even proud that she was engaged in an activity that wasn't entirely frivolous. She was a writer. She had published a novel and hoped soon to publish another. She detailed to Maud an incident that had occurred one day at the club. She had been relaxing on the cool shaded veranda when a man approached her and engaged her in conversation. He had heard from talk around the club that she was about to go to camp with her husband and asked her about her preparations. He was poised to give her suggestions of

---

6   Trix Kipling, letter to Maud Diver, 30 July 1896.
7   Ibid.
8   Ibid.

ways to pass the time, but Trix assured him that she had plenty to do to occupy herself. Nonetheless, the kind man urged her to take up needle work. He recommended fret work as a fine resource for a woman in camp. Trix was annoyed by the man's presumption and condescension. She did not need to take up stupid, senseless stitching; she was writing fiction for publication. She and her correspondent Maud were not like other silly women. They were serious writers. In fact, as she prepared for camp in July 1896, Trix was imagining yet another novel, a third. Writing stories was a source of pleasure and pride, although she modestly and repeatedly asserted that the joy of it was 'utterly even ludicrously out of proportion to the worth of the thing'.[9]

While Trix was writing her light entertainments and completing her comic novel, a group of British women novelists were introducing changes to the English novel. During the years between Trix's first and second novel, 1890–1897, a 'New Realism' about the relations between the sexes appeared in fiction, featuring a rebellious heroine, the 'New Woman'. This 'New Woman', drawn in opposition to the innocent virgin or the angel about the house, was clever, ambitious, independent, and plain-spoken. She challenged age-old ideals of femininity and maternity. She wanted power, autonomy, and a place in public life. She spoke frankly about taboo subjects including sex, male promiscuity, and venereal disease. Dissatisfied with her lot in life, she refused to accept marriage and motherhood as her only destiny. She challenged social norms in order to fulfil herself—emotionally, sexually, artistically, and politically. She forcefully articulated her anger at the inequities women suffered. These heroines talked, often to excess.[10]

'New Woman' novels often began with an innocent and trusting heroine marrying a man she hardly knew. She was immediately confronted with the severe limitations of wifely duty. The new bride, possessing few political rights and oppressed by an unsympathetic husband, became disenchanted with her role as a wife and explored other unconventional and temporary ways to find fulfilment. At every turn, she was frustrated and thwarted. Eventually, she was forced to conform to her society, often with a better-chosen second husband. In

---

9 Ibid.
10 Jane Eldridge Miller, *Rebel Women: Feminism, Modernism and the Edwardian Novel* (Chicago: University of Chicago Press, 1997).

the end, these exceptional women either had to conform to the demands of their societies and accept traditional feminine roles or they had to accept life as misfits or outcasts. Alternative but terrible options were always available—renunciation, self-sacrifice, madness, and suicide.

Novelists discovered that there was no way to portray women as happy and satisfied outside of their domestic roles. Even when these novels included fierce indictments of society, and of marriage in particular, they concluded by returning their heroines to the domestic sphere, thus unintentionally supporting old-fashioned values and age-old roles. With nowhere to anchor their rebellious heroines, they usually took them shakily home. These conclusions felt contradictory to the story just concluded and were deeply unsatisfying.

Working mostly within the traditional novel form, women novelists portrayed the real lives of women in often shocking detail. Sarah Grand in *The Heavenly Twins* (1893), Emma Frances Brooke in *A Superfluous Woman*, (1894), Ella Hepworth Dixon in *The Story of a Modern Woman* (1894), Mona Caird in *The Daughters of Danaus* (1894), *Nobody's Fault* by Netta Syrett (1895), and *Gallia*, by Menie Muriel Downie (1896) described women's psychological pain as well as their physical experience of sex and childbirth. Though criticized as primitive in style and brutal in tone by male critics, many of these novels were sensational best-sellers. Sarah Grand's *The Heavenly Twins* (1893), a long polemical novel with surprising twists and turns, was a huge and scandalous success.

Nowhere does Trix mention any of these novels, authors, or their daring subjects, but it seems very likely that she read *The Heavenly Twins* and *The Beth Book* by Sarah Grand. Grand's novels were published by Heinemann, a well-known publisher (and soon to be Trix's publisher), and they were widely read. It would be surprising if she did not know of the recent trends in feminist fiction and had not read some of these novels, even though they were very different from her own fiction and the fictions of her brother and her best friend. Trix had to be aware of the ongoing struggle for women rights, especially the dramatic fight for the vote for women. Trix made only one mention of the suffrage movement in a brief postscript to a letter to Maud. 'I loathe Suffragette methods—& think they are retarding & degrading the cause of women thereby—but lonely women of independent means—widows or maids who pay taxes—ought in common fairness to have votes'.[11] Trix's objection is to methods; she does not address the larger issue of the denial of the vote to married women. As always, she makes a case for a specific instance while ignoring the larger issue of women's rights. Similarly, she never questioned the role of the British in the rule of India nor the relations between the ruling British class and the many castes of Indians.

The novels Trix does mention are by older, well-known, and mostly male novelists—American short story writer and novelist Bret Harte, French novelists (Trix could read French easily but not speak it) and short story writers, Pierre Loti, Paul Bourget, Guy de Maupassant, Victor Hugo, Alphonse Daudet, Alexandre Dumas, and Henri Greville (pen name for Alice Marie Celeste Durand); English novelists, Henry Seton Merriman, William Thackeray, Thomas Hardy, Jane Austen, and, of course, Dickens; and the Scottish novelist Samuel Crockett.

It seems likely that Trix was reading many contemporary novels, especially those written by women and those set in India. She mentioned Flora Annie Steel's mutiny book, *On the Face of the Waters* (1896), novels by Edna Lyall, Mary E. Wilkins, and Marie Coselle, and she indicated a familiarity with the current India-based writers whose stories appeared in the same magazines as her own. When Maud's first imperial romance novel was rejected, Trix recommended a more serious and less 'modern' type of publisher, indicating her knowledge of current trends in publishing. She encouraged Maud to persevere and sympathized with her disappointment.

> Don't you feel inclined to try somewhere else dear—when you have the M.S. all ready it seems to me such a pity not to. Who are the people who publish Edna Lyall's books? Not that you are in the least Edna Lyallish—but they at any rate like stories dealing with moral purposes & high endeavor. I would certainly try getting another opinion on it if I were you. One refusal is nothing—though don't I know how cast down a 'No thank you' makes one feel—Heart up dear friend & try again—As to title I prefer A Labour of Love! You know.[12]

Maud, like Lyall (the pen name of Ada Ellen Bayly) and many others was writing in this high moral vein, publishing hugely popular romantic

---

11 Trix Kipling, letter to Maud Diver, 5 March 1908.
12 Trix Kipling, letter to Maud Diver, 5 December 1896; Edna Lyall is the pseudonym of Ada Ellen Bayly (1857–1903), an English novelist.

tales. Trix often supplied the titles for Maud's stories and permitted her to use the title of her own first novel, 'The Heart of a Maid'. Maud's early stories—'Sunia: A Himalayan Idyll', 'A Brahman's Honour', 'A Moment's Madness', 'Feet of Clay', and 'When Beauty Fades' were published in the same magazines as Trix's stories.

Maud's early romantic tales had high moral purpose as well as elevated language, ornate description, and intense feeling. 'Sunia: A Himalayan Idyll', one of Maud's first published stories was published by *Longman's Magazine* in 1898. The story begins with this dramatic description of the scene. 'The pearly glimmer of dawn was over the mountains; the far-off snows looked indescribably pale and pure against the dove-like tones of the sky'. Into this landscape is introduced a girl

> The face was a pure oval, with flower-like curves of cheek and chin, and eyes of that rare pale brown which is only found among true Hill folk, and that none too frequently. A flower-like silver ornament in one of her delicate nostrils seemed set there with coquettish intent to accentuate its exquisitely tender curves. The soft fullness of her lips suggested passionate possibilities, and the scarlet of betel-nut upon them made an enchanting incident of colour amid the dusky tints of her face and dress.[13]

A brave Englishman saves this girl from being mauled by a huge shaggy bear. After securing the prize, he:

> found himself brought to a standstill by two brown arms, that clung about his boots, whilst a voice from the earth blessed him fervently and fulsomely after the fashion of the East. Stooping, he had raised the girl to her feet, with reassuring words, and, in so doing, had looked upon Sunia's face for the first time—a sensation no man would ever be likely to forget.[14]

At the dramatic conclusion of the story, the girl offers up her arm to the fatal bite of a poisonous snake rather than allow its venom to harm the man she worships and adores. Their love is never spoken.

---

13   Maud Diver, 'Sunia: A Himalayan Idyll', *Longman's Magazine* (1898). Maud Diver's novels when she began to publish them a decade later, were imperial romances, daring in their depiction of inter-racial love affairs but conventional in most other ways. Her first novel, *Captain Desmond, V.C.*, was published in 1907. Her subsequent novels, *The Great Amulet*, *Candles in the Wind*, *Far to Seek* and many more made her a global bestseller in the first half of the twentieth century.

14   Ibid.

Trix criticized her friend's stories, often warning her against overwriting. She praised 'Sunia' for its picturesque drama. She advised about pacing, delicacy, character development, and foreshadowing. She based her criticism on her own very specific and personal reactions to the text, not based on any theory of writing. Sometimes she was pleased simply by the style of a novel. Sometimes she read for the swing and sweep of the story and ignored the style. Inconsistencies didn't trouble her, but her lack of formal literary training did. She confessed to Maud, 'I wish I did know anything of the theory & technique of writing—I grope for it so very vaguely—I was thinking the other day of the things chiefly trifles that I think important to remember when one writes & I wrote them down & send them to amuse you'.[15]

When, years after publishing her first novel, Trix decided to attempt a second, she ignored traditional romance plots, new feminist trends, and her own satiric gifts, and looked backward. She returned to the safety and familiarity of a story from a decade earlier, one of the anonymously published *Plain Tales from the Hills* from 1886. The new novel, *A Pinchbeck Goddess*, was an expanded version of this brief and not especially memorable piece. Trix had been turning this plot of elaborate disguise over in her mind for a long time.

A Pinchbeck Goddess[16] has, as its central character, an imposter, a woman who takes on an actual disguise. When she first appears, she is young, unmarried, disdainful, and frigid. Her name is Madeline. When we meet her again, she is older, widowed, loud, and vulgar. Her name is Winnie.

The Introduction of the novel begins on shipboard, where *The Heart of a Maid* left off. A young woman is traveling from Bombay to England after a mortifying defeat. Madeline, almost thirty years old, is returning to England to be with her tyrannical Aunt Agatha after an unfortunate season in India. She was raised an orphan by this terrible aunt, who had monitored her every thought. Thus, she had learned to conceal her real thoughts and fabricate false ones. An older lady had taken her to India for a year with the intention of finding her a husband. Madeline had stubbornly and disdainfully resisted these matrimonial schemes, which she found humiliating. After driving away all the men who had

---

15 Trix Kipling, letter to Maud Diver, 1 May 1897.
16 J. M. Fleming (Alice M. Kipling), *A Pinchbeck Goddess*; dedicated 'To My Brother'.

approached her, she had become morbid and bitter. Having made poor use of her natural beauty, she returned home with no hope for the future. She had been the author of her own defeat. As she arrives in England, she learns that her detested Aunt Agatha has died.

In Chapter I, the scene and characters abruptly change. Without explanation, a new set of characters is introduced in a new setting. Winnie and Janet are unpacking in Simla, the summer hill station for the British in India. Winnie is the opposite of Madeline, who was a 'dowdy frump'. Winnie is a pinchbeck (sham, spurious, counterfeit) goddess. Winnie's husband has died, and she has a six-year-old daughter she has left behind in England. She is a vulgar woman who dyes her hair, wears makeup, and ornaments herself with gaudy jewels.

A large cast of female characters take their places in the novel. Nancy Ivey is a sweet young girl, who loves Noel Curtis, who loves her in return but whose prospects are uncertain. Lilian is an ungenerous wife with an unhappy temperament, whose husband disciplines her by being cold, distant, and silent. There is a corresponding cast of male characters. Gilmour, an eligible and charming man, is attracted to Winnie, despite her paint and diamonds. Strutham-Ingram is also drawn to Winnie. Carelessly, she encourages him. When he proposes to her, while out riding, she regrets that she had encouraged him and blames herself for toying with his feelings. Sholto Adare loves Nancy Ivey and proposes to her on horseback. Not knowing how to respond, she consults her mother, who encourages her to accept the proposal. Even though she does not love him, she seriously considers marrying him. He is rich. Noel Curtis, a young man unsure of his financial future, loves Nancy but postpones making his feelings known.

Winnie goes to parties where she dances and flirts. She is obviously looking for a second husband to replace her first. Gilmour pursues Winnie against his own better judgment. Even though she is a painted woman with a child, he cannot help but love her. He, like everyone else in this society, believes Winnie to be an adventuress.

There have been some hints that Winnie may be Madeline. A reader, vigilant for more clues, has her suspicions confirmed at this mid-point, when Winnie refers to her past and her Aunt Agatha. It is clear now that Winnie is Madeline.

Nancy still does not know how to respond to Sholto's proposal. She knows that she does not love him. Plagued by indecision, she wonders how a young girl makes this choice. Should she follow her heart or the advice and encouragement of family and friends? Happily, Curtis relieves her of this dilemma by declaring himself. Nancy is able to reject Sholto and accept the man she really loves. But she could easily have accepted Sholto. No one tells her not to, and many encourage her to.

Lilian, who had bitterly excoriated her husband for his cold, unresponsive, punishing treatment, is suddenly transformed by pregnancy. Just the promise of motherhood overturns her perverse nature.

When Winnie attends a fancy-dress ball, where Madeline had been a disaster, she is a vulgar triumph. She is, by her own design, foolish, gaudy, and indelicate. Gilmour is sickened by the performance. But he loves her in spite of everything. When he proposes, Winnie tells him the story of her imposture. She confesses that she is not a widow but a 'spinster in a wig'. She had been a dour creature, but now she will sparkle. She is amazed that Gilmour was attracted to her, insisting that he was drawn to the tinsel and show. He protests. She explains that she had purposely made herself disagreeable. At last, she will be happy. She will marry Gilmour, who loves her and whom she loves.

The structure of the novel is purposefully confusing. The Introduction—the Madeline chapter, which is psychologically complex and intriguing, hangs suspended. It stays in a reader's mind, but uneasily and uncomfortably. A reader is tempted and then encouraged to think that Madeline is Winnie, but this supposition is not confirmed for many chapters. Trix artfully delays the revelation.

But once the identification is confirmed, the imposture exposed, it remains troubling. It feels oddly unmotivated and implausible. If Madeline wants to find a husband and make a good marriage, it would have been far more reasonable for her to return in a simple, artless pose and to win her man with this real and lovely self. Revenge for Madeline's humiliation seems the most plausible explanation for her disguise, but Winnie never assigns this as her motive. She is trying to find a husband, but it is unclear why she tries in this self-denying and possibly self-defeating manner. She seems to be proving something, but it isn't clear if what she is proving is that she can be attractive to men, that she can undo her past defeat, or that she can make fools of the men whom she encouraged to humiliate and reject her.

The heroine runs cold and then hot. If Madeline's excessive coldness repels men, then Winnie's excessive heat should also turn them away. She should attract men and especially the right man only when she arrives at her true correct temperature—warmth. But the hero of the story, Gilmour, loves Winnie in spite of her imposture. He sees the real her behind the disguise. This is difficult for a reader to accept, as a reader cannot see the real her. She never reveals herself and she seems not to know who the real her is. How can she know that Gilmour is seeing the real her when she doesn't seem to know who she is? Where May of *The Heart of a Maid* knew exactly who she was and what her limitations were, Madeline/Winnie seems not to understand herself or her actions. Her first act of make-believe ends in unanticipated failure, her second in unwarranted success. She is surprised by both.

The opening chapter of the novel—the history of Madeline's failure—is the most compelling part of the novel. Trix feelingly described Madeline's original discomfort at being paraded on the marriage market. During her early seasons at Simla, Trix felt humiliated, exposed, and in peril of having the accept a proposal she was not ready to entertain. Thus, she understood this feeling well.

The minor character Lilian is also especially well-drawn. Lilian, like May in *The Heart of a Maid*, has an ungenerous and unhappy temperament. She is married to Gilbert, a cold, undemonstrative man who disciplines her with silence and distance. When she is desperately lonely and unhappy, she wonders, 'Did other women feel like this? Did they, too, sit at home doing little services for their husbands while they half hated them? That was wicked, but it was the truth; Gilbert was hateful'.[17] Neither Lilian nor Gilbert changes, but Lilian is happily transformed by becoming a mother.

Lilian's insupportable marriage resembles May's miserable marriage to Percy. Trix was especially deft at portraying these very troubled unions. Pregnancy and childbirth cure both Lilian and May and suggest that Trix believed becoming a mother had transformative power.

---

17   'Chapter 10' in ibid.

Both *Pinchbeck* and *Heart of a Maid* feature perverse characters, Madeline and May—women who thwart their own happiness by being stubborn, unyielding, and headstrong. Trix supplies little explanation for why they are so contrary and difficult. It is not the fault of society or of the institution of marriage. It is the fault of the women themselves. These women were brought up away from their mothers. May in *Heart of a Maid* has a living mother, who only wants to marry her off and is (she believes) partly responsible for the death of her baby. In *Pinchbeck Goddess*, Madeline's mother is dead, and she is raised by an evil aunt, also dead by the time of the main action of the novel. So, both girls are deficient in feeling because they did not have maternal love. They suffer from 'mother want'. This inner deficiency is all that is provided to explain their unhappy temperaments.

At the end of *Maid*, May vows to change. She will bend her ungenerous and unyielding nature into a better shape. This will not be pretence but will be a true alteration of her character. But a reader never gets to see this change. The novel ends before the transformation can be attempted. At the end of *Pinchbeck,* Winnie/Madeline is allowed to drop her masks to reveal her genuine self. She claims that beneath the disguises is a loving woman who will marry successfully. A reader does not get to see this softened creature but must accept on faith that behind the two artfully constructed masks is a woman of genuine feeling.

The heroines of Trix's two novels are, first, a woman with an unhappy and ungenerous nature who promises to change in a future that never arrives, and second, a woman who disguises her true nature under two false fronts and claims, but never exhibits, the sweet nature beneath. The happy natures are a frail promise and an unpersuasive assertion. A truly loving, caring, generous nature is something Trix was unable to envision with sufficient clarity to write. The angry nature that a reader feels behind both of these characters is something Trix did know well and did present well. But this was as far as she could go. She could not or would not explore where this anger came from and what its more damaging consequences were. But she clearly situated the problem as internal, not coming from the external society.

What is most remarkable about May is that she does not disguise her feelings at all. She tells Anstruther from the start that she does not love him and does not believe she ever will. Despite this icy confession,

Percy marries her. Later in the novel, she does not disguise her furious, ferocious anger at the death of her baby. She never pretends. At the very end of the novel, she considers changing her character, not disguising it, but really experiencing an alteration of character. But she is unable even to imagine this change clearly, and thus a reader never gets to see it. Total lack of pretence, while satisfying in itself, seems to lead nowhere, to a dead end. May is left literally adrift.

Winnie, on the other hand, only pretends. Her first pretence as Madeleine is the result of feeling demeaned as an object. Her response to this humiliation is to become cold and forbidding. While self-defeating, this response feels sensible and understandable. Winnie's second disguise is not only unhelpful but also baffling. She returns in an ugly, garish costume, which, while disgusting most men, does not deter Gilmour, the one man she wants to attract. Gilmour ignores the gaudy disguise and unexpectedly and unreasonably loves her in spite of it. But she seems merely lucky. Gilmour's love is an undeserved surprise. She could easily have ruined her chances a second time.

In her fiction, Trix always placed the blame for women's unhappiness on the inner nature of the women themselves. She never blamed her society or its institutions. Trix's unwillingness to think deeply or to write fully and truly about her society's treatment of women resulted in a double loss. First, she damaged her own novels by giving her heroines insufficient motivations and by giving her plots inadequate conclusions. And second, she failed to write the (possibly wicked satiric) novels about thwarted female expectations that she could have composed with pleasure and perhaps success.

As soon as Trix completed the novel to her own satisfaction, she began, with help from her mother and father, to search for a publisher. Rudyard had shepherded *The Heart of a Maid* through publication, but this time the task fell to her and her parents. She submitted *Pinchbeck* to several publishers and entered into prolonged negotiations for the best possible deal. She accepted an offer from Watt, who submitted it unsuccessfully to *The Queen*, *The Pioneer*, and *The Gentlewoman* for serial publication. After waiting a long time for Watt to place the novel, she removed it from him. She then sent it on to the well-respected publisher, Heinemann, hoping that they would accept it. And on 5 December 1896, four months after submission, Trix was happy to report to Maud, 'My news is that the

"Pinchbeck" has been accepted in a kind of a sort of a way'.[18] Heinemann had written to her, 'I have read Mrs Flemings' M.S. & although it has quite the qualities of a good story, it is I fear somewhat out of date in its treatment. I think it would be better handled by a firm less determinedly modern than mine—However, if Mrs Fleming wishes me to publish it in preference to some one else I would do so, because the book is entirely charming & its publication so creditable'.[19] He agreed to take it on, offering to publish it in a cheap form and with no royalties. Compared to the 'New Woman' novels Heinemann was publishing, it certainly was 'out of date'. Trix hesitated but soon agreed to this unspectacular offer, preferring to have *Pinchbeck* published by a good and well-known firm rather than to get more money from some obscure house.

Trix's second novel, *A Pinchbeck Goddess*, was finally published on 12 February 1897 and then republished in March by D. Appleton and Company, a division of Heinemann. It appeared under the name 'Mrs J. M. Fleming (Alice M. Kipling)' and was dedicated 'To My Brother'.[20]

Well before the novel was published, Trix found fault with it and worried about the flaws that others would find. She had shown the novel in manuscript form to her parents and, having incorporated their suggestions and corrections, was sure of their approval. She felt certain of Maud's good opinion as well, but confessed, 'I'm rather shaking in my shoes & a few snubbing or scathing notices feel at present about all I have to hope for'.[21]

As soon as the novel was published, Trix nervously awaited the reviews. When they arrived, she reported them to Maud.

> I've had four little reviews thus far—the best & longest being in 'The Scotsman' [...] The general treatment in 'A Pinchbeck Goddess' in entirely original & possesses a brilliance that defies comparison' — Each character is excellent in its way— [...] The 'Daily Telegraph' is very down both on me & Simla 'A tale almost wholly devoted to Simla life, or rather Simla frivolity, for what is so elaborately described can only by a stretch of language be called life! — She confines herself to trifling incidents & to dialogue for the most part so vapid that the average man will probably wonder why an artist should thing such babble worth recording— This

---

18   Trix Kipling, letter to Maud Diver, 5 December 1896.
19   Ibid.
20   J. M. Fleming (Alice M. Kipling), *A Pinchbeck Goddess*.
21   Trix Kipling, letter to Maud Diver, 5 December 1896.

budget of inane chatter serves no artistic purpose. It yields no instruction & affords but the slightest modicum of amusement'. There. Observe the joys of publishing a little book! And did you ever hear of the 'Morning Leader'? I never did—It's been good enough to devote half a column— signed D. Pitkethly — chiefly to finding fault with Pinch — but with this comforting conclusion. 'For Mrs 'Fleming, despite her fatal gift of quotation, her brilliant small talk, her very ordinary love affairs, her commonplace colonels, majors & aides-de-camp, has just that grace of narration that saves her novel from collapse'. Also I am invited next time to 'make a nobler use of her undoubtedly rich resources'.[22]

"Vanity Fair" of all papers gave me an amazing notice & says of Winnie, "a wittier more delightful person I have not made the acquaintance of for many a long novel [...] a real & very charming woman"—There— that made me purr like anything!'[23] But 'Bookman' took her to task for the improbable plot, 'which has some common place smartness in it & nothing much better'.[24] 'How lucky I've been not to have heaps more reviews like that,' she reported light-heartedly to Maud. But Trix herself worried that the novel 'was as dull as a vanilla wafer & not half as crisp!'[25]

While negotiating with publishers to get *Pinchbeck* into print and then waiting for publication and reviews, Trix considered her next fiction. 'I've written of frivols in India & now I want to write of the other side of the shield,'[26] she wrote confidently to Maud. She wanted to write something new and different. She was done with frivolity.

She had in mind two novels, both featuring widows. One was tentatively titled 'Conquering Shadow' and was, in her own estimation, a fearfully gloomy tale. The other, titled 'Their Husband', was, in her opinion, even more disturbing. Trix had dark plots on her mind, featuring heroines with some experience, not innocent virgins. When thinking about publishing her third, more serious novel, she became worried that it would shock her 'petty prim Mamma-in-law'[27] and planned to publish it under a pseudonym.

---

22 Trix Kipling, letter to Maud Diver, 15 March 1897.
23 Trix Kipling, letter to Maud Diver, 1 May 1897.
24 Trix Kipling, letter to Maud Diver, 28 June 1897.
25 Trix Kipling, letter to Maud Diver, 26 June 1897.
26 Trix Kipling, letter to Maud Diver, 28 June 1897.
27 Trix Kipling, letter to Maud Diver, 30 July 1896.

She was especially stuck over one novel she had titled 'A Stopgap'. This novel included what she referred to as the 'sex question'. The sex question the novel posed was a very specific sex/marital quandary, not one of the larger issues of sexual freedom and equality being posed by the feminist novelists of the period. Trix's widowed heroine, Hester, after the death of her beloved first husband, makes a very particular bargain—a convenient second marriage without sex—and then is surprised and distressed when the husband insists on revising the arrangement. She resists accepting the new terms, but because of her love and loyalty to the living and the dead, she feels she must yield. Trix got as far as, 'Then Viola [the child] dies & her death sets H. free & she does--'[28] There Trix stopped. Like May in *The Heart of a Maid*, the heroine is free in the end, but to go where? The conditions of the marital bargain and the eventual breakdown of trust are unique and personal. They are not posed as representative of anything larger or more significant. The plot touches on sex but shies away from making any larger claims about male power and betrayal or female submission and loyalty. Feminist novels of the period questioned the sexual double standard, encouraged female sexual exploration, and castigated men for their sexual freedom and self-serving moral code of conduct. Trix moved near to these issues but never engaged them.

> I've written at great length—could one write such a story—or is it best left alone? The notion of it is a woman who has spent all the passionate love of her nature on one object—& whose spirit suffers cruelly from the bondage of the flesh. I think one could do it without making Forbes seem a brute—or Hester an idiot. Tell me honestly what you think—I've only actually written the first three chapters—I think it would be better if I could [...] finish some of the ten stories begun—half done & projected [...] but Hester sticks in my mind somehow. I fear I must write her to get rid of her—You must be nearly worn out with all this![29]

The first three chapters of the novel have not survived. Trix was unsure if she could make the man tolerable in his selfishness and the woman sympathetic in her submission. And, as before, she was unable to fashion an appropriate and satisfying ending. She abandoned this novel.

---

28 Trix Kipling, letter to Maud Diver, 26 January 1897.
29 Ibid.

She had in mind the plot for another novel for which she had many possible titles, all of which she hated—'Lighthearted', 'A Chosen Fate', 'A Far Cry', 'Overseas Alone', 'While Others Dance & Play'. At the centre of the novel is a bride who comes to India with pleasant expectations and is overwhelmed by the loneliness, dreariness, heat, and lack of civilization. She has a baby who dies, and after much suffering, she herself dies of cholera. In a final scene, her husband drives her body swathed in a waterproof sheet in his bamboo cart and feels irritated as the dreadful thing jolts and bangs over the rough roads. When the sheeted bundle shifts, he almost swears at it. 'Am I too horrible?' Trix asked Maud of this brutally vivid and emotionally complicated image.[30]

While she was full of plots, characters, and titles, she could not manage to settle on any one idea. She wanted to do something different, to tell a possibly disturbing tale. She fretted and dithered, writing to Maud, 'My comfort in not writing now is that I feel as though 'Lighthearted' or 'A Chosen Fate' or whatever the name of my new novel will be was simmering in my head & would be none the worse of the little delay'. And she added, 'Remember that I wrote it [Pinchbeck] more than two years ago & should never care to do anything so frivolous again.[31]

She was 'chock a block with notions for stories long and short' but unable to work any of them out. Trying to organize herself, she made herself a list called 'Many Intentions' where she wrote down all her projected stories, three novels—'Conquering Shadows', 'A Stopgap', and 'Her Womanhood;' four longish short stories — 'The Indian Girl', 'Verona's Summer', 'Under Changed Skies', and 'Where Hooghli Flows'; and heaps of short stories, some of which had been on her mind for years. Four of them were half written—'The Last Theft', The Little Footprints', 'Janie's Man', and 'Rubbish Games'.[32] Six more were very clear in her mind. But she was unable to begin most of them, no less finish any one of them.

She seriously considered her Indian story, titled 'Where Hooghli Flows', which was set in old Calcutta more than a hundred years in the past, but abandoned it as hopeless. She stopped working on 'Rubbish Games', a story about children, because she recognized sadly that she

---

30   Trix Kipling, letter to Maud Diver, 28 June 1897.
31   Trix Kipling, letter to Maud Diver, 1 May 1897.
32   Trix Kipling, letter to Maud Diver, 12 August 1897.

really didn't have enough contact with children to describe their ways and create their words.

Moody and dissatisfied, Trix wrote a lot, but completed little, and approved of less. Although she complained of her inability to get down to work and compared her laziness always unfavourably to Maud's dedication, she was, in fact, writing many pages. She just wasn't satisfied with any of them. More than ever, she deprecated her own modest efforts compared to Maud's progress. 'Your novel nearly twice as long as mine & in its whole scheme & structure is as an eagle compared to a canary bird! You soar while I cheap & twitter'.[33]

Reporting for the *Pioneer*, not dithering over fiction, was easy. After one of her experiences in camp, she submitted 'A Journey in the Jungle', a charming account of her time in the northwest provinces and the Kingdom of Oudh. It was published unsigned in the 21 February 1897 issue of *The Allahabad Pioneer*.[34] The piece, which recounts a long march on untrodden roads through high jungle grass, includes several sweet and fey observations, characteristic of Trix's writing. Always fond of animals, Trix described 'a dear elephant with charming manners and a fondness for sweet biscuits, who evinced no displeasure when his tail was bent into a loop'. Trix found him, 'breakfasting on half a haystack, and finding it rather monotonous'. She paid special attention to her own pampered terrier, who accompanied her on the trip and who, when fording the winding river Ool, 'was forced to swim, with great injury to her feelings, and a marked improvement to her complexion'. Trix complained about the unreliable promises she had believed about the abundance of game she would meet. 'We had been told that we should find ourselves in a sportsman's paradise, with geese and peafowl at every turn, a cloud of duck fluttering up from each *jhil*, quail and black partridge as common as butterflies and deer a very likely probability. But the game resembled the promised jam in Wonderland—'Jam to-morrow and jam yesterday but never jam to-day!' Wishing to conclude on a positive note, or being pressed by her editor to conclude on such a note, she ended her breezy report with this picture of Indian well-being. 'It was pleasant to see a fine potato field near a well, healthy neatly trenched plants that would be ready to dig in about a month.

---

33 Trix Kipling, letter to Maud Diver, 30 July 1896.
34 Trix Kipling, 'A Journey in the Jungle', *The Allahabad Pioneer*, February (1897).

Pleasanter still it was to notice, during a detour through a village, that the children's naked little bodies displayed comfortable curves, that the women wore ornaments, that the ribs of the cattle were not in evidence, and that not one person asked for alms'.[35]

But her sad thoughts prevailed. Trix missed her more literary friend Sibyl Healey, who had recently returned to England. She sorely missed Maud, who had also returned to England and was living at Middle Bourne, Farnham in Surrey. Her dearest friends were worlds apart from her. In 1897, without the encouragement of her family and friends, Trix was dependent on Jack, whose approval and appreciation were always less than enthusiastic. Although Trix never openly complained about the tepid reception of *A Pinchbeck Goddess,* she could not have been happy that the novel caused so little stir. Trix had laboured long and hard on *Pinchbeck,* a story that had been in mind for more than a decade. Trix always disavowed her ambitions, deprecated her literary gifts, and minimized her distress over her poor reviews, but this modest pose served to hide a very real ambition. After the cool reception of her slight second novel, Trix was determined to write something more serious, but she found it difficult to finish her stories and wavered over the plot of her next novel. One story she did complete (possibly 'Ricochet') she could not sell. When her publisher, McClure, delayed and demurred over accepting her stories, she felt, 'fathoms five in depression'.[36] This phrase may have been a typical dramatic exaggeration, or it may have been a description of her mounting feelings of despair.

She repeatedly berated herself for sloth, comparing her laziness with Maud's steady application. 'My dear you are bound to succeed your energy & perseverance are so splendid—your letters always make one feel such a lazy lump—With ten times your leisure & opportunities for writing I just do nothing—while you go steadily quietly on'.[37]

Jack, who might have provided some little support, was at the time more needy than she. In the spring of 1897, he was going through a particularly bad time, suffering from a variety of physical complaints, which only exacerbated his worst personality traits. He was plagued by lumbago and insomnia and troubled by poor vision. Anxiously, he paced up and

---

35 Ibid.
36 Trix Kipling, letter to Maud Diver, 16 March 1898.
37 Trix Kipling, letter to Maud Diver, 26 January 1897.

down about the house, looking dreary and depressed. Granted a six-week leave from active duty, during which he was forbidden to use his eyes, he depended on Trix to read aloud to him for hours. Reading endlessly to Jack prevented her from writing her stories and delayed her replies to Maud's letters, but she felt a brute if she didn't try to relieve his misery.

After eight years of marriage, Trix was accustomed to Jack's temperament and to how often he annoyed her past irritation and into angry words. Writing to Maud, she complained mildly and often humorously about Jack's health and his moods, but she did not detail her many serious dissatisfactions. She lamented that she hardly saw her nieces and nephews and the many children she loved, but she did not describe this loss fully. 'It's a little unkind of Fate that I who am so fond of children have to get on without ever seeing my own nephews & nieces & the friends children—like your Cyril & Nettie's Kathleen that I feel belong to me too!'[38]

In May 1897, she wrote this unusually thoughtful and revealing letter to Maud.

> The lack in my life that a childless woman who loves children must feel— is a thing that I daren't let my thoughts dwell on—I have so much to thank God for that it would be wickedness itself to fret for the one good gift withheld. But the thought of squirrel [Maud's son, Cyril] & other darling children fills me with loving envy. But indeed I'm thankful for the health & strength that enables me to go into camp & be Jack's constant companion & more thankful than words can say for his unfailing love & goodness which seems to strengthen as the years go on. I do so despise & disagree with the modern notion that marriage kills love—all that is best worth having in love grows & strengthens & it's such a beautiful & wonderful thing that the chance attraction which begins at a dance or in the most frivolous surroundings possible should become the strongest & best feeling in two lives—I have a dread sometimes that Jack will feel lonely when we get old & miss children then—but sufficient unto the day & he certainly does not miss them now.[39]

It was extremely unusual for Trix to write so seriously about Jack and her feelings for children. Even with Maud, she rarely broached these sensitive subjects. Although she often complained about Jack's most irritating traits—his morose silence and stubbornness—she never

---

38   Trix Kipling, letter to Maud Diver, 1 May 1897.
39   Ibid.

complained about his larger deficiencies and his possible betrayals. Here, she acknowledged her unhappiness about being childless but refused to dwell on this deep sorrow. She reminded herself and Maud that her marriage had its strengths and that Jack loved her unfailingly. But in these words of reassurance there is a shimmer of anxiety. She was grateful to be able to be with Jack in camp, but also concerned that were she not able, there could be a problem. Similarly, having failed to give Jack children, she dreaded what that could mean in the future.

Bedevilled by health issues which did not resolve, Jack applied for eighteen months furlough beginning in November 1897. Trix was thrilled with the idea of going back home so soon again. She had been in England in 1895. She was hopeful that the change in scene would improve Jack's health. Her own good health was not an issue. Her greatest pleasure was her expectation of being with Maud, who would be at last on the same continent. She wrote cheerfully to Maud, of having 'beautiful visions of our being at some dear little Scotch sea side place & getting you to come & stay with us. Our men should golf while you & I would watch Squirrel [Maud's son, Cyril] paddling & digging & talk!'[40]

When the furlough came through in early 1898, Trix and Jack returned to the Fleming home in Scotland, where Jack's two sisters lovingly looked after their brother. Relieved of Jack's constant care, Trix sank into herself. Dutifully, she stayed by Jack's side at his grim family home, and later, when he was well enough to travel, she miserably accompanied him on a golf holiday to St Andrews. Living with the stiff and unsympathetic Flemings in cold and damp Edinburgh, Trix became more and more depressed. Through the spring and summer, as Jack's health steadily improved, Trix's spirits declined.

Trix's fantasy of a sea-side holiday never became a reality. Never did Trix chat with Maud while Squirrel dug in the sand. Instead, in the fall of 1898, while in Edinburgh with the Flemings, Trix fell into deep despair, refusing to speak, eat, or move. To the Fleming family, this breakdown seemed sudden and unexplained, a complete surprise and shock. She had hidden her feelings well. She had given few indications to her parents, her brother, or her friend Maud of the true state of her mind. But her stability, always fragile, had been crumbling for some time.

---

40 Trix Kipling, letter to Maud Diver, 28 June 1897.

8. Breakdown

I can see Trix as she holds herself rigidly together, sitting with her mother in the drawing room that had been hastily engaged for her at the Royal Palace Hotel. The towering red-brick pile in Kensington was far less grand than its name promised, but Trix didn't notice or care where she was. She sat in stony silence, as her mother tried to cajole her into tasting food or sipping water. She didn't want to answer her mother's nagging questions—What was the matter? How did this start? What could she do? She didn't want to take the sips of tea and spoons of broth that her mother kept trying to force between her tight lips. She didn't want to talk, or eat, or even be where she was.

Trix had been sent from the Fleming home in Edinburgh to the London hotel at her mother's insistence. The Flemings had been alarmed by Trix's odd and disturbing behaviour while she and Jack had been visiting with them in the fall of 1898. Trix had seemed fine when she arrived, but soon she was restless and anxious, pacing about the floor and twisting her hands in nervous motions. Then, as the weather grew cooler, Trix became angrier and angrier, marching back and forth and talking furiously and uncontrollably. Unable to stay still, Trix moved nervously about. When at rest, she sat motionless, staring into space. The Flemings were shocked by these inexplicable and violent changes. They had never encountered anything like this and felt helpless to do anything about it. The Kiplings, when they were alerted to Trix's behaviour, were equally stunned, but they were ready to take control of the situation

.Alice, fiercely protective of her child, asserted her maternal authority, assumed responsibility, and demanded that her child be removed to her care. Jack and his sisters, who had been horrified by Trix's behaviour and scandalized by her speech, were relieved to send her away. Trix was swiftly transferred to her mother in London, arriving like a hastily dispatched parcel, at the doorstep of the Royal Palace Hotel.

Alice was confident that Trix would recover once in her mother's care, but Trix remained deeply distressed. Alice repeatedly tried to calm and console Trix, but her improvised efforts made little difference. Eventually, Alice was forced to admit that Trix needed help. Insisting that there was nothing seriously wrong with Trix, Alice refused to consult a medical expert. Instead, she called in Dr Robert F. Colenso, neither a trained physician nor a mental health expert, to diagnose and dose the patient. Dr Colenso believed in the healing power of diet and massage, a gentle treatment that was reassuring to Alice. Eager to placate the worried mother, he agreed that the patient was suffering from a mild temporary malady, and Alice, eager to believe this generous diagnosis, trusted to time and patience. Trix continued to alternate between stony silence and wild raving. Sensitive doctors treating these kinds of symptoms were accustomed to assign benign diagnoses—hysteria or neurasthenia—and to prescribe gentle treatment.

But in the winter, when Rudyard heard the details of Trix's condition, he stepped in to take charge of the situation. After confirming the reports he had heard of Alice's resistance to professional care, he insisted that proper diagnosis and treatment be found for his sister. He enlisted the help of Alfred Baldwin and other relatives, who had had some personal experience with mental disorders. When he finally visited Trix at the hotel, he found her, to his horror, sitting in a rigid posture, staring icily into the distance. While Alice fretted and fussed to no constructive end, Rudyard tried to find out what was going on in Trix's troubled mind. Alice and Rudyard sensed from Trix's repetitive gestures and mumbled words and sounds that there was one fixed idea whirling around and around in her restless mind. But neither one could discover what this fixed idea was.

Rudyard's alarm at Trix's condition was compounded by his frustration with Alice, who denied and dismissed all suggestions that Trix was seriously ill. She remained implacable and obstructive to finding proper medical help, insisting that she could care for her daughter alone. Although Rudyard recognized that Alice's stubborn denials were endangering Trix, he also recognized that he could not disregard her opinions. He needed her cooperation. He was enraged that he had to use his energies to pacify his mother, while his sister was in real peril. Rudyard advised the doctors that 'the main point is not to flutter the mother'.[1] Rudyard's own diagnosis was no different from the doctors'—melancholia and depression.

Trix expressed one constant emotion—fierce anger at Jack. She refused to see or speak to him and insisted that she be allowed to remain separate from him. When she was informed that he was planning to visit, she became agitated and anxious. Trix's rage at Jack and her barely intelligible mutterings about Jack suggest that he had betrayed her and perhaps replaced her. Jack remained a tall, strikingly good-looking man, especially in uniform. He spent a fair amount of time separated from his wife in places where infidelity was common and grass widows abundant. Jack may well have found other objects for his affections. Or Trix may have felt abandoned or in immediate danger of being replaced. Trix, who had been abandoned in the past, feared this eventuality more than anything else, and having it in front of her as a real or imagined possibility could well have precipitated her collapse. She was unwavering in her fury at Jack and her absolute refusal to see or speak to him.

With her family's intervention and some medical advice but without any legal formulation, Trix was allowed to separate from her husband.

With Alice in charge, in the beginning of December 1898, Trix was treated at a London Clinic again by Dr Colenso. Despite his own dubious qualifications, he called in a respected mental specialist, Dr George Savage, President of the Medico-Psychological Association of the Neurological Society, the editor of the *Journal of Mental Science*, and author of *Insanity and Allied Neurosis* (published in 1884).[2] Dr Savage's medically approved treatment hardly differed from Dr Colenso's—rest, quiet, and not too much sedation. Dr Savage found Trix deep into melancholia and depression and recommended quiet and isolation. She was obstinately refusing to respond when spoken to, show her tongue when asked to, or take food when offered it, and thus she was forced to eat, to take milk and medicine. This was the standard cure of the time—being fed, massaged, and kept quiet. Dr Colenso feared her becoming 'noisy or listless', either of which might require committing her or moving her into a private asylum where she could be discreetly

---

1   Rudyard Kipling, letter to Alfred Baldwin, 18 November 1898. Dalhousie University; also in *Letters*, ed. by Pinney, vol. II, p. 353.

2   Dr George Savage was consulted by the Stephen family to treat Virginia Woolf in 1904.

looked after. However, as she became calmer and more obedient, she was allowed to remain where she was. Noisiness meant not simply constant chattering but chattering that had an unseemly perhaps obscene character to it. Trix's wildly shifting moods continued to move from rigidity and mutism to restlessness and constant uncensored talk. After a few weeks, Dr Colenso reported to Jack Fleming that his wife was getting better, that she was sleeping and napping as required. Although she had been forced to take food and would not speak when addressed, she had for the first time given the doctor her pulse. She still refused to show her tongue. Dr Colenso reassured Fleming that he would not put Trix in an asylum unless she had 'acute mania'.

At the end of December, Trix was slightly better. She ate her meals and took pleasure in her walks. Although she felt less apathetic and more animated, she told Dr Colenso that she did not think she would ever feel the same again. The sympathetic doctor supported Trix's adamant refusals to see Jack. He responded to Jack's repeated requests to have his wife restored to him by tactfully recommending patience and restraint. He advised Jack that neglecting his wife altogether for a while would be more likely to bring about a return in her affections than insisting on visiting her. Dr Colenso allowed that Trix might soon be well enough to travel abroad, but suggested her father, not her husband, as her travel companion. But other crises erased the possibility of foreign travel.

In early February, while Trix was in a clinic in London, news arrived that Rudyard and his six-year-old daughter Josephine were both gravely ill with lung inflammations or pneumonia in New York. Alice, anxious about Trix, now had Rudyard and her granddaughter, Josephine, to be concerned about. She sent Lockwood to London to fetch Trix home to Tisbury, and together the three waited for word about the two patients. On 6 March, Josephine died. Rudyard, kept ignorant of his favourite child's death until his own health was restored, was devastated when he finally learned of his loss. Trix was well enough to understand the tragedy that had just befallen Rudyard and wept when she heard of her niece's death.

The grieving grandparents settled their ailing daughter into The Gables, their modest grey stone and red-tiled house. Alice encouraged Trix to eat, to walk about the garden, and to sit at the bay window and look out at the cornfield in the distance. Trix continued to vacillate between mutism and 'almost constant talk—and oh—my dear—nearly all nonsense,' reported Alice. When Trix returned to her own bright self, as she did during parts of the day, Alice felt hopeful. But Trix would suddenly change and 'drift away into a world of her own, always a sad one'.[3] Trix's moods continued to shift as a new doctor—Dr N. R. Gowers, another respected specialist in nervous diseases—was called in.

Dr Gowers arranged a lady companion for Trix, Miss Ross. But, as before, Alice protested, jealously guarding her role as Trix's sole caretaker and protector. When Dr Gowers suggested that Trix go away with Miss Ross, 'Mrs Kipling was on the verge of frenzy at any suggestion of such a thing—Mr K. yielded to his wife's excitement, although he was agreeable'.[4] Dr Gowers noted that Trix displayed extreme mental excitement or rather intellectual activity, which those who knew her considered excessive in degree, even for her.

Miss Ross stayed for two months at Tisbury, after which she left, persuaded that Trix could do just as well without her. Alice was keen to see her go. Alice, who became nervous and agitated when parted from Trix, was determined not to be separated from her. When the two were left undisturbed, they both calmed.

In returning to her parents' home, Trix was doubly blessed. She distanced herself from her immediate marital suspicions by separating from Jack. And she was returned to the childhood she had never had. This was her chance to satisfy her 'mother want', to compel her mother to take care of her. Some combination of fragility and strategy brought her to Tisbury. It was a situation that both mother and daughter accepted, welcomed, and, in fact, prolonged. It was the treatment designed by Trix and Alice together, and it was the perfect treatment for Trix.

Shortly before her breakdown, in mid-1898 when she was slipping into depression, Trix had been working on a story she eventually entitled 'Her Brother's Keeper'.[5] She referred to it as her 'loony story'. The plot focused on Mrs Mary Addison, a middle-aged English woman living in India who confronts, disarms, and calms a violent madman. He is also English, her countryman, the 'Brother' of the title. By the end of the story, Mrs Addison has talked the dangerous madman back into calmness, cleverly drugged him so that he can be restored by sleep, and returned

---

3   Alice M. Kipling, letter to Georgiana Burnes-Jones, 6 March 1899. University of Sussex.
4   N. R. Gowers, letter to Jack Fleming, 15 November 1899. University of Sussex.
5   Alice Fleming, 'Her Brother's Keeper', *Longman's Magazine*, June (1902).

him to the prospect of sanity. She deserves the praise of the doctor who credits her with having surely averted murder and mayhem. While Trix was working on the story in Scotland, she complained to Maud that it was 'bald & dull' and was undecided about its title, considering 'The Beginning of a Friendship' and 'The Strength of her Weakness'.[6] The story, written more than six months before her own breakdown, described the treatment Trix believed most salutary for controlling madness—compassionate maternal care. Amazingly, Trix prescribed the treatment for her own disease—Alice's tender care—months before she required and received it. Recovering at The Gables, Trix reworked her loony story, deciding on the title 'Her Brother's Keeper'. The title tantalizes with a promise of revelations about her actual brother Rudyard but does not in any way deliver. When she was satisfied with the story, she submitted it to *Longman's Magazine*, where it was published in June 1902.

The treatment that Trix received was the standard practice of the day. It was also standard for doctors to address all important communication and correspondence to Jack or Rudyard. Trix herself was always spoken of as a person without rights, without a voice in her own diagnosis and treatment.

At the time, there was no effective treatment, proper diagnosis, or even name for what ailed Trix: fluctuating states of manic activity and deep depression. The standard cure for these ills—established by Dr Silas Weir Mitchell, the pre-eminent American specialist in nervous diseases, and adopted in England—was enforced passivity, infantilizing rest, and a fattening regime. Dr Weir Mitchell believed in removing the patient from familiar surroundings, enforcing rest, and reducing outside stimulation.[7] This regimen suited Trix, who was happy to be removed from India, Jack, and the constant socializing of Anglo-Indian life. Trix was always described as suffering from a disease of the nervous system. Terms like manic, catatonic, or insane were never used in describing her condition. The doctors were very tactful in their language when speaking or writing to Jack and Rudyard. When communicating with Alice, they were even more circumspect.

From November 1898 to June 1899, and from April 1900 to September of that same year, Trix was a complete invalid, without the ability or the desire to read or write. But during the interim periods and later, she was

---

6   Trix Kipling, letter to Maud Diver, 28 June 1897.
7   Charlotte Perkins Gilman's story 'The Yellow Wallpaper' describes the dire effects of this infantilizing treatment on a young female patient.

decidedly well and remarkably productive, writing dialogues, stories, and poems. She worked on two sustained projects in this period—a group of poems conceived and composed in concert with her mother and eventually published as *Hand in Hand*[8], and one hundred pages of comic dialogue featuring a married couple named George and Mabel.[9] The poems were often sad, lamenting the loss of love in marriage, while the dialogues were hilarious, presenting a comedy of marital miscommunication and incompatibility. Trix's poetry from this period featured several clever and devilish parodies, which were not included in *Hand in Hand*. The dialogues and the parodies were especially brilliant, Trix at her very best. When her mood was good, it was very, very good.

Trix's poems in *Hand in Hand*, twice as many as her mother's, were grouped under various headings: Verses, Sonnets, Indian Verses, Pieces of Eight: A Garden Series, A Thoughts Series, and Echoes of Roumanian Folk Songs. One of Trix's poems, 'Where Hugli Flows', expresses affection and even nostalgia for Calcutta, where she had lived with Jack. These are the first and last stanzas of that poem:

> WHERE HUGLI FLOWS
>
> Where Hugli flows, her city's banks beside,
> White domes and towers rise on glittering plain
> The strong, bright sailing ships at anchor ride,
> Waiting to float their cargoes to the main,
>   Where Hugli flows.
>
> Yet years hence, when the steamer's screw shall beat
> The homeward track, for us without return,
> Our bitter bread, by custom almost sweet,
> We shall look back, perhaps through tears that burn
>   Where Hugli flows.

Among the daughter's verses were many sweet lyrics and one good sonnet, called 'Love's Murderer'. The poem described the loss of love between a husband and wife. As in most of her novels and stories, Trix placed the blame for the lack of love on her heroine. Reading her poetry as autobiography, which is difficult not to do, she blames herself for the problems in her marriage. If Jack had strayed and caused her to fear abandonment, she took responsibility for it. She had never loved him as she should have. She had trusted his love to sustain them both, as he

---

8   *Hand in Hand: Verses by a Mother and Daughter* (London: Elkin Mathews, 1902).
9   Trix, unpublished George and Mabel dialogues, in Lorna Lee, pp. 171–266.

had promised when he proposed. This may have been the final blow for Trix—that Jack, whose reassurance she had relied on, had betrayed her.

> LOVE'S MURDERER
> Since Love is dead, stretched here between us, dead,
> Let us be sorry for the quiet clay:
> Hope and offence alike have passed away.
> The glory long had left his vanquished head,
> Poor shadowed glory of a distant day!
> But can you give no pity in its stead?
> I see your hard eyes have no tears to shed,
> But has your heart no kindly word to say?
>
> Were you his murderer, or was it I?
> I do not care to ask, there is no need.
> Since gone is gone, and dead is dead indeed,
> What use to wrangle of the how and why?
> I take all blame, I take it. Draw not nigh!
> Ah, do not touch him, lest Love's corpse should bleed!

'Love's Derelict' takes up the same subject, but it puts the blame squarely on the husband (Jack)—the master who has cast her out, alone and forgotten.

> LOVE'S DERELICT
>
> I who was once full freighted for the sea,
> Strong timbered, with my ivory canvas gleaming,
> Now drift a battered hulk, all aimlessly,
>   Sun-shrivelled waveworn, useless tackle streaming.
>
> The water washes, like dull sobs in dreaming,
>   Across the soaked planks that were the deck of me;
> I keep no course, who steered so faithfully,
>   And bear no cargo, who had riches teeming.
>
> Love's Derelict am I, Love's Derelict,
>   Wrecked by his hand, by him flung to disaster;
> Drifting alone, through merciless edict,
>   Alone, cast out, forgotten of my master.
>
> Strong prows of purpose pity as ye pass
> Love's Derelict, Love's Derelict, alas!

'Memory' suggests not only abandonment but infidelity, another woman who stole her husband's love. It also contains a recurring element in Trix's verse and prose—the death of a child.

> MEMORY
> I am she who forgets not,
> The other women forget, and so they can be happy,
> But I am always wretched, because I must remember,
> And Memory is so sad.
>
> I had a dream of Memory,
> Her two hands held two sorrows;
> One sorrow was a sword,
>
> A sword to pierce my heartstrings,
> The memory of my daughter, the little one who died.
> One sorrow was a snake,
> A snake to sting my bosom,
> The memory of the woman, who stole my husband's love.
>
> I am she who forgets not,
> And Memory is so sad!

During the period when Trix was writing these sad lyrics, she was also composing a long (100 pages) series of humorous dialogues, featuring a husband not unlike Jack Fleming—remote, rigid, and inaccessible—and a wife somewhat like herself—talkative and busily engaged in vapid domestic chores.[10] The dialogues, similar to the Mr and Mrs Brown sketches that appeared in the *Pioneer* years earlier, were written as comedy. Trix's actual married life with Jack had ceased to be a comedy and had become a near tragedy of reciprocal incomprehension. The fictional wife, Mabel, was a silly, self-deluded, chattering fool, while George, the husband, was a silent, sulking critic. Using only dialogue, Trix created a portrait of a dry, dull, dissatisfying, and often contentious marriage.

The misalliance between George and Mabel resembled the implacable division between the talkative and effusive Trix and the silent, suffering Jack. If Jack had married Trix in the hope that her vivacity and chatter would energize and entertain him, he had found instead that those traits irked and irritated him. Her lively talk did not revive and revitalize him, as he had hoped, but simply overwhelmed and oppressed him.

---

10 Ibid.

Similarly, if Trix had married Jack in the belief that his calming influence would balance her volatile moods, she was deceived and disappointed. He was not calm; he was remote.

Over time, Trix recognized that Jack's stalwart and hearty demeanour and his stolid silence were not strength and calm but a show of strength to mask depression and physical frailty. Her own ebullience, her ancient defence against being overlooked and abandoned, only caused Jack to retreat further into depression. Jack's silence and unresponsiveness led Trix to feel ignored and alone. These dissatisfactions, while never directly mentioned in the dialogues, form its unspoken background.

Trix mined her own experience as a married woman living in India to paint a clear picture of the occupations available to a proper English wife. Mabel does needlework, writes letters, and attempts to keep a diary. She is busy with the social calendar, attending dinners and weddings, buying gifts, and sending Christmas cards. She drinks tea with friends, where she gossips about other friends—their clothes, their manners, their lovers, and their indiscretions. She plays golf and rides. She borrows books from the library. She attends tennis matches, horse races, and dances. She has her photographic portrait done. She is a member of the Amusement Club. She spends time ordering, reworking, and arranging her hats, her dresses, and her jewels. She goes to visit friends at hill stations in the hot weather without her husband. She travels with her husband on the survey, staying in rustic camps. Her life is an endless round of ordering dinners, keeping the servants up to the mark, and going to the club with her husband.

But Mabel is a fictional creation. She is talkative, indiscreet, envious, and mean. She is utterly insensitive to her effect on others and totally unaware of their feelings towards her. She treats her one friend, Amy, with disdain and derision. She hardly notices her husband or his attitude towards her. He is, for the most part, completely out of patience with her. While she chatters endlessly, he hardly attends, and when he does, it is with criticism, correction, and irritation. She constantly upbraids him, usually about things that are her own fault, accusing him of her failings and mistakes. George, she complains, is always 'grumbling and fault-finding and making things uncomfortable'.[11]

Trix assigned to Mabel a few of her own experiences and traits. Mabel tells Amy Forbes, her one friend, that all through her first season

---

11   Ibid., p. 204.

she was called 'Rose in June'. She claims to have mesmeric power. She passed an ambulance course in Simla ages ago and is competent to render First Aid to the Injured. But this is not a self-portrait; no one ever described Trix as selfish and insensitive, although many, including herself, described her as a chatterer.

Trix's portrait of George, the silent and suffering husband, is deftly created from what he does not say and from what Mabel says in response to him. Throughout the first sixteen dialogues, which are actually monologues, George says nothing, although his remarks can be inferred from Mabel's replies. Mabel refers to his funny teasing ways, which she makes light of and dismisses. She accuses him of just sitting there, looking cross, and sulking, while she does all the work. When she dismisses George's complaints without a thought, she is making a mistake. He is not teasing her or joking with her. He is in a state of constant annoyance and irritation with her. He may in fact be in a state of impotent, explosive rage. He mostly smoulders.

In 'Keeping a Diary', Mabel laments that George wouldn't be interested in reading her diary if she kept one. 'You never take an interest in anything I do, George, and it is so disheartening!'[12] 'A Cheerful Giver' presents more of Mabel's carping about her husband's poor temper: 'I never knew anyone like you for saying a pleasant thing disagreeably, and it is a habit you should fight against, dear, for it makes the people round you very unhappy'. She continues, 'It's no pleasure to me to talk to a man in a raging temper, very much the reverse, I don't wish ever to speak to you again'. At the end, she says, 'I'm simply worn out making suggestions for you to carp at'.[13] He has not raged or been in a temper; he has simply disagreed, repeatedly and reasonably.

When her friend Amy excitedly discloses that she is engaged to be married, Mabel all but ignores this important news. She is busily intent on sorting through her own dresses. After hardly allowing the giddy girl to speak, Mabel concludes, 'It's been so sweet to hear you pouring out all that is in your heart, and you know how lovingly I sympathize. Do come to lunch to-morrow, there's a dear, and we'll really settle about the pink satin'.[14]

---

12   Ibid., p. 234.
13   Ibid., p. 236.
14   Ibid., p. 219.

In 'Character Delineated', Mabel visits a palm reader who reports that she is 'very talkative'. Mabel objects to this, insisting that she is much too thoughtful to be talkative.

In 'The Joys of Camp', Mabel describes, in happy anticipation, the pleasures of roughing it and the welcome change from the usual round of silly social obligations. When she is actually in camp, she complains about sleeping out in the open, rising and dressing in the cold before dawn, and the general boredom and discomfort of rustic living.

In the final monologue, 'The Pleasure of his Company', George finally speaks. Sounding very like Mabel, George complains to his wife as they prepare to attend a party at the home of a friend. He criticizes her too youthful dress, her too bejewelled and ornamented person, her lack of a proper shawl, her elaborate and frizzy hair 'fringe', her slowness, and lateness. He blames her for not knowing the proper address and for arriving first too early, then too late at the party. He warns her not to sing, prolong the party, or keep him up late. He is unhappy with the food, the drink, and the cheap cheroots he will have to smoke. In general, he is almost as unpleasant as she.

While Trix was writing these dialogues, she was also working on 'A Christmas Minstrel'—a story in which an unsympathetic husband and wife barely tolerate each other's company. As the husband sits and composes a holiday poem, the wife sits across from him and knits. When he reads out his lines, she invariably and unenthusiastically approves. He views her handiwork 'with indulgent scorn'. She finds his verses tiresome, while he concludes, 'Who would believe the amount of time and trouble you women spend over trifles!'[15] Throughout the dialogues, husband and wife ignore or denigrate the occupation of the other.

Another story from the same time, 'A Sympathetic Woman'[16], takes place on shipboard. Mrs Seymour, a sought-after young woman, engages in conversation with a number of her fellow passengers who easily confide in her. Mrs Seymour, without distinguishing one speaker from another, makes only one reply to everything she is told—'I know'. She is perceived as the most caring, compassionate and sympathetic companion by all, although she speaks only these same two words.

---

15 Alice Fleming, 'A Christmas Minstrel', in Lorna Lee, p. 287.
16 Alice Fleming, 'A Sympathetic Woman', in Lorna Lee, pp. 288–96.

Trix submitted several other stories to publishers, but they did not meet with success. The long series of George and Mabel monologues may have been submitted for publication to *The Pioneer*, where Trix's earlier Mr and Mrs Brown dialogues had been published. A long, connected series of humorous pieces, they would have been difficult to place. They were never published.

Trix was especially comfortable and confident writing dialogue. It seemed to flow out of her with great ease. She was particularly deft at allowing a character to damn herself with her own words, displaying an almost absurd lack of self-knowledge. Repeatedly in her stories, she portrays one character who chatters heedlessly on about one inconsequential thing or another. The chatterer has no regard for her audience, rushing on impetuously with details. The listener rarely listens, but is preoccupied with his own concerns, out of patience or out of sorts with the chatterer and her silliness. Rarely did Trix create conversation that actually portrayed two people trying to communicate with each other. On the contrary, Trix presented talk as standing in the way of communication, one person stringing words together while the other person tries not to be bothered by the noise.

When Trix was feeling strong, she was able to concentrate and work steadily and productively. Alice allowed her the time and space to write in private.

Intent on keeping Trix close, Alice stayed home with her when she was indisposed or tired. When the two were together at home, they happily cooked meals and baked sweets to entertain friends. Both Alice and Trix were comfortable in the kitchen and delighted in foreign recipes and new kitchen devices. After purchasing a new griddle, they experimented together making waffles and potato cakes. While they both enjoyed creating food, neither one was particularly interested in eating it.

When Trix felt well, Alice encouraged her to visit with friends she and Lockwood had made in the neighbourhood. With a fine understanding of her daughter's tastes, Alice suggested an introduction to William and Evelyn de Morgan, a distinguished artistic couple, he a ceramicist and novelist and she a painter working in the Pre-Raphaelite style. Trix was agreeable when Alice arranged a visit with Evelyn de Morgan. At first, Alice accompanied Trix when she ventured out to meet Evelyn, but soon Trix was able to go alone to make visits to Evelyn's studio, where her many large and colourful canvases hung high up on the walls. After a while, Trix felt comfortable walking about the studio, studying the paintings at her leisure. Evelyn walked beside her, describing the allegorical sources and meanings of the crowded and colourful paintings. When Trix asked for complete explanations of paintings that especially attracted her, Evelyn generously showed her verses she had written to accompany some of her allegorical and mythological works. And, to Trix's surprise, Evelyn confided that the verses had been written in something of a trance. Evelyn, like Trix, harboured a hidden enthusiasm for spiritualism. Although Evelyn's husband William supported and shared her interest in the spiritual world, Evelyn found it easier to keep her spiritual interests private. Trix understood and sympathized with this deception. She had kept her interest in automatic writing and crystal gazing to herself. Here was Evelyn, an educated and artistic woman who, like herself, responded to poetry, painting, and spirits. Evelyn, she discovered, was a perfect friend.

Trix went again and again to Evelyn's studio, drawn to both the painter and to the paintings. Evelyn's art spoke to her, actually called forth poems from her. When Trix entered Evelyn's studio, she looked at the paintings on view in the studio, paintings in progress or recently completed paintings leaning up against the walls. When she found a painting or sculpture that moved her, she allowed herself to gaze steadily at it and to fall into a trance-like state. In this state, Trix produced verses. She was inspired by Evelyn's bust of 'Medusa' to write a brief poetic response. Its short and simple structure suggests that it was written automatically—quickly and while in an altered state.

> MEDUSA
> Is there no period set: Is pain
> eternal?
> Still through the eons must her
> vipers sting?
> For all Eternity the anguish burn?
> An endless circle, endless
> suffering!
> Beauty has lit heaven, shut deep
> in Hell.[17]

---

17 Alice Fleming, unpublished manuscript in the archives of the De Morgan Centre, Wandsworth.

While Trix was recovering in Tisbury, Evelyn painted 'The Thorny Path' (1897), 'The Valley of Shadows' (1899), 'Love's Piping' (1900), and 'Victoria Dolorosa' (1900). These are the paintings Trix saw in the studio and was drawn to. Evelyn's painting 'The Valley of Shadows' presented allegorically the fate of the soul at death. The painting provoked Trix to write these lines:

> Dark is the Valley—the Valley of Shadows
> Weary of heart and of life is the King—
> He sits among ruins, and thorny the meadows,
> The meadows unfruitful, forgotten the Spring.
> A green snake is keeping the Palace's portal,
> The lizard is warder of the desolate halls,
> And wine has no savour, and Love the Immortal
> Seems fading at even, as fast as the light falls.
> O, Dark is the Valley, the Valley at even,
> The King's brow is clouded, the King's heart is black,
> His down-gazing eyes give no glance to the Heaven,
> Where angels are winging their homeward-bound track—
> Sure in this dark hour at brink of the grave
> The Slave seems the Monarch, the Monarch the Slave[18]

Alice kept Trix close, protected her, and provided space and privacy for her. Trix was calmed by her mother's care and once calmed, was able to create serious poetry and humorous prose. Alice located an appropriate friend for Trix, and Trix was able to make a close connection to an exceptionally talented woman. While maintaining her reputation as emotionally fragile, and thus sustaining her position as a daughter in need of maternal attention, Trix was remarkably productive in her work—writing verses and dialogues—and remarkably successful in her personal life, making an important new friend.

At the end of December 1900, Trix was considered well enough to take a trip. It was recommended that she travel to Italy with her parents. Travelling with her husband was not considered. Arrangements were made for Trix and her parents to tour Genoa and Florence. Protected and guided by her mother, Trix toured art galleries and churches. She went to concerts and the opera and visited with her parents'

---

18   Alice Fleming, in *Evelyn de Morgan: Oil Paintings*, ed. by Catherine Gordon (London: De Morgan Centre, 1996).

acquaintances. When meeting new people or familiar friends, Trix was her old performing self. She recited, did imitations, flirted, and flattered.

While she was in Florence, she was introduced to Lady Walburga Paget, wife of the British Ambassador to Florence and later to Rome. In 1893, when her husband retired to Britain, Lady Paget bought the Torre di Bellosguardo—a beautiful villa perched above the city, south of Florence. She was living there when she heard about Trix, a beautiful young woman who, she was told, shared her interest in psychic matters. She invited Trix to visit her at the splendid villa, high above the domes and towers of Florence. Trix accepted the invitation and made her way up a perilous hill to meet the titled lady. The gracious older woman eagerly told Trix about her adventures in the spirit world, and, bringing forth her own crystal ball, demonstrated her skill in discovering visions in the crystal. When Trix described her automatic writing, Lady Paget sympathetically encouraged her to continue with it or to return to it, if she had sworn off it. The generous words of this older aristocratic lady, like the friendship of Evelyn de Morgan, were a comfort to Trix. Her own family was distressed by her interest in the world of spirits and made it known that they feared it was a bad influence on her mental health.

One evening in Florence, while dining out with her parents, Trix was introduced to Mrs William James, wife of the famous American philosopher. Mrs James seemed to know who Trix was. Although the Kiplings were only vaguely aware that Trix was the subject of gossip, they uneasily gleaned from Mrs James's conversation that Trix's fame had spread. Mrs James had heard of Trix as an exceptional young woman traveling with her parents. She understood that Trix was in the process of getting a divorce, a piece of information that was apparently generally known.

The grounds for the divorce were unclear, but Mrs James believed that the strong support of her parents indicated that the grounds were serious. Mrs James speculated that Trix, who had been separated from her husband for two and a half years, had sufficient cause to undertake this serious step and also had the encouragement of her father, who had apparently never liked the husband, and the approval of her mother, who had recently grown suspicious of him. The Kiplings learned that many others in their circle had heard the rumours Mrs James reported.

They were chagrined to learn that their daughter was the subject of talk, especially since the talk was untrue. At this time, no divorce proceedings had been initiated or were even being seriously considered.

Trix returned from the Italian tour feeling triumphant. She settled back into her routine with her parents at the Gables, feeling not simply well but frisky. She was eager to return to her poetry writing. Britain was abuzz with the upcoming coronation of King Edward VII, and Trix imagined the patriotic drivel that might appear from the country's poets. With her ear for verse and her spirit of play, she composed a series of witty and sly parodies. Published as 'Odes for the Coronation' in *The Pall Mall Magazine* of May 1902, these light verses were deliciously daring.[19] She poked fun at William Butler Yeats with a parody of his 'Lake Isle of Innisfree', titled 'The Pavement Stand of Westminstree'. This is the opening stanza:

> I will arise and go now, and go to Westminstree
> And a campstool take there, that's very strongly made:
> My gold watch will I doff me, for fear of pickpocketry,
> And meet with my fellows unafraid.

Disagreeing with Rudyard's stance on the Boer War, Trix aimed her critical barbs at her brother's war poems, especially at his 'The Islanders'. Her poem, 'The Milenders', mocks his exalted tone. These are the last four lines of the poem:

> Till the Eve of the last great Battle, till the Dawn of the first great Peace
> Neither corn nor the freight nor the cattle, neither import nor export cease,
> And the strong calm School of Nations, full fed, full feeding, fulfilled,
> Takes the Rule of its Obligations as the Powers have surely willed![20]

While the parody of Rudyard is clever, it is not cruel. Trix had a perfect ear for her brother's verse. No one else knew as well as she how to imitate his voice.

---

19   Alice Fleming, 'Odes for the Coronation', *Pall Mall Magazine*, May (1902), pp. 29–34.
20   Alice Fleming, 'The Milenders', in 'Odes for the Coronation', *Pall Mall Magazine*, May (1902) pp. 32–33.

In a more sympathetic tone, Trix wrote this parody of Rudyard's beloved poem 'If', which he had written in 1895. Trix's parody dates from the period of the Boer War 1899–1902, while she was in Tisbury with her parents.

> IF
> 'O god, why ain't it a man?' –RK
> (To a young C. O. now enjoying complete exemption)
>
> If you keep your job when all about you
> Are losing theirs, because they're soldiers now;
> If no Tribunal of C.O.s can flout you,
> Or tilt the self-set halo from your brow;
> If you hold forth, demand your soul's pre-emption,
> And play up conscience more than it is worth,
> You'll win your case, enjoy 'complete exemption',
> And—at the usual price—possess the earth.
>
> If you can take from college and from city
> Culture and comfort all your conscious days,
> Take all and render nothing, more's the pity,
> But cunning preachments of self-love, self-praise;
> Exempt you are, forsooth, and safely nested,
> Above your priceless pate a plume of white,
> Protected by this symbol all detested,
> Your worst foe—self—is all you need to fight.
>
> If you can claim to follow Christ as Master
> (Tell us when he shirked service or grim death),
> How dare you plead for freedom from disaster,
> And, wrapped in cotton-wool, draw easy breath?
> If you evade—not touching with a finger –
> The heavy burdens other young men bear,
> We dare not breathe the ugly word 'malinger'
> For fear, perchance, your craven soul we scare.
> If girls in uniform do not distress you,
> If you can smile at verbal sneers made plain,
> If you don't wince when soldier friends address you,
> Proffer bath chairs, and greet you as 'Aunt Jane',
> Then rhino hide is nothing to the human,
> Holier than they are, grudge ye not their fun,
> But, laddie, realise the average woman
> Gives heartfelt thanks that you are not her son.[21]

---

21 Alice Fleming, 'If' (1902).

When not imitating other peoples' verse, Trix worked hard to find a publisher for *Hand in Hand,* the volume of verse she had written with Alice. Writing to Elkins Mathews in February of 1902, Trix enquired politely if he would be interested in publishing a volume of verse by a mother and daughter, not mentioning at first that they were the mother and sister of Rudyard Kipling. When he agreed to publish the book, Trix continued to correspond with him about the work in progress. She had suggestions about all aspects of the book—its length, size, paper, margins, and typeface. On her own, she arranged to have the book published in America by Doubleday at the same time that she was negotiating with Mathews in London. And finally, she proposed that Lockwood should design a drawing for the volume. She pursued this project with great determination, responding immediately to every request from her publisher. Her correspondence with Mathews, written with respect and care, is in every way sane and sensible.

Fig. 26 The front cover of *Hand in Hand*.

Hand in Hand: Verses by a Mother and Daughter was published anonymously and printed in London by Elkin Mathews in 1902.[22] The slender volume contains 31 poems by Alice Kipling, 'To My Daughter', and 63 poems 'To My Mother' by Alice Macdonald Fleming. The little book bears all the earmarks of a labour of love. A frontispiece illustration in a photogravure by Lockwood Kipling was the father's contribution to the family collaboration. Lockwood's illustration depicts a seated woman in classical draperies, her right hand lightly resting on the shoulder of a girl who kneels beside her. It was an open secret that the authors were near relatives of Rudyard Kipling, but the critics agreed that the poems stood on their own merits and needed no outside help.

During the period referred to as Trix's breakdown, from the late fall of 1898 to the early fall of 1902, Trix was not at all times in a state of mental collapse. In fact, for much of this period, she was calm and content. Once she recovered from the initial shock of Jack's suspected infidelity, was allowed to separate from him, and settled into a domestic routine with her mother, she was unusually productive. Alice fussed over Trix during this period and was nervously protective of her. Although Alice's tardy attention could never fully repair the damage of her earlier neglect, it did prove useful. Alice provided Trix with a safe place to recover, where she could be free of whatever anguish and distress Jack was causing and whatever demands he was making. Alice successfully calmed and quieted Trix, allowing her to concentrate and write. Trix rarely wrote this much and would rarely write anything for publication again.

In the early months of 1901, Trix's doctors as well as her brother reported that she was quite sane. When she travelled to Europe with her parents in the spring of 1901, she charmed everyone she met. When she corresponded with Elkins Mathews in 1902, she was in full command of her faculties.

Thus, in 1902, Trix was faced with a choice. She could pursue permanent separation or divorce and remain in England under the protection of her parents, or she could return to married life with Jack in India.

Although she had been mostly content in the care of her parents, she did not wish to maintain the fiction of madness, which would

---

22   *Hand in Hand: Verses by a Mother and Daughter* (London: Elkin Mathews, 1902).

have allowed her to remain with them. She was not insane. Permanent separation or divorce, which would bring public shame and scandal not only on her but on her family, also troubled her. She was loath to cause her family even more distress. Trix was always quick to accuse herself of wilfulness and ingratitude, and she was afraid not only of public censure but also of her own self-recriminations. Added to all of this was her suspicion that, after four years, Alice was growing weary of tending to her. And finally, Trix recognized that she was growing weary of Alice's anxious care.

Jack offered another possible future—domestic life back in India. Jack had been constant in his desire to have Trix return to the marriage. He had not abandoned her but, on the contrary, had badgered her to return. In response to Jack's pressure, Trix, more than once, had made plans to return to India, then cancelled the arrangements and remained in England. She had put off for as long as she could what she knew was inevitable—the return to Jack and India. The alternatives were not possible. She was not mad and she would not pursue divorce.

After four years, Trix had somewhat recovered from the sting of Jack's perfidy. His repeated insistence that she belonged back in India with him assured her of his continuing attachment. Thus, in September of 1902, Trix relented and complied with Jack's wishes. After more than two years of good health, good spirits, and a clear mind, she agreed to leave her parents in Tisbury, return to Calcutta, and resume her married life.

With Alice's cooperation and encouragement, Trix had given herself almost four years of what was essentially a separation from Jack.

9. Psychic Research

Trix returned to India, not simply resigned but resolved to salvage her marriage to Jack. She resumed her life in Calcutta, which she described as 'the sun-scorched and dust-laden city where flame flowered trees shed petals like sparks without pity to fire every breeze'.[1] There, she worked to convince Jack of her stability and reliability. She had been alienated from him for almost four years. To reassure Jack, Trix undertook her household chores and social obligations with special fervour. She tended carefully to her house and her husband, but still she had energy to spare.

Trix had been full of ideas for novels and stories before her breakdown and had written and published many poems and stories during her time in Tisbury. But she did not return to fiction or verse. Her large store of untried, unfinished, and unworkable fictional ideas simply slipped away. From time to time, she recalled with some pride how she had once submitted her work to publishers, dealt competently with editors, and gloried in seeing her work in print. Instead of returning to writing, she revived her interest in the psychic world.

On a steamy summer morning in 1903, Trix rose early and, still in her dressing gown and slippers, padded softly up to her writing table and wrote a letter to Alice Johnson, the research officer and secretary of the British Society for Psychical Research (SPR) in London. She explained that she had learned of the Society from having read and been deeply moved by *Human Personality and its Survival of Bodily Death*, written by the Society's founder, the late Professor Frederic Myers of Cambridge University.[2] Rarely shy, Trix introduced herself and described her

---

1. Trix Kipling, 'Letter to William de Morgan' (1908), in *William de Morgan and his Wife*, ed. by A. M. W. Stirling (New York: Henry Holt, 1922).
2. Frederic Myers, *Human Personality and its Survival of Bodily Death* (London: Longmans, Green & Co., 1903).

interest in psychic research. She explained that she had practiced automatic writing—which she called 'pencil writing'—since 1893, for her own amusement and in spite of her family's discouragement. She added that she was able to see visions in a crystal and enclosed ten lines of automatically written verse. In her letter, Trix described herself as a healthy, cheerful woman, thirty-five years of age, who sometimes became conscious of beings and influences not patent to all. She wondered if this frame of mind should be checked or encouraged. She confessed that her own people hated what they called 'uncanniness', and that she was obliged to hide from them her keen interest in psychic matters.

Trix further explained that her automatic writing often came to her in childishly simple verse. While jingling in rhyme, the verses were rarely trivial in subject. Their most striking feature was the rapidity with which they came to her, swiftly dictated and without erasures. Her hand moved so quickly that she seldom knew the words as they were being formed. Trix added, 'I have never been in surroundings that encouraged this interest, I have never been mesmerized, I have never attended a séance, for the idea of anything connected with paid mediumship is peculiarly disagreeable to me. I only discovered by accident five years ago, that I have the clairvoyant faculty'.[3] Trix waited for Miss Johnson's reply.

Earlier that summer, Trix had become absorbed in Professor Myers's unusual work of spiritual science. In mid-day, when it was too hot to do anything but lie down and dream, Trix stretched out on her couch and read Myers's book describing his theory of the survival of the soul after death. Myers was a classical scholar and poet as well as a researcher into the subliminal mind, trance-like states, and telepathy—a word he coined. Myers's suggestive and seductive work contained his thoughts on the mysteries of psychical phenomena and set forth his innovative psychological and metaphysical theories. As the title of his book suggests, Myers wished to prove the survival of the spirit after the death of the body. He postulated that this could be confirmed by communications from the spirit world.

Trix was not alone in being attracted to Myers, his book, and the society he founded in 1882. At the end of the nineteenth century, the

---

3   Trix Kipling, letter to Alice Johnson. 'On the Automatic Writing of Mrs Holland', *Proceedings, Society for Psychical Research*, 21 (1908–09), pp. 171–74.

Society for Psychical Research was a respected British organization, the American branch of which had been founded by the philosopher and psychologist William James. Myers's book, which captured Trix's imagination, attracted many to the Society for Psychical Research (SPR), including numerous famous academics, philosophers, scientists, and writers. Members of the society included Sir Oliver Lodge, physicist, Lord Rayleigh, physicist and Nobel prize winner, Gerald, second Lord Balfour, classical scholar and philosopher, Prime Minister Arthur James Balfour, Gilbert Murray, Greek scholar, Henri Bergson, philosopher, Prime Minister William E. Gladstone, 'Lewis Carroll' (author of *Alice in Wonderland*), Alfred Lord Tennyson, John Ruskin, and Sir Arthur Conan Doyle. The Society appealed to the fashionable, the respectable, academics, aristocrats, and royals.

Although Trix knew little about The Society, she familiarized herself with its immediate history and worked to understand its avowed aim—defending orthodox religion against the two main currents of thought threatening it. One current was a hunger for new and exotic forms of religious belief to supplement Christianity, including a revival of interest in the Rosicrucians, the Masons, and the theories of Emanuel Swedenborg in Europe, and the rise of Mormonism (founded in 1830) and Christian Science (founded in 1872) in the United States. A second opposing current included Darwinism, materialism, and agnosticism and the anti-religious tendencies of the day, which denied the existence of the soul separate from the body and maintained man's soul-less descent from distant non-human ancestors. The SPR represented a formidable backlash against these two powerful trends. The founders of the SPR proposed to subject the claims of these opposing belief systems to rigorous scientific exploration in the hope that they could cast serious doubt on them.

Myers and the founders of the SPR believed in the existence of the soul and were deeply desirous of answering the question, 'If man had a soul, could that soul survive bodily death?' Myers and his followers wished to prove survival after death as a state of being that man could look forward to as a sign that the universe was a benign and friendly place. They hoped through careful experiment to be able to demonstrate that immortality was a scientific fact, that natural science might rationally encompass the supernatural.

While serious intellectuals were endeavouring to test the claims and counter claims of the foundations of religion, Darwinism, and spiritualism, many frauds and fakers were exploiting the keen public interest in these theories for their own spurious ends. Spiritualism was a popular entertainment at the time. Phonies of all kinds took advantage of the credulous, describing inexplicable psychic phenomena and inventing dramatic stories of communications from the beyond. The popularity of spiritualism posed a challenge to science, if not to common sense. The fascination with the supernatural occasioned derision on the one hand and uncritical enthusiasm on the other. From the beginning, intimations of fraud sullied the reputation of the spiritual movement. The SPR endeavoured to distance itself from the numerous table-turners, spoon benders, and fakers who had recently appeared to take advantage of the fad for psychic entertainment. The society was especially eager to distinguish itself from the Theosophical Society founded by Madame Helena Blavatsky, a clever and charismatic charlatan who proclaimed herself the founder of a new religion, Theosophy, and wrote its bible, *Art Magic*.[4] The high-minded Victorians of the SPR engaged in psychic experiments from what they believed were pure scientific motives. While self-deception might have existed in the researchers of the SPR, calculated deceit did not.

Psychic phenomena were not new to the Kiplings. Alice and her younger sisters often boasted playfully that they had second sight, while Trix, sometimes playfully and sometimes seriously, believed herself to be especially open to occult experiences. Rudyard was drawn to extraordinary religious expression, Freemasonry, and other forms of psychic experience. He described the state of artistic creation as a kind of trance. He claimed that 'the pen took charge' as he wrote stories about Mowgli and animals, which later grew into *The Jungle Books*. He advised, 'When your daemon is in charge, do not try to think consciously. Drift, wait and obey'.[5] This state of artistic inspiration resembles the state of hypersensitive passivity thought to be conducive to receiving psychic messages. Many of Kipling's stories, possibly conceived in this way, also have uncanny and supernatural elements to them. ('At the End of the Passage', 'By Word of Mouth', 'In the House of Suddhoo', 'The

---

4 Madame Blavatsky, *Art Magic* (1876).
5 Rudyard Kipling, 'Chapter 8', in *Something of Myself*.

Strange Ride of Morrowbie Jukes', 'The Phantom Rickshaw', 'The Sending of Dana Da", 'The Mark of the Beast', 'The Return of Imray', and more.) Thus, Trix was not alone in the family for being receptive to the supernatural.

For some time in private, Trix had indulged in automatic writing and crystal gazing, believing that she was successfully hiding these occupations from her family and friends. During her time in Tisbury, she had shared with her new friend Evelyn de Morgan her interest in spiritualism, although she had not shared it with others and was unaware that others knew about it, which, it seems, they did. When Trix had visited Florence, she had been encouraged by Lady Walburga Paget to resume her crystal gazing. The spirit world had, for some time, been beckoning to her.

When Trix sat at her writing table in the early morning, corresponding with her friends, she often felt her hand move of its own accord, inscribing letters intended not for her usual correspondents but for people unknown to her. These curious movements and messages made her uneasy. She tried to ignore them or avoid them by dropping her pen, leaving her writing table, and taking up needlework or knitting until the force had spent itself. If her hand was not actively engaged at some other task during these times, it clenched itself and made the motion of writing in the air. Resisting these movements exhausted her and caused her to suffer cruel headaches. But after a while, Trix became more comfortable with these strange movements and, instead of discouraging them, relaxed into them and allowed her hand to move of its own accord. At the same time, she also began more seriously to seek visions in her egg-shaped crystal ball.

When she casually or accidentally mentioned these activities to Jack, he was not pleased. When Rudyard learned of Trix's continued participation in psychic activities, he became alarmed. He was worried that psychic research might have an untoward effect on his sister's precarious mental health. Rudyard, aware of his own susceptibility to spiritualism, warned Trix away from it precisely because he well understood its powerful attractions. Trix recognized that it would be wise to keep her renewed interest in spiritual matters to herself, and she tried to do so.

Trix scoured Myers's book *Human Personality*, trying to locate a person to contact in order to express her interest in psychic matters and to describe her own psychic abilities. Eventually, she found the name of the secretary of the SPR, Alice Johnson.

Miss Johnson, as a representative of the SPR, responded to Trix's letter with interest. She was especially intrigued by Trix's potential for receiving messages from the 'other side'. She described Trix's exceptional abilities to the other members of the SPR and explained that, as Trix's family objected to psychical research, she wished her name not to be mentioned in public. She was therefore given the name 'Mrs Holland'.

Miss Johnson, a natural scientist from Newnham College, was a trained researcher, vigilant against shoddy and ill-substantiated data. Like most other members of The Society, she was eager to find appropriately serious and qualified mediums and considered Trix to be ideal, as she had literary ability, a dramatic imagination, rapid perception, and a fine discrimination of character. Most importantly, Trix was a woman of integrity. Before locating Trix, the SPR had found few mediums whose honesty they could rely on. They had unhappily learned that psychic talent often manifested itself in decidedly shady characters. Mediums like the notorious Eusapia Paladino embarrassed their sponsors and brought discredit to their research. William James in Boston had been fortunate to discover an honest and respectable medium, Mrs Leonora E. Piper, who was later paired with Trix for a number of psychic experiments.

Thus, the SPR was delighted to be contacted by Trix, a medium of ability and integrity. When they suggested that Trix send her automatic scripts to them, she readily complied. Over some weeks, Trix sent many pages of writing but received little encouragement, until she sent a script that included the name and address of a woman in London. Trix had conjured the name and address from the air, but 'Mrs A. W. Verrall of 5 Selwyn Gardens, Cambridge' was the name and address of a lecturer at Newnham College and a leading member of the SPR.

Miss Johnson and members of The Society were very excited about the inexplicable appearance of this name and address and believed it indicated a connection between the two women. To exploit this valuable connection, Miss Johnson designed experiments that paired Trix (Mrs

Holland) with Mrs Verrall to discover 'cross-correspondences' between their two texts.

'Cross correspondences' were being carefully studied by the SPR to investigate communication between immortal souls and living mediums. The SPR submitted for study the theory that fragmentary utterances from one script, when put together with the fragmentary utterances of another script, supplemented one another and expressed a complete idea only partially expressed in each. This complete idea was trying to be communicated by a person or group of persons from the beyond who had invented this plan of cross-correspondences expressly to meet the objections of sceptics and unbelievers. This theory rested on the belief that an active intelligence was constantly at work in the present and was not a mere echo or remnant of individuals of the past.

More easily acceptable was the theory that information contained in alleged messages from the 'other side' were not actually communications from the dead but resulted from telepathy among living mediums. Messages received from the 'other side' were actually the product of the automatists acting under the impact and implied direction of the situation. Eager to act out the characterizations which they had taken upon themselves, they produced the desired results.

Although Trix was not privy to the exact nature of the experiments she was participating in, she submitted her scripts to The Society, assured that they were useful evidence. Trix never asserted a belief in the theory of cross-correspondences, never claimed to be in contact with the dead, or to communicate with spirits, but she was aware and proud of her own sensitivity to perceptions and influences that were outside of normal consciousness. She knew she had a remarkably keen memory. Most of all, she wanted to communicate, to be understood, and to transmit and receive thoughts and feelings over distance and time. Throughout her life, she felt she had failed at communicating to those she most earnestly wished to reach, and this failure was a continual sadness to her. (She was also able to transform this sadness into hilarious dialogues of marital discord. Miscommunication can be a tragedy, but it can also be a joke.)

Many people involved with psychic research had suffered a terrible sudden bereavement, a secret love, or a hidden relationship. While Trix had not suffered in these ways, she had experienced a prolonged bereavement, a childhood of exile and loneliness. In Trix's scripts, she conveyed her old yearning to be heard and understood, her ancient unanswered cry for her mother. Many of Trix's scripts sounded like a wail of pain from a bereft child.

Trix sent scripts to Miss Johnson steadily from September 1903 to January 1904—filled, like her conversation, with quotations from poetry, fiction, and drama as well as classical literature and mythology. Early in the morning, before the bustle of the day began, Trix crept softly to her desk, settled herself into her chair, and, as instructed, tried to make her mind blank in order to receive messages from Frederic Myers and Edmund Gurney, former leaders of the SPR. Leaning forward with her pen or pencil, she bid these spirits to come to her. When the spirits came, she felt her hand move, saw the letters form, and wrote until the spirits passed. Although she felt she was conscious during her writing, on several occasions she partially lost consciousness, and, on one occasion, when she shut her eyes, she felt as if her right arm were the only part of her body not asleep. At times, she felt so sick while writing that she had to get up from her desk and leave the room. At times, she found that being interrupted at her writing gave her a jarred and dizzy feeling. But at other times, when she concluded her writing, she felt refreshed and alert.

She had been directed to write every day, and for a brief period she seated herself at her desk and waited for the spirit to come to her at eleven each morning. But she found that she preferred writing earlier in the day when she was less likely to be disturbed. She wrote at this early hour once a week, not once a day. Trix thus arrived at a schedule of weekly sessions, where, as the dawn broke outside of her tall windows, she sat alone and called to the spirits. Most often, what came to her, as she cleared her mind and closed her eyes, were sad thoughts about the difficulty of communication between souls living and dead. Her waves of classical and mythological references rode on an undercurrent of pure personal lament.

Sometimes, Trix, under the control of Mr Myers, wrote in a sloping, pointed, and continuous hand, using a pen. At other times, under the control of Mr Gurney, she wrote in a bolder, more upright, often disjointed style, using a pencil. Under the influence of both Myers and Gurney, she dwelled on her difficulties and discouragements. The various texts do not make it clear who exactly is describing these troubles. It could be Myers or Gurney or Trix herself, who is 'sending a message', 'dictating feebly', or feeling powerless and impotent.

This appeal is typical.

'If it were possible for the soul to die back into earth life again I should die from sheer yearning to reach you—to tell you that all that we imagined is not half wonderful enough for the truth . . .'.[6] Trix detailed the troubles:

> The nearest simile I can find to express the difficulties of sending a message—is that I appear to be standing behind a sheet of frosted glass—which blurs sight and deadens sound—dictating feebly—to a reluctant and somewhat obtuse secretary. A feeling of terrible impotence burdens me—I am so powerless to tell what means so much—I cannot get into communication with those who would understand and believe me.[7]

Miss Johnson, who edited and commented on the scripts of both Mrs Holland and Mrs Verrall, wrote that 'the reader who compares the general character of the two scripts can hardly fail to notice the emotional nature and the note of personal appeal in the utterances of the Holland-Myers [Trix] as contrasted with the calmer, more impersonal, and more matter-of-fact tone of the Verrall-Myers'.[8] In concluding her impressions of the first phase of Trix's involvement with the SPR, Miss Johnson focused on Trix's painful efforts to be recognized by the spirits from beyond in laments like this: 'It is such a passionate craving sometimes that I find myself crying out: "If I could help you—Oh! If I could only help you!" while I write'. Trix reported that the writing 'often brings a very sad impression of great depression with it—a feeling as if some one was calling to deaf ears'. Trix recalled:

> a feeling that sometimes comes in connection with the script—a feeling that some one, somewhere, urgently and passionately desires to be understood, or reported even without understanding, and that no mental strain on my part can adequately respond to this demand. This feeling has been strong enough to make me cry and to make me speak aloud. I do not often dwell upon it. I frequently control it, for it seems to me perilously akin to hysteria; but it is a very real part of automatic script.[9]

Trix, struggling to receive and transmit Myers's words, cried aloud, 'If I could only reach you—if I could only tell you—I long for power and

---

6   *Proceedings of SPR*, 21 (1908–09), p. 179.
7   Ibid., p. 208.
8   Ibid., p. 239.
9   Ibid., p. 240.

all that comes to me is an infinite yearning—an infinite pain. Does any of this reach you—reach any one—or am I only wailing as the wind wails—wordless and unheeded'.[10]

In her automatic writing for the SPR, Trix reported Myers's and Gurney's anguished yearnings across the infinite beyond to transmit messages. Then she sent her transcriptions across thousands of miles, from India to England.

'Wailing as the wind wails' recalls the feelings of Trix's sad childhood. As a lonely little girl, Trix longed for contact and consolation, writing imaginary letters and composing imaginary scenes of reunion, reconciliation, and revenge.

Later, as a misunderstood and unappreciated wife trying to reach her unresponsive husband, she experienced similar feelings, which she cleverly transformed into comic dialogues of miscommunication. As a cautious and conflicted fiction writer, she tried, without complete conviction, to write what she deeply knew and felt, the bitter alienation and frustration of women's lives. 'Wailing as the wind wails' is how Trix had often, perhaps always, felt. Automatic writing gave her permission to weep and wail on schedule and on paper. It also held out the promise of being useful to researchers.

For five months, week after week before dawn, Trix let herself slip into an altered state, somewhere between waking and dreaming. She sought out this trance-like state, encouraged it, and repeated it.

After January 1904, she wrote with less regularity, but continued her correspondence with the SPR. Then, in April 1904, she stopped her correspondence for almost a year, because, as she explained to Miss Johnson, when she was interrupted during her writing, she experienced a terrible jarring feeling. This feeling did not justify the uncertain results she obtained from her writing. The greater problem during this time was that Trix didn't have the privacy she needed to write undisturbed. She was not in her own home in Calcutta but traveling on the continent with her husband. On 15 February 1905, Trix resumed the correspondence with the SPR, sending Miss Johnson a poem which she had written in January of 1905. She explained her long silence in part by describing the troubling sleepiness and faintness that had accompanied her recent writing. She

---

10   Ibid., p. 222.

had also been discomfited by a trance she had fallen into, during which she had spoken automatically for about a quarter of an hour.

Trix omitted from this explanation Jack's strict prohibition against her correspondence with Alice Johnson. Jack claimed that he was protecting Trix's health from the extreme agitation caused by her psychic activity. But he was also protecting his own reputation among the British ruling class, who looked on psychic activity with extreme disfavour. On more than one occasion, Jack had cause to suspect that, despite his strictures, Trix was continuing the correspondence. When he was especially troubled by doubts, he interrogated Trix cruelly. On one occasion, when he wrung a confession of disobedience from her, he extracted a promise that she would put an end to the correspondence. Trix tried to honour this hard promise, but the impulse to write was irresistible, and she resumed her writing in February 1905, continuing with complaints about the difficulties of communication. 'The Veil remains the Veil. The Door will continue to have no Key...', and 'We feel as if only one sentence reached of twenty that we strive to send'.[11]

During the spring and summer of 1905, Trix, with Jack's approval, made arrangements to travel alone to England in the fall. What Jack did not know and would not have approved of was that her plans included a meeting with Miss Johnson, the woman who had been an important part of her world for the preceding two years, who had received not only her scripts but also her private thoughts and feelings.

In early October 1905, Trix travelled past Oxford Street to busy Hanover Square, then to number 20, the headquarters of the Society for Psychic Research. Eager and excited to have her first meeting with Miss Alice Johnson, she arrived at the appointed hour at the impressive Regency building. At the double pillared entrance of the brick façade, she was greeted by Miss Johnson, a woman slightly older than herself. Together, the two women climbed the wide ornamental staircase, lit from above by glowing glass panes. Miss Johnson ushered Trix into a formal drawing room and directed her to a comfortable chair. Having seated Trix, she then seated herself opposite, under a large portrait of man with a trimmed grey beard, high forehead, and keen gaze. Trying to look at Miss Johnson, Trix found herself drawn to the man in the

---

11   Ibid., p. 249.

painting, who seemed familiar to her, but whom she could not identify. She could not take her eyes off the portrait and stared so fixedly at it that she feared she might fall into a trance. She could hardly listen to what Miss Johnson was saying to her. Before the interview could begin, Trix anxiously asked Miss Johnson, 'Who is that man? I'm sure I've seen him before. I know him quite well'. Miss Johnson explained that he was Frederic Myers, the dead man whose spirit Trix had been struggling to hear and report. Once Miss Johnson had identified the portrait, Trix recalled having seen it reproduced in one of Myers's books.[12]

After identifying the portrait, Trix spoke calmly with Miss Johnson for two and a half hours. Wishing to appear amiable and tractable, Trix held herself still and silent to listen to the Miss Johnson's reports of the society's progress and purpose. But when her chance to speak came, she rushed on enthusiastically to describe the details of her writing process. She happily supplied the sources of her many classical allusions and poetic quotations. When Miss Johnson questioned her repeatedly about the possibility that she may have heard, seen, or read names, dates, or photographs that appeared in her scripts mysteriously and spontaneously, she struggled to reconstruct all the books she had read and photographs she had seen, and agreeably entertained all the possible explanations Miss Johnson suggested for their appearance. Trix found Miss Johnson cautious and reticent in her speech and careful to avoid any indiscretions about the experiments in which Trix was participating.

Miss Johnson recognized that Trix often produced in her automatic scripts names, places, and images, which, when shown to her later, were unknown to her. Miss Johnson was impressed by this failure of Trix's supraliminal (conscious) mind to recognize something well known to her subliminal (unconscious) mind. Later scripts of Trix's confirmed the process by which ideas and impressions recorded by the subliminal mind emerged in automatic scripts, although they were unavailable to the supraliminal mind. Myers and others recognized that the dreaming mind similarly had access to impressions and images not available to ordinary consciousness, and which the waking mind found surprising, unbelievable, and often unacceptable.

---

12   Ibid., p. 266.

Trix met Miss Johnson several more times in November, cheerfully providing whatever information was requested of her. At one meeting on 16 November, Trix arrived at Hanover Square and was taken by surprise to be introduced to a woman she had never seen before. This was Mrs Verrall, Trix's immediate cross correspondent. Trix and Mrs Verrall, who had never met nor communicated directly before, were escorted up the grand stairs under the skylight and into an austere drawing room, seated at separate desks, and instructed to write scripts while sitting together in the same space. The experiment was meant to determine if propinquity had any influence on the correspondences in their writings. The experiment proved that it did not. From November to June, Trix returned many times to Hanover Square to sit as a subject in psychometry experiments for the Society, exchanging rings, gloves, and other trinkets to test for influences emanating from objects. While these experiments produced largely negative results, they nonetheless constituted useful data for the Society.

Through November and December of 1905, while Trix travelled back and forth from London to Tisbury and to Edinburgh, she faithfully sent scripts to the Society. In February 1906, Trix began two series of experiments with Mrs Verrall, which she found especially difficult, as they produced faintness almost to stupor. She tried writing in the evening, sitting in a hard, straight chair away from her table with no support for her arms or head, rather than in the morning to see if this helped, but she continued to feel so sleepy she fancied she might fall into a trance. Miss Johnson encouraged her to continue writing, and, despite discomfort, she kept at it.

Miss Johnson, when evaluating the evidence provided by Trix and other mediums, was a scrupulous and prescient investigator. Writing on subliminal reminiscences, she suggested explanations that were entirely reasonable and that resemble the results of modern neuro-scientific experiments. She posited that the recrudescence of memories that have completely lapsed from the normal consciousness is common and is not to be attributed to a supernormal cause. Events, although seemingly forgotten, have been recorded and retained, and are often reproduced in dreams, hallucinations, and recovered memories.

When not visiting London, Trix stayed with her parents in Tisbury. She felt it was her duty when visiting The Gables to try to entertain

Alice, and she generously chattered away to her frail and unhappy mother. On this trip to England, Trix was surprised to be invited to stay at Wilden with her wealthy Aunt Louisa and Uncle Alfred Baldwin. Trix had never before been invited to visit Wilden or to spend time with the grand Baldwins. Trix was suspicious that Louisa, a devout Christian, had heard of Trix's involvement with the Society for Psychic Research, and had invited her expressly to dissuade her from pursing her impious pastime. If she tried to influence Trix, she was unsuccessful. Trix remained devoted to her friends in the SPR.

The high point of Trix's visit to England was a large house party she attended at Clouds, the Salisbury home of her parents' closest friends, the Percy Wyndhams. The Wyndhams were members of an elite social group called 'The Souls', who cultivated high aesthetic and cultural values and practiced unconventional and liberated morals. The members of the group pursued superior social pleasures, disdaining the vulgarities of racing, card-playing, and gossip. The Wyndhams' home, a grand gothic-style mansion, was the setting for many gatherings of intellectual excitement and romantic intrigue. The interior of the house was designed by Kipling family friend, William Morris, and the walls were hung with paintings by Trix's uncles, Edward Burne-Jones and Edward Poynter.

Trix arrived at Clouds to find that the many distinguished guests included twenty adults, several cheerful adolescents, and numerous raucous children. At her arrival, Trix was shown to her own lovely bedroom. When she came down to luncheon in the elaborately decorated dining room, she was delighted by the informal festive meal. Later, at the formal dinner, she nervously wondered how she could speak with any of the many famous men. When she was seated between Sir Oliver Lodge and Mr George Wyndham, she did not know which way to turn and felt 'like the donkey between two bundles of hay'.[13] She was especially eager to talk to Sir Oliver Lodge, who resembled a great sage with his fine brow and long beard, but she was intimidated by his formidable reputation. Lodge was a revered scientist and author of many books who had been, since the 1880s, interested in detecting and transmitting electromagnetic waves. Along with Marconi and Tesla, he was an early experimenter on

---

13 Trix Kipling, letter to Maud Diver, 4 September 1906.

the transmission of radio signals and wireless telegraphy. For Trix, he was of special interest as a former president of the SPR (from 1901-3) and a close friend of the late Frederic Myers.

At dinner, Trix wished to speak with Lodge, but feared he would try to talk to her about electromagnetics. She was relieved when he engaged her in conversation about the psychic realm. When he asked about her automatic writing, she enthusiastically described her part in the cross-correspondence experiments and was surprised and flattered to learn that Sir Oliver knew about her. Delighted by his familiarity with her work, Trix described how effortless automatic writing was for her, how it came to her unsummoned and with swiftness and ease or not at all. Lodge was surprised, telling Trix that most mediums who had attained proficiency had done so only after a great deal of study and effort.

Gerald Balfour, a distinguished SPR member, who was present at the party, asked Trix if she would attempt crystal gazing as an after-dinner entertainment. She readily agreed and gave a dramatic performance, while Balfour cooperatively held the crystal for her. When Lodge prepared to leave the house party, he went out of his way to search Trix out. In saying goodbye to her, he repeated his praise of her powers, assuring her that they were a great deal rarer than she imagined. He earnestly begged her to faithfully continue the experiments—however dull they might seem—for the sake of science. She promised to continue her writing, a pledge she meant to redeem.

At their last meeting, 28 May 1906, Trix and Miss Johnson discussed the results of the new set of experiments, which had been scientifically tabulated for correspondences and were more compelling than earlier experiments. Nonetheless, the cautious Miss Johnson wrote that the cross correspondences of Mrs Holland and Mrs Verrall had not produced 'really good evidence of supernormal knowledge'.[14]

She concluded that the results of the cross-correspondence experiments were too slender to support the hypothesis of supernatural communication. The many experiments were seen as promising and worthy of consideration, but not proof of any supernatural communication. Miss Johnson concluded that 'the same normal though

---

14   Alice Johnson, 'On the Automatic Writing of Mrs Holland', *Proceedings, Society for Psychical Research*, 25 (1911), p. 391.

obscure psychological processes with which we are all familiar in dream and reverie are also at work in automatic writing'.[15]

After her last meeting with Miss Johnson in Hanover Square, Trix returned to Tisbury to rejoin her mother, who was anxiously worrying over the deteriorating health of her sister Agnes. Through most of the spring, Aunt Aggie—wife of the painter Edward Poynter—had been in failing health. While Aunts Edie and Louise had nursed their sister in her final months, Alice had only rarely gone to comfort her sister. After several months lying in bed, often unconscious, Aggie died on 12 June.

Trix had already booked her passage back to India, when Agnes died, and, although she recognized her mother's sorrow, she could not postpone her departure. She left her mother on the day of Aggie's funeral, 16 June, and boarded the P. & O. Somali in London, as she had planned. Abandoning her grieving mother gave Trix a fierce headache, which lasted for the first three days of the voyage. But soon, Trix's head cleared, and she felt well enough to read, devouring Sir Oliver Lodge's book, *Life and Matter*,[16] which convinced her that telepathy was an actual phenomenon. For most of the journey home, she felt unusually well. She made new acquaintances and resumed a friendship with an old dancing partner from Simla days. The weather was perfect all the way to Port Said with sapphire seas, fresh breezes, and lovely cool nights full of stars. East of Suez, the seas grew rougher, but the lovely beginning of the voyage made Trix feel rested and restored. In the past, Trix had suffered on the long sea voyage, but this trip was a delight. Despite the heat and the rolling of the ship, Trix never missed a meal.

She arrived in Bombay on the morning of 8 July, but she still had to endure the long, hot trip to Calcutta. This, too, was easier than before, especially because Jack had made special efforts to make her comfortable. He provided an electric fan for her railway carriage, had hired a new Victoria with rubber tires for her overland journey, and had even purchased her favourite tooth-paste.

When Trix finally arrived in Calcutta and saw Jack, she was alarmed. He was thin and white, and worry creased his face. He told Trix that he had been unable to shake off a constant low fever, and that it had worn him down. She could see that the fever had also exacerbated his usual

---

15   Ibid., p. 283.
16   Oliver Lodge, *Life and Matter* (London: Williams and Norgate, 1905).

depression. Despite his low energy and low spirits, he had managed to engage a new house at 7/1 Loudon Street—a large three-storied structure on the corner of Loudon and Shakespeare Streets, in the heart of 'White Town'. It was ochre-yellow stucco with green shutters, fancifully etched windows, and a lush walled garden in the rear. Trix was charmed by the asymmetry of the house and its many small rooms and impressed by the vast, forty feet long drawing room. She made plans, which she eventually carried out, to make the small rooms into a suite of separate bedrooms and dressing rooms for herself and Jack. She needed a place where she could sit alone and be undisturbed in the early hours of the day, when she resumed her automatic writing.

The house was two blocks away from the Saturday Club, where Trix and Jack dined, played tennis, swam, and met with friends. The club, named for the day of the week on which the mail arrived from abroad, was a gathering place for the British. It featured formal reception areas, rooms for billiard tables and squash courts, two dining rooms, four bars, and a large hall for dancing parties. Behind the main building were lawns for tennis courts and tables for outdoor dining. In a separate building, a large marble swimming pool was housed beneath a vaulted glass skylight.

The house and the club were ideal for socializing, but Jack hardly felt social. Added to his usual complaints was a new one—varicose veins, for which he required surgery followed by bed rest. After recovering from the operation, he continued to be in poor health and low spirits. Trix felt she was constantly battling it, like 'David slinging pebbles at the Goliath of his habitual depression'.[17] Although she knew how useless it was to try to dispel his black moods, she couldn't stop herself from trying. She endeavoured to think only resolute and cheerful thoughts, refusing to let Jack's despair drag them both down. Faithful to the pledge she had made to Sir Oliver Lodge, in early August, Trix returned to her writing for the SPR, rarely missing a week. As always, she filled her scripts with literary references—Shakespeare, Dante, Ovid, Milton, Swinburne, Shelley, Poe, and classical myth. But she wailed and worried less in these later writings than she had before. Trix continued writing regularly on Wednesday mornings through 1907 and into early March 1908. Though

---

17 Trix Kipling, letter to Maud Diver, 17 October 1907.

Trix took her promise seriously, she had her doubts about the results of her scripts. She confided to the de Morgans, the only people to whom she ever mentioned her automatic scripts, that while the writing went on fairly regularly, it was dull when she read it over. Nonetheless, she faithfully sent her writing—secretly—to the patient readers at the SPR, and she modestly claimed that 'they sometimes found things that seem to count'.[18] As before, her texts were compared with Mrs Verrall's and with several other mediums for cross correspondences.

During the rest of the day, while enduring the extreme climate—alternating periods of insufferable heat and pounding rain—she ran the household and did her part in the social and sporting activities Jack was able to pursue. As always, she read great amounts of contemporary and nineteenth-century fiction. She read current novelists as well as Thackeray, Austen, Balzac, Flaubert, and Maupassant, and had a remarkable memory for everything she read. Although reading constantly, Trix wrote almost nothing. She tried her hand at drama, composing a slight entertainment for children. In September 1906, the play 'The Smuggler's Cave', or 'Old Mother Midnight', was performed in the puppet theatre at the home of her friends, the Mackails. In the program, the author of the play, Alice Fleming, identified herself with the anagram Alice F. Le Ming. James M. Barrie, creator of *Peter Pan*—who Trix described as 'a very shy bird'—was in the audience, but he hastily flew away before Trix had a chance to talk with him.[19]

This was all that Trix produced. She did not compose stories, plan novels, or submit essays. She confessed to Maud, 'Don't I know the 'stuck' fits in writing—(I'll forgive you if you suggest that I appear hardly to know any others!) I think you have wonderfully few of them as writers go'.[20] Trix wrote and published nothing, while Maud continued to publish one story after another. At the same time, Rudyard, at the age of forty-one, was awarded the Nobel Prize in Literature in 1907. Trix did not openly lament the end of her own writing career, contrive excuses for abandoning it, or express envy of the international fame of her brother. Trix's friend Redney Coates felt that Trix poured all of

---

18   Trix Kipling, 'Letter to the de Morgans' (1908), in *William de Morgan and his Wife*, ed. by A. M. W. Stirling (New York: Henry Holt, 1922).
19   Trix Kipling, letter to Maud Diver, 18 September 1907.
20   Ibid.

her extensive energy into her long and charming letters, which were absolutely 'Trix on paper'. This explained why there was so little of 'Trix between covers'.[21] If Trix regretted that she was spending her energy on letters and scripts and not on fiction, she did not complain about it.

When it was too hot to concentrate on anything, she entertained herself with numerology—reading character from names. In the languor-inducing heat, she made calculations for her own amusement, by replacing the letters in names with numbers and then supplying the characteristics associated with the numbers. She made calculations for herself, for Maud, and even for Maud's fictional characters. Evelyn, one of Maud's heroines, is calculated at 7+5+3. Neptune and Mercury are her planets, sea green and slate blue her colours. She is magnetic, full of life and go, apt to be intuitive and sometimes mystic and occult. She is imaginative, plucky, often not overly scrupulous, tender-hearted, generous, and easy going—up to a certain point when she will fight like a tiger cat. Trix passed her time in this silly and harmless way.

While Trix kept up a steady correspondence with good friends back in England, including Maud and Redney Coates, she had only a few sustaining friendships in Calcutta. Like most English women in India, Trix had little experience with 'natives', and no friends among Indian women. Indian women tended to keep to themselves, and British women resisted interfering with this tendency, which nicely coincided with their own. But in the fall of 1907, Trix made the acquaintance of a woman lawyer named Cornelia Sorabji. With financial help and special pleading from her friends, Cornelia had been educated at Bombay University and at Somerville College at Oxford, where she was the first woman to take the Bachelor of Civil Laws exam. She became a social reformer and legal activist, advising and championing purdah women denied access to the legal system. She petitioned the India Office to provide women with a female legal advisor in provincial courts and, to that end, travelled throughout India to the provinces of Bengal, Bihar, Orissa, and Assam. Trix met her at the start of her long and distinguished career and was impressed with her exceptional education, extensive reading, wide social circle, fascinating personality, lovely sense of humour, brilliant mind, and mystical spirit. Trix was proud and pleased to have

---

21   Trix Kipling, letter to Maud Diver, 6 May 1908.

formed this friendship, and was especially gratified when, after she had introduced Mrs Sorabji to Maud Diver, the two women collaborated on a book, *The Englishwoman in India* (1909).[22]

Trix remained devoted to her old friend Maud and wrote to her faithfully on a fortnightly schedule. Maud, who had published stories in the same magazines that had accepted Trix's early efforts, was just beginning her long and successful career as a novelist. Trix read Maud's early novels *Captain Desmond, V.C.* (1907), *The Great Amulet* (1908), and *Candles in the Wind* (1909) in rough drafts and gave specific suggestions as well as general advice. Trix criticized her friend's work with great confidence. She had a sure sense of how a novel was structured, how a character was developed, how sympathy for a character was maintained, damaged, or destroyed. She praised Maud's insight, her wonderful character studies, her splendid writing, her powers of invention, and her steady application. She disliked overwriting and was especially firm when discouraging Maud from over-praising her characters. She begged Maud to not rub in the best qualities of her most beloved characters, and when Maud was unable to adhere to this advice, Trix sweetly chided her. 'I smile at your tendency to put sugar on the top of the butter […] yet you have struggled bravely against that inclination to over sweetness!'[23] When a reviewer in *The Times* wrote that Maud's novels were 'not quite literature', Trix tried tactfully to explain this criticism to Maud.

> Well to the best of my often expressed belief you cannot do full justice to your work if it goes to the printers hot from your hand. You ought—on completion—to lay it aside for at least 3 months & think of something else—Then bring a rested brain & a fresh eye to bear upon it & make your final corrections & eliminations—Your gift of language & your power of realizing & loving your characters have of course contributed greatly to you success but like all good gifts they need guarding & controlling— Had you brought a new cool eye to bear on Candles you would have toned down some of the over praise of Lyndesay— […] You remember how years ago I used to risk your wrath by begging you to turn the limelight off Theo—It's the same sort of thing—Trust your readers a little

---

22 Cornelia Sorabji and Maud Diver, *The English Woman in India* (Edinburgh: William Blackwood and Sons, 1909).
23 Trix Kipling, letter to Maud Diver, 6 May 1908.

more & don't rub in your best beloved characters too much—You only do it with your special favourites –

I think leisurely re-reading would have made you cut out one or two of the scenes between Lyndesay & Videlle—Holding down the loud pedal too much rather expresses what I am trying to say—As for 'efflorescence of diction'—I notice—when reading Candles en masse that—owing to your wealth of words every noun has almost inevitably one adjective—& often two or three & that does give rather a piled up effect—Also—since we are dissecting things, be wary that your sentences don't grow too long –[24]

After reading a published edition of *Captain Desmond*, Trix wrote that she was 'proud to think I had a finger in the beginning of such an admirable pie!'[25] She went on with praise for many specific improvements she had herself suggested earlier. She discouraged Maud from trying to turn *Captain Desmond* into a drama, citing the considerable difficulties of having a play produced without the aid of a cooperative actor manager, leading lady, or wealthy backer. She cautioned Maud how situations which can be delicately developed in the leisure of a novel must be rushed and coarsened to suit the stage.

Maud's second novel, *The Great Amulet*, published in 1908 by William Blackwood & Sons, was dedicated 'to Trix Fleming in Memory of Dalhousie Days'.[26] This dedication, memorializing the teenage friendship between the two girls, expressed Maud's gratitude to her old friend for her extensive help in the writing of the novel. Trix had written detailed suggestions about the shape and tone of the novel, mostly suggesting cutting, pruning, and toning down. She repeatedly recommended restraint and time for reflection and revision. When Trix read the plot outline of Maud's third novel, *Candles in the Wind,* she responded with a long letter of specific, chapter by chapter, suggestions. Maud had many reasons to be grateful for the editorial help of her friend.

During these years, Trix was occupied by tending to her pleasant home and her gloomy, grumbling husband. Jack's continual depression weighed heavily on her, and although she had devised methods for easing his suffering and sparing herself, she had to continually steel

---

24 Trix Kipling, letter to Maud Diver, 6 December 1909.
25 Trix Kipling, letter to Maud Diver, 9 April 1907.
26 Maud Diver, *The Great Amulet* (Edinburgh: William Blackwood & Sons, 1908).

herself against Jack's fears and forebodings. Writing to Maud, she put the best face she could on the extreme differences between herself and Jack.

> I suppose it is Nature's intense care for the next generation that insures married people always having widely differing tastes. It prevents the race from getting groovy—if your husband were as book loving as you are Cyril would not be the dear many sided lad he is—& if I had been privileged to have babies Jack's practicalness & order & punctuality would have been greatly blest to them.[27]

By this time, Trix had accepted the deep divide between herself and Jack, and although she tried to find the good in the disparity of their tastes and interests, she did not find much. She lamented that she not been 'privileged to have babies', but she never explained exactly why she had been denied the 'privilege'. She was simply unaccountably and sadly childless. Trix maintained her health and her spirits during this last stay in India. She was proud of herself for having fared so well where many other women had suffered in mind or body.

In March 1908, as Jack's army service was terminated and she prepared to leave India for the last time, Trix suspended her writing for the SPR and busied herself with the details of closing the house and packing up her things. She was no longer afraid of the hardships of the journey back to England and had learned to accept the difficulties cheerfully. Knowing it would be her last Indian railway journey and her last long ocean voyage, she was prepared to be uncomfortable and even sick. But when, in mid-summer, she boarded the ship for the final voyage home, she was quite well, and after 24 hours on shipboard, she was able to shake off her few worries and laugh as she chased her dinner plate across a rocking table. She was well enough to write her first script in several months on 23 July, from shipboard.

As an officer of the Indian Army in permanent civil employ to the Survey of India, Jack had served faithfully for many years. Fleming's career, a steady rise from Captain through Major to Lt. Colonel, was unspectacular. He advanced, but slowly and never to a position of prominence. His stint as superintendent 2nd Grade in the Survey of India in Upper Burma lasted but a brief time in 1900 due to his ill health. Receiving his first commission in 1902, he was based in Calcutta first in

---

27 Trix Kipling, letter to Maud Diver, 4 September 1906.

charge of Engraving and Drawing, then in charge of the Photographic and Lithographic Office, then in charge of the Survey General and Mathematical Instrument Office, and finally as Superintendent of the Map Publications Office.[28] He studied military history and wrote an ambitious volume, *The A.B.C. of the More Important Battles of the Eighteenth and Nineteenth Centuries*, which was unfortunately never published. His undistinguished career can be accounted for by his own physical ailments as well as Trix's mental problems, both of which required long and frequent home leaves. Jack and other Fleming family members suggested that Trix's occult activities compromised his advancement, but this contradicts Trix's many assertions that she kept her activities to herself, protecting Jack from being associated with anything that might be considered improper or unsavoury. Jack's own depressive personality coupled with his many physical complaints were sufficient to keep his career from flourishing.

When his service ended, he and Trix travelled amiably together on the continent—to France, Spain, and Italy. They returned to England in the late summer of 1908.

In the fall, Trix had her long-anticipated visit with Miss Johnson in Hanover Square. After describing her most recent script from the voyage home, Trix considered Miss Johnson's newest proposal—a new series of cross-correspondence experiments with Mrs Verrall and Mrs Piper, an American medium discovered by William James. Trix accepted the invitation and promised to set aside time to write weekly automatic scripts.

In the spring of 1909, Trix and Jack visited friends in Torquay, then returned to Edinburgh, where Trix tried to make herself comfortable at 8 Napier Road. Never happy under the sunless Scottish skies, Trix tried to content herself with Jack and the Fleming family.

She paid frequent visits to Alice and Lockwood at The Gables in Tisbury. Alice, who had grown more and more isolated, was delighted to have Trix with her. She rarely ventured out, and few of her neighbours cared to call on her, having been alienated by her sharp tongue. When Trix came to visit, Alice insisted that they not be separated, installing a cot in her room for Trix. Used to her mother's anxious hovering from her previous visits, Trix accepted Alice's conditions and manipulations.

---

28 Office of the Superintendent of Government Printing, India, *The Quarterly Indian Army List* (1896–1912), Calcutta, British Library, London.

Alice called her an angel. Lockwood, still active and social in his retirement, had deepened his friendships with his neighbours. When Trix came to The Gables, he was happy to give over Alice's care to her, while he dined out with friends. Like Alice, he was full of praise for his daughter.

Whether in Edinburgh or Tisbury, Trix faithfully wrote her automatic scripts. Between 25 November 1908 and 19 May 1909, she produced twenty-two pieces of script. When she could get to London, she continued to meet with Miss Johnson, going over her scripts and identifying the many obscure allusions and references. Trix's scripts were compared with scripts from Mrs Verrall and from another medium, named Mrs Forbes—not from Mrs Piper, as originally proposed. The comparisons encouraged Alice Johnson to entertain a more audacious interpretation than she had ventured previously. She put forward as a possibility the existence of an independent intervention, an active designing intelligence constantly at work in the present and coming from departed spirits from the other side. But, as an honest investigator, Miss Johnson reported all of the very compelling objections to this theory. 'The weakness of all well-authenticated cases of apparent telepathy from the dead is, of course, that they can generally be explained by telepathy from the living'.[29] She concluded that spirit agency had not been proven conclusively.

Whether the result was deemed supernatural or telepathic, the evidence supporting it was supplied by Mrs Holland, and that evidence was extremely useful to the Society. Trix was considered an important medium by the SPR, and to be valued by the members of this society was sustaining for Trix. In India, she had been surrounded by people, including her husband, who offered her little intellectual stimulation or affirmation. They failed to notice her gifts, praise her efforts, or make use of her energy and enthusiasm, while the members of The Society—university-trained, knowledgeable in literature, philosophy, and the sciences—respected and esteemed her efforts. Here was an audience who appreciated her talents.

Trix's contribution to the SPR—many hundreds of pages of automatic writing—took a shape that elegantly combined her fluid writing with her emotional longing. As a medium for the departed spirits of Frederic

---

29   Alice Johnson, 'On the Automatic Writing of Mrs Holland', *Proceedings, Society for Psychical Research*, 25 (1911), p. 375.

Myers and Edmund Gurney, she poured out scripts in which she repeatedly, monotonously begged for communication, understanding, and connection. She allowed herself to fall into a state of feeling that was familiar, if painful to her—that depressed her spirits, often to tears, but provided an outlet for her yearning. In this dreamy state, Trix experienced feelings that were unavailable or unacceptable to her in her normal waking state. She opened herself up to the 'obscure psychological processes with which we are all familiar in dream and reverie',[30] as Alice Johnson described them. Through these psychological processes, called primary process thinking or free-association, Trix found a way to express her feelings of longing, isolation, and disconnection. If a psychoanalyst, rather than a psychic researcher, had listened to or read her scripts, she might have offered Trix some insight into her longing and perhaps some relief from it. But Trix found relief just in being able to express her yearning and have it heard and valued.

Through the SPR, Trix designed a therapy for herself that allowed her to experience painful states and feelings again and again and perhaps gain some mastery over them. It is as if, ten years before Sigmund Freud published *Beyond the Pleasure Principle* in 1920, which explained how the repetition compulsion was useful in restoring control to a traumatic situation, Trix had made the same discovery for herself. Freud postulated that by repeating the traumatic event, one might control an unbearable situation and establish a more favourable outcome. In hoping to reach the departed spirits of Edmund Gurney and Frederic Myers, Trix hoped to substitute happy contact and conversation for devastating separation and silence.

It was a wonderful coincidence that Trix and the SPR found each other, that Trix's particular talents and the SPR's needs so neatly dovetailed. Trix gave herself permission to dream her way into emotional release and relief by reassuring herself that she was participating in scientific research. She more or less stumbled upon this therapy for herself, without being aware that her psychic trances were acting as a form of psycho-therapy.

Trix's experience, while hardly ordinary, is not utterly strange or unique. The connection between psychic experience and mental

---

30   Ibid., p. 283.

illness is more than a coincidence. The medium, like the mad woman (and the inspired poet) has fluid boundaries between conscious and semi-conscious states—trances, automatic writing, crystal gazing, and subliminal suggestion. For Trix, being a medium was an acceptable way of using her tendency to go into dream or trance-like states by giving in to it with an avowed scientific purpose.

When Trix sat at her desk with pen in hand in the early morning, she was not herself. She was a medium, a conduit for the words of departed spirits. She was free from personal responsibility and could express shocking and dreadful thoughts. As if she were in a dream, she could see, hear, and report visions that were obscure, obscene, and insane.

Frederic Myers, whose book first inspired Trix, had worked productively in two disciplines—psychic research and mental health research. In the 1880s, he published a series of articles on the abnormal and the supernormal, focusing on the subliminal as it emerged in trance states and dreams. Anticipating Freud, Myers believed that behaviour was only partly controlled by the conscious mind and that ordinary consciousness was just a small part in a larger mental process that goes on outside of awareness. He posited the existence of the subliminal mind, similar to Freud's unconscious and Carl Jung's collective unconscious.

Myers and other neurologists, alienists, psychologists, psychoanalysts, and philosophers—including Jean-Martin Charcot, Hippolyte Bernheim, Sigmund Freud, and William James—were investigating the uses of trance, dissociation, automatic writing, double consciousness, dream, and other altered states as clinical tools for assessing a subject's susceptibility to hysteria, as therapies for mental distress, and as mechanical means of reducing agitation. Hypnotism was studied for its use in the diagnosis and treatment of mental disorders. Dream interpretation, free association, and Freud's primary process psychoanalytic technique depended on establishing access to the patient's unconscious mind. Dream or trance-like states were especially helpful in releasing inhibitions, uncovering hidden motives, and exposing unacceptable desires. Freud's early psychoanalytic cures for mental disease depended on hypnosis and trance-like free association to make known to patients their repressed and unacceptable memories, thoughts, and feelings, and thereby relieve their hysterical symptoms.

Psychic researchers, like alienists, recognized the hypnotic state and other altered states of consciousness as elevated states of inspiration. But, unlike mental health professionals, they were not interested in these states to relieve mental suffering but to reveal the existence of the soul. Mediums and the spirits they heard or embodied in trance were studied with interest and enthusiasm by researchers into the new psychical sciences, in order to provide proof of the existence of the immortal soul.

Myers, who was trained as a scientist, wanted the experiments he designed to provide hard evidence, not be reliant on faith, belief, or received religious teachings. One of Myers's favourite theories was that the influence of science on modern thought was not confined to this life alone but could be carried on into the next. The experiments Myers designed, which were carried forward by the SPR, were meant to lead to evidence of an afterlife. But, instead of demonstrating the existence of the eternal soul, the research provided evidence of communication between living minds—telepathy. Thus, Myers's disciples followed the evidence where it led, concentrating later experiments on telepathy.

Many of Freud's techniques—hypnotism, free association, dream interpretation, and transference—depended on an active sympathetic collaboration between the doctor and patient. Transference, occurring in the intimate relationship between analyst and analysand, included the possibility—perhaps even the inevitability—of hidden transmissions. The spiritual resemblance between occult communications and transference is even more striking when transference is described as a haunting return. Through transference, the patient re-experiences, for example, a first love. All subsequent loves conform to this stereotype of one's first love. Every succeeding love is thus a ghostly repetition, a revenant, a reincarnation of the first love.

Like the analytic patient, the medium creates visions or forms words in concert with his or her experimenter. The medium's suggestibility and connection to his or her experimenter produces the visions or creations. Myers posited direct contact between individual minds through telepathic communication, a subliminal collaboration.

Spiritualists, like other scientists, wanted to provide proof—hard evidence for the existence of an afterlife. Psychoanalysts similarly wanted to develop a science of the mind, a medical specialty in which observable symptoms could be catalogued, diagnoses could be standardized, and treatment results could be verified. Philosophers, psychologists, and psychic researchers all considered dreams, hypnotism, automatic writing, crystal gazing, trances, and speaking in tongues as important areas of mental activity that could be studied and measured with scientific accuracy to reveal the unknown workings of the human mind.

At the time, the conjunction of these fields of enquiry seemed plausible to many serious, intelligent, and educated people. This may seem odd now, studying trance-like states for insight into potential cures for mental disease and as proof of the existence of the soul. But, at the end of the nineteenth century, as much that had been invisible came to be explained and harnessed for human benefit—radio waves discovered in 1887, x-rays in 1895—areas of the unknown and unseen were open to scientific enquiry. The existence of the soul might be demonstrated by scientific measurement, while advances in technology—the telegraph and the telephone, entangled as they were with theories of spectral communication—at times seemed haunted. Myers, Lodge, and other members of the SPR were interested in detecting and manipulating invisible waves—magnetic, electric, radio, and psychic. All were equally mysterious at the time. Radio waves and emanations from the immortal soul were equally valid phenomena for study. The need to prove the utility of magnetic waves and the desire to prove the existence of the invisible soul were not considered opposite realms of study—one pure science, one pure superstition—but were part of a spectrum of invisible and mysterious occurrences.

Trix, who knew none of these theories, discovered the benefits of automatic writing almost by chance. She had indulged in automatic writing as a pastime in secret for some time. Once she had connected with the SPR, she persisted with it to provide evidence for the existence of the soul after death. She was drawn to it, and certainly remained attached to it, because it eased the strain on her mind.

During the seven-year period of Trix's active involvement with the SPR, she steadied herself and repaired her shaky marriage. She travelled from India to England several times, ostensibly for her health, although threats to her health may have been convenient excuses so that she could separate from Jack, leave India, stay with her parents in Tisbury, and visit with members of the SPR in London. In general, this was a period of good health and good spirits. Trix tried to keep her automatic writing a secret from Jack and Rudyard, although Jack discovered the secret several times and Rudyard may well have suspected it. She knew they considered it unhealthy for her, 'Whereas,' she reported to Maud, 'I have felt so much better & more practical in my mind since I read Mr Myers' "Human Personality" in 1903 & realized that the automatic writing I have tried to suppress for years is a well known thing & not necessarily dependent on imagination or "hysteria."'[31] Alice Johnson, with whom Trix corresponded during her years of psychical experimentation, was convinced that Trix's interest in the research in no way contributed to her mental illness and, on the contrary, exercised a healthy influence over her mind. It appeared to Miss Johnson that Trix gradually freed herself from various nervous fears and obsessions and came to have a sense of much greater security in the universe.

During the years that Trix worked with the SPR, the nervous disorder that had felled her earlier remained in abeyance. She maintained a clear mind and remained sceptical, forthcoming, and enthusiastic about her contributions to the Society. Psychical research, despite the fears of Rudyard, Jack, and her parents, did not compromise Trix's mental health. On the contrary, immersion in psychical research channelled and checked Trix's distress and helped her to maintain her mental balance for a long period of time.

This stable period came to an abrupt end in December 1910.

---

31   Trix Kipling, letter to Maud Diver, 26 June 1906.

10. Relapse and Exile

In October 1910, while Trix was living in Edinburgh with Jack, Alice was diagnosed with Graves Disease (hyperthyroidism). As soon as Trix heard the diagnosis, she went to be at her mother's bedside. Through October and early November, Trix went back and forth between Edinburgh and Tisbury to tend to her mother, feeding and dressing her as well as entertaining her with constant jollying talk. In mid-November, when Trix was at St Andrews accompanying Jack on the golf course, she received a telegram from her father calling her home. Lockwood, recognizing that Alice was nearing the end, summoned Rudyard home as well. Trix went immediately to Tisbury and was at her mother's side when Rudyard arrived at The Gables on 19 November. Both children were present on 22 November 1910, when Alice died.

Trix chose to remain with her mother's lifeless form, helping the nurse to lay out her body. After she had done all that could be done, she begged the nurse to leave her alone with the body. Staring down at the mother she had never had enough of, she thought how beautiful she looked with all the lines of age and pain removed from her face. Calmly and tenderly, Trix touched her mother's cool cheek for the last time. Whatever was left of Trix's 'mother want' was to be her final portion.

Believing that Rudyard would want to take a final look at his mother, Trix went down the stairs to fetch him. When she entered the library, she expected to find Rudyard limp with grief. Instead, she found him on his feet, furiously tearing up papers. Having come upon him unawares, Trix tried to make sense of what she saw. She assumed that he had gotten possession of their mother's keys, had opened the cupboard, emptied its contents, and was in the process of destroying private family papers. Surprised and frightened (and perhaps not seeing or hearing with complete clarity), Trix weakly protested against her brother's violent actions. Looking more attentively at the papers in Rudyard's clenched hands, she thought she saw the will that her parents had discussed with her a few months earlier. She tried to stop Rudyard from destroying the document, but he said, "Oh, Death invalidates this', and threw himself snarling over the torn papers'.[1]

Trix had felt all right as she had nursed her mother in her final illness and even as she had watched her die, but several days after her mother's death, she became excited and nervous. She couldn't stop pacing about the familiar rooms, talking, shaking, and screaming. Over and over again, she saw Rudyard tearing up papers. She became increasingly suspicious and angry at him, hurling furious accusations and terrible words. Rudyard tried to calm her but was unable to control her. Jack, who was also present with the rest of the family, didn't even try to exert his influence. Rudyard assumed the responsibility of managing his sister. While he took charge of Trix, Carrie took over the details of the funeral.

Lockwood, old, weary, and devastated by the loss of his beloved wife, was initially comforted to have his children stay on at The Gables. But after a week of witnessing Trix's mounting fury and distress, Lockwood no longer found any solace from having her near. On the contrary, she upset him and unsettled the rest of the household. Feeling helpless and heart-broken, Lockwood encouraged Jack to take his wife away to Salisbury. Jack carried Trix off, then abruptly returned with her a few days later. He had been unable to manage her and was relieved to deposit her back with her family. He went on alone to London, but a week later he was recalled by Rudyard. Trix had become even more difficult. Jack dutifully returned, but he soon recognized that he could do nothing to contain Trix's outbursts. Unwillingly but not entirely unhappily, he left Trix again with her father and brother at The Gables. Trix, carried hither and thither, seemed not to care where she was.

Once more, the family was forced to acknowledge that Trix was in need of serious medical help. Alice was no longer available to take charge of the situation, as she had done when Trix first broke down. Thus, Lockwood, Rudyard, and Jack when he was available, had to work together to devise a plan for her care. Lockwood and Rudyard were sympathetic to Trix, recognizing how deeply she felt the loss of

---

1   Trix Kipling, letter to J. H. C. Brooking, 26 November 1941. Texas A&M.

her mother, but Jack hardly shared in this loss. He simply wanted his wife speedily restored to good health and to him. When Jack, as Trix's husband and legal representative, asserted his authority, Rudyard and Lockwood were helpless to protest or interfere, although they complained vigorously about him to each other. Rudyard, who had never liked Jack, was unusually nasty about him, referring to him as 'carking Jack! that sleeplessly cantankerous invalid'. Rudyard was thankful that Jack wasn't demanding his marital rights as well as his legal ones and suggested, 'It's change and firm sympathy the poor child wants and above all change, and—low it be spoke—the assurance that J. will not descend on her and tell her to "pull herself together."'[2] Rudyard tried to persuade Jack to look after his own precious health, always his primary concern, and leave Trix's care to Lockwood and himself. He wanted Jack to leave, preferably to another continent.

After just a few weeks, Trix's mental state was characterized as a 'breakdown'. Lockwood wrote to Edith Plowden on Christmas day, one month after Alice's death, 'I am in deep water just now with my darling Trixie's break down [...] There are difficulties of all sorts, but they've got to be overcome. The worst is the husband who would give a brass monkey depression'.[3] Lockwood tried to be optimistic about Trix, recognizing that, as in all these cases, there were times of progress and times of regression. The trouble was Jack, who, wretched, pessimistic, and sleepless, was little help in finding treatment and a suitable nurse for Trix. Lockwood wrote to Edith Plowden that Trix 'has had a nervous breakdown and is in a sad state, but I trust will soon be better. It is not so bad as her first some years since [...] Col. Fleming left on Tues. for Scotland. She seems to get on better with me alone'.[4] Certainly Lockwood and Rudyard got on better without Jack.

Trix's moods shifted back and forth, while Rudyard and Lockwood at The Gables considered the best treatment for her. Jack, on his own in London, consulted Dr Lang, Dr Munro, and Dr J. P. Williams-Freeman of Weyhill House to recommend treatment and nurses for Trix. Dr

---

2 Rudyard Kipling, letter to John Lockwood Kipling, January 1911. University of Sussex.
3 John Lockwood Kipling, letter to Edith Plowden, 25 December 1910. University of Sussex.
4 John Lockwood Kipling, letter to Edith Plowden, 23 January 1911. University of Sussex.

Williams-Freeman offered Jack a secluded place for Trix to stay should she need a quiet situation in which to recuperate, an offer Jack soon accepted.

Trix, when calm, still liked to curl up in a comfortable chair and read. She liked strolling around the garden. One afternoon, Trix returned to the house after a walk in the fresh air and found what looked like a conference in progress. She had left the house bright and cheerful but was puzzled to see Rudyard and Lockwood engaged in talk with a woman she had never seen before. She soon recognized that what was taking place was an interview with a prospective nurse for herself. She disliked the woman immediately and was indignant that, without her approval, the woman was being considered for a position. Trix was repulsed by the woman's looks and said so plainly. She felt no need to behave or speak decorously. Lockwood sent the woman from the room and dismissed her with dispatch. Trix was now beyond good manners. But she was not beyond self-will, and she maintained her right to choose her own companion.

Trix might have recovered not only her manners but her mind if no other calamities had occurred. But, a little more than two months after Alice's death, on 3 January, a fresh disaster overtook her. Trix was away from The Gables, under treatment at Weyhill House in Andover, when she was told that Lockwood, while visiting the Wyndhams at Clouds, had been felled by a sudden heart attack and had died. Far from the family and removed from the scene, Trix had to absorb this new and terrible loss alone and from a distance. Following doctors' orders, she remained at Weyhill House. She never saw her father's body, did not have any part in the preparations for his funeral, and did not attend his burial service.

She had been improving under the care of Dr Williams-Freeman. But the news of her father's unexpected death sent her sadly back into herself. Barely able to accept the loss of her mother, Trix was unable to absorb the shock of this second blow. When Jack visited her on 1 February, the day after Lockwood's funeral, he found her body shrunk and her mind wandering.

It was not a straying husband, a childless marriage, a literary disappointment, or psychic influences that caused Trix to break down, but the death of her parents that finally undid her. If Lockwood had survived to mourn Alice's death with her, and comfort and reassure her, she might have recovered, but the double loss was simply too much for her to take in.

While Trix was constrained at Weyhill House, Carrie took charge of all the funeral and financial arrangements. The breaking up of The Gables and all its contents was left in her competent hands. Trix was not aware of what was happening, although later, she accused Rudyard and Carrie of cheating and robbing her, taking for themselves valuable furniture, embroideries, carpets, and silver, while she was out of the way and incapable of objecting. Although Rudyard and Carrie denied any wrong-doing and intimated that Trix was simply mad, she remained steadfast in her belief that, while she was in residence at Weyhill House, Carrie took advantage of her absence to remove precious items from The Gables. Carrie was especially assiduous in destroying documents, burning personal papers and family letters, including Trix's. Anything she deemed possibly embarrassing or damaging she destroyed, claiming that she was 'simplifying'—her word of explanation for the destruction of material she deemed unsuitable for public scrutiny.

Trix's most damning allegation was that Carrie had destroyed Lockwood's will. Trix asserted that the will, which was never found, would have left to her a larger share of her father's estate. Trix supplied the name of the solicitor at Salisbury to whom Lockwood had gone to draw up the will, in which she claimed, 'everything he possessed of money and furniture went to me, and only his books, MS, and pictures to his wealthy son!'[5] As no will was ever found, it was determined that Lockwood died intestate, an unusual circumstance for a man of his position. Thus, Lockwood's estate was divided evenly between his two children, a fair arrangement but hardly commensurate with their relative wealth and need. Rudyard was by now a rich man. Without consulting Trix, Rudyard and Carrie carried off all of the books, furniture, and household effects from the Gables. When these items were evaluated, their worth was deducted from Rudyard's share of the proceeds of the estate. This seems a fair arrangement, but there is little doubt that Trix was ill-used.

Rudyard defended himself and Carrie against Trix's accusations by asserting that Trix was irresponsible and delusional. And Trix was not in

---

5   Trix Kipling, letter to J. H. C. Brooking, 17 July 1945. Texas A&M.

a perfect state of mind at the time. She was kept out of the way and was unable to defend herself. Rather than accept the obvious explanation that Trix's mental state was due to the almost simultaneous deaths of her parents, Rudyard positively attributed Trix's mental illness to the spiritualists. Rudyard held them responsible for 'the wreck of her mind'. His idea was that 'the soul-destroying business of "Spiritualism" affected her mind much more profoundly and permanently than anyone dared to say when the trouble first began'.[6] He was convinced or convinced himself that all the delusions that attacked her after their parents' deaths were caused by her association with psychic research.

Rudyard's belief that spiritualism was responsible for Trix's illness is not only unsubstantiated but inconsistent with her state of mind during the preceding years. Better than anyone, he knew the suffering she had endured as a child, as the daughter of Alice, and, later, as the wife of Jack. Blaming the spiritualists allowed him to exonerate the family by locating the source of Trix's troubles outside of the home. Trix's longest and most serious period of involvement with psychic research was, in fact, one of her healthiest. Her engagement in automatic writing served not as an irritant, but rather as a self-prescribed form of therapy and solace. That the deaths of her parents should cause her to break down is completely reasonable. Trix was deeply attached to her mother, never had enough of her, and, with her death, knew that she would never be able to make up the loss.

Trix now felt utterly alone, adrift in the world. Her parents were gone, the house in Tisbury, which had been her refuge, was broken up. She felt that her brother had betrayed her, and her husband had abandoned her. She was returned to the helplessness and loneliness of her childhood, once again feeling like an unwanted parcel deposited here and there. Her mostly empty journal contains this entry for the entire year 1911 'Widowhood—Father died Jan 4th. Orphaned and deserted by both Brother & Husband—I ought to have died—And Colonel F[lemin]g mourned for her—six lovely months at most—'[7]

Trix almost disappears from her own story at this point. Others took charge of her, decided where she lived, for how long, and with whom.

At first, Trix remained miserably at Weyhill, which she referred to as 'Weyhill Prison', near Andover in Hampshire. Recognizing Trix's

---

6 Rudyard Kipling, letter to Elsie Macdonald, 3 June 1927. Texas A&M.
7 Trix Kipling, Journal (1911). Carl A. Kroch Library, Cornell University.

extreme reluctance to receive visits from Jack, Dr Williams-Freeman at Weyhill discouraged his visits and recommended constant vigilance and self-restraint. When she had been there only a few months, Fleming made enquiries to the Lunacy Board about having Trix certified as incompetent. He did not proceed with this when Trix's doctors deemed her capable of managing her own affairs.

Rudyard seriously objected to having his sister certified. Writing to Fleming in March of 1911, he expressed his reluctance to have Trix certified for sentimental reasons and because 'It jars on one'.[8] He urged Fleming not to be precipitous, reminding him that Trix's attack had, by then, only lasted three months. Trix was unaware that such a move was even being considered at the time.

Over the years, Jack's plans for Trix alternated between having her put entirely out of the way and having her completely restored to him. When Jack was not hatching plans to have Trix certified and sent to an asylum, he was pestering her doctors about being able to approach her more closely. He tried several times to convince the mental specialists that she was certifiable, but, on the contrary, each time they said that, while she was run down and sensitive, she was unusually brilliant and well balanced. When Jack insisted on his rights as a husband, Trix's doctors gently but firmly turned him away. Discouraged but not deterred, Fleming continued to visit his wife about once a month, receiving, more often than not, violent and furious outbursts from her. Jack's persistence inspired even Rudyard to feel kindly toward him. Rudyard, with greater compassion than usual, reassured Jack that in the majority of mental cases the patients turn for a while against those who are nearest to them.

Patients like Trix posed a dilemma for mental doctors. They were reluctant to have patients certified and sent to asylums, they were eager to protect fragile and vulnerable patients, and they needed to be responsive to the often inappropriate requests and suggestions made by family members. Dr George Savage, President of the Medico-Psychological Association and of the Neurological Society, and Dr Williams-Freeman at Weyhill House tactfully balanced these competing interests, keeping Trix out of an asylum, protecting her from being molested by her husband, and responding gently to the wishes and whims of her family. Although Trix felt that Jack had abandoned her, he

---

8   Rudyard Kipling, letter to Jack Fleming, 13 March 1911. Texas A&M.

never did. He visited her with regularity and made repeated attempts to see her and speak with her. On several occasions, he made special trips to visit the Divers, attempting to learn from Trix's most intimate friend, Maud, what Trix was thinking and feeling. Maud, who knew more than anyone else, did not share what little she knew with Jack. Trix's complaint that he mourned for her 'six months at most' reflects her suspicion that he sought out the company of other women after only this short period of time. She may well have been correct.

Tussles among Trix's doctors, her husband, her brother, and the Macdonald sisters continued for years. In the early years, when Trix seemed to be improving, Jack considered moving her closer to his family in Scotland, while the Kiplings and the Macdonald sisters tried to settle her in London, closer to them. With a hired companion, Trix travelled from place to place, sometimes with her husband, sometimes with friends, to hotels, lodgings, or private houses, while her mental health fluctuated. All places were the same to her—featureless and cheerless places of exile. Hired companions and nurses came and went. Meant to help her, they mostly oppressed her with their constant presence. She hated sharing a bedroom and loved 'open windows & drawn back curtains & one only attains the real blessedness of sleep in one's own atmosphere—Own books near one & the best thoughts one is mistress of as canopy & shield'.[9]

She was often dull and muddled, unresponsive to the treatments of her doctors, but she rallied from time to time, giving her family hope that she might recover.

Animosity between Rudyard and Jack waxed and waned, but mostly waxed, as Trix's illness dragged on. Rudyard complained to Jack that he didn't know what was happening with Trix and often didn't know where she was or why. His offers to visit her or have her visit him repeatedly came to nothing. When Rudyard did visit Trix in Scarborough in July 1913, two years into her illness, he found her much improved—steadier, more communicative, and less self-absorbed. He took her for a drive and a walk, during which she talked and behaved in an appropriate manner, remarking on things with discrimination and penetration.[10] Following this visit, Rudyard proposed another visit, which did not take

---

9   Trix Kipling, letter to Maud Diver, not dated; probably early 1920s.
10 Rudyard Kipling, letter to Jack Fleming, 13 March 1911. Texas A&M.

place—possibly because John, Rudyard's son, came down with mumps. Later planned visits were also cancelled, suggesting reluctance from either or both parties. Added to the stress caused by Trix's condition was the continuing discord between Jack and Rudyard about the distribution of Lockwood's estate.

As Trix was moved about from place to place, she was, from time to time, taken to London where she was evaluated by new doctors. In mid-1914, she was seen by Dr Craig and Dr Bartlett, neither of whom was reassuring about her progress. Dr Maurice Craig, who took charge of her care at this time, was a well-respected medical psychologist, author of a textbook on *Psychological Medicine* (1905). He, like Dr George Savage and the many other doctors who had seen Trix, offered the standard treatment of bed rest, quiet inactivity, and regular intensive feeding.[11]

In 1914, while Trix was oblivious to world events, Jack began to investigate the possibility of joining up to serve in the First World War. He was sufficiently serious about this plan to consider where he might place Trix if he should be posted abroad during a tour of duty. Rudyard considered the idea of middle-aged, retired Fleming serving on active duty as completely deluded and daft. Rudyard recognized that the plan to have Trix certified and safely in an asylum was primarily to ensure Fleming's peace of mind and not to secure Trix's best treatment. To prevent this, Rudyard repeatedly offered to take over Trix's care himself, proposing to find a place for her within easy motoring distance from his home. Jack repeatedly turned these offers down. Rudyard feared that having Trix certified would definitely close all hope of her recovery and would be deeply resented by her. Jack ignored Rudyard's suggestions and objections and continued investigating asylums for Trix and pursuing plans for military duty.

Toward the end of 1914, another prospective caretaker entered the fray—Miss Winifred Holt, daughter of the American publisher Henry Holt and a tireless do-gooder. While Trix was in London being examined by Drs Craig and Bartlett, she was introduced to Miss Holt and met with her several times. On one occasion, Miss Holt invited Alice Johnson, Trix's friend from the SPR, to join them at the Sesame Club on Grosvenor Street. Trix arrived profoundly depressed, inert, and mute. Nonetheless,

---

11 Both Drs. Savage and Craig treated Virginia Woolf.

'Miss Holt, believing that the one chance for her was to be rescued from her husband, made great efforts to persuade her to accompany her back to America and was on the point of engaging a passage for her'.[12] Miss Holt, together with Miss Johnson, even consulted a lawyer about the legal situation of removing Trix. But in the end, the scheme failed, as Trix was unable to cut herself loose. She was paralyzed by fear that she would be considered wicked and ungrateful for abandoning her marriage.

The long horror of the First World War passed Trix by, as she lived secluded from the world and indifferent to its upheavals. News of the death of Rudyard's son, John, in September 1915 at the battle of Loos in France either did not reach her or did not touch her. Rudyard's grief over the fate of his young son and his continuing hope for his return kept him occupied for the next two years. He was thus much less engaged in the long-standing debates about Trix's treatment.

When Jack was refused active service, as Rudyard knew he would be, the issue of transferring Trix's care was dropped for a while along with the prospect of certifying her. But, when Jack visited Trix and found her peevish and distant towards him, he again considered sending her to an asylum. During a period when Trix seemed to soften towards him, Jack moved her to 8 Napier Road, the family home he had inherited at his mother's recent death. He soon regretted this decision. Trix was not an agreeable wife. On the contrary, she was often agitated and angry. After only a month in the house, she became obstreperous and, in a fit of temper, cut off her hair. Disgusted with Trix's behaviour, Jack sent her away again, moving her from Worplesdon to Carlisle, Keswick, Blackpool, and St Andrews. Trix endured these frequent moves without complaint. The one happy event of this period was the arrival of Mary Sinclair. Mary was hired to look after Trix as her personal maid. Along with Minna, another personal maid, Mary became half of what Trix humorously and lovingly referred to as the 'prickly pear [pair]'. These two women remained Trix's trusted and faithful servants for many years.

In 1917, at his wits' end, Jack arranged a family conference with Rudyard and Carrie to discuss what to do with Trix. At this meeting, Rudyard suggested that Trix come to stay for a while with him and Carrie

---

12   Alice Johnson, 'Mrs Holland' (1934). W.H. Salter Archive, Wren Library, Trinity College, Cambridge.

at Dudwell Farm, up the road from the Kipling home, Bateman's, in Burwash. This plan was approved, and an extended visit was arranged.

On 19 September, Trix, with her latest companion Mrs Postle, set off for Dudwell Farm. Rudyard looked forward to the visit, but Carrie decidedly did not. Grudgingly, Carrie carried out her duties as hostess to her sister-in-law. But she had little good feeling towards Trix, whom she found simply selfish and self-centred. She was convinced that Trix should be able to control her behaviour by sheer will power. By the end of September, her small sympathy for Trix had dwindled away to nothing. Compounding her displeasure was Rudyard's obvious delight in his old intimacy with his sister. The two took long daily walks, even in the frigid weather. Trix was happy in the familiar company of her brother but was oppressed by the cold both inside the house, where the fires seemed to give out no heat, and outside, where the Sussex chill actually frightened her.

After more than two months of having Trix as his guest, Rudyard, at Carrie's repeated urgings, wrote to Fleming asking that he remove Trix from Dudwell after Christmas. Eventually, after much back and forth, Rudyard allowed that she could stay on through February. Although Carrie grew more and more jealous of the attention Trix received from Rudyard, she continued to take care of her sister-in-law. It wasn't until 12 March that Trix and Mrs Postle left Bateman's for Blackpool, arriving back at Napier Road in early April.

Fig. 27 Trix's passport, renewed in 1919.

During the spring, summer, and fall of 1918, Trix was in deep distress. Often, she couldn't even get herself out of bed. When she was urged to get up, she went limp with resistance, groaned, and screamed. Late in the fall, she became violent—furiously smashing glass, hurling hatpins, and outraging everyone in the household. In early 1919, when Jack was unable to curb her fury, he sent her away to Pitlochrie, north of Edinburgh, where she continued her riotous behaviour. When she returned to Edinburgh at the end of June, she was as difficult and disruptive as before. She threw her diamond rings to the floor, kicked and stomped on them, trying to destroy them. These were the rings she had proudly displayed during the early months of her engagement. Now, they reminded her not of Jack's love and faith, but of Jack's heartlessness and betrayal. From June through the middle of August, Trix kept herself coldly apart from Jack, while he made plans to send her farther away—to Jersey.

During the years from 1917 to 1919, Jack tried numerous times to return Trix to the house in Edinburgh and reintroduce her to family and marital life. Trix either immediately defeated these attempts or engaged in prolonged wranglings and refusals, punctuated by dramatic violent acts—hurling sharp objects, breaking glass, and destroying ornaments. Trix found Jack utterly insensitive to her feelings of physical revulsion against him, based on her belief that he had again been unfaithful to her. Repeatedly and callously, Fleming tried to reclaim Trix, then gave up and sent her away, first to visit her brother at Dudwell Farm, then to Pitlochrie, and finally to Jersey. When thoroughly defeated and resigned to a bachelor life, Jack made plans to sell the family home.

During these years, when Trix was actually with Jack, she was either violently angry at him or silently tolerated him. She believed he had betrayed and forsaken her, failed to protect and care for her during her grief at the sudden double loss of her parents. Whenever he tried to touch her, she reacted with revulsion and rage. Her doctors repeatedly warned Jack not to attempt to renew intimate contact with his wife. His attempts to possess Trix were a series of abject failures.

In 1920, Jack sent Trix into her most prolonged and lonely period of banishment—mostly in Jersey, with infrequent trips to the Brittany coast (1920-1924). There, she resumed her correspondence with her old and dear friend, Maud Diver. In her few letters to Maud in the 1920s, she shared little of her thoughts and feelings. She reported on books she had read and responded with her usual precise critical judgments to the drafts of the novels the prolific Maud continued to send to her. Her critical faculties were as sharp as ever. She was full of praise for her friend's continued productivity but never referred to her own vanished writing career.

As before, the medical establishment did what it could for Trix, ordering the standard benign treatment of rest, quiet, isolation, feeding, and a minimum of sedation. They protected her from her husband's demands, discouraged his visits, and refused many of his attempts to remove her from their care. But they also protected her conventional and easily embarrassed family by keeping her out of their way.

This period of thirteen years, from 1911 to 1924, was a dark time in Trix's life. She had no say in where she went or what happened to her. Alone with her own sad thoughts, Trix was only barely aware of all the decisions that were made about her. Like the unwanted bundle abandoned on the doorstep, Trix was once again being shifted about by others.

It is likely that Trix needed to be sent away after the deaths of her parents. She not only needed constant attention, but she also embarrassed her family by her unruly behaviour and unrestrained speech. A more sympathetic family might have found ways to keep her at home, to tend to her with patience and compassion. When Trix had broken down in 1889, she had had her mother to care for her. This time, with her parents gone, she had no one willing to make the sacrifices necessary to tend to a difficult and demanding patient. Rudyard was occupied with his fame, his writing, and his family—especially the loss of his son. Carrie, always unsympathetic to Trix, was unwilling to take on the onerous burden of her permanent care. Jack, back in Edinburgh after his long tour in India, was eager to resume a normal life. Under the influence of his family, who never approved of Trix, and with the active participation of his sister Moona, he was encouraged to consider his own interests and pursue his own pleasures, which he did.

Trix wrote almost nothing about her feelings during her years of banishment. Only long afterwards did she try to describe what had happened to her. Years after the events, she made it clear that she had felt misused, doubly deserted by her brother and husband.

At different times, Trix blamed different people for abandoning and abusing her. She was initially incredulous that Rudyard, who had shared her early losses, did not understand and sympathize more fully with her feelings of orphanhood at the time of their parents' deaths. She blamed Carrie for Rudyard's lack of empathy. Similarly, she blamed Jack's favourite sister, Moona Richardson, for Jack's callousness. At one time, she shifted the blame entirely onto Rudyard and Carrie, asserting that they had boycotted her and had exercised their poisonous influence on Fleming. Much later, in a desire to exonerate Jack, she shifted the blame entirely onto his controlling and influential sister, Moona. 'Moona was to blame for the fight I fought between 1911 and 1924 for sanity and liberty, and she always ruled her brother, barely 16 months older! RK of course treated me as an outcast then'.[13]

Trix claimed that she and Fleming had been 'on normal affectionate terms' until her breakdown at age forty-two. 'There was no other woman then—though of course there was later—but that was not my fault—I had not one to turn to or appeal to—& perhaps he took my resignation for indifference—I know his sister influenced him unduly—but after 21 years of married life I had some claim'.[14] Trix accused Jack of being indifferent to her, although he made many awkward attempts to get close to her. During most of her illness, she treated him as if he had wounded her, betrayed her, and coldly rejected her. While she confessed that he was the only man she ever had any real feeling for, she did not characterize that feeling as love or desire. During the period of her exile (1911-1924), Jack lived his own life.

> Until 1916, when his mother died, he lived with her in his childhood home. After his mother's death, his elder sister practically annexed him and did her best to write me off the slate [...] His sister and her friends gave him all the social life he needed, and 'pick-ups' at the Empire the emotional outlet he preferred, and there was nothing left for me. And we had been happy and normal man and wife for 21 years. I suppose my illness (I was very thin and wan) revolted him and he broke the habit of being married and never wanted to resume it.[15]

---

13 Trix Kipling, letter to J. H. C. Brooking, 25 October 1945. Texas A&M.
14 Trix Kipling, letter to J. H. C. Brooking, 28 July 1945. Texas A&M.
15 Trix Kipling, letter to J. H. C. Brooking, 25 October 1945. Texas A&M.

Trix continued that Jack was 'tired of Holy Matrimony' and would have put her away if he could have.

Anxious to exonerate her brother and husband from blame for her years of exile, Trix consistently blamed Carrie and Moona. Women—her mother and Mrs Holloway—had been the villains in Trix's early life. Later, she added Carrie Kipling and Moona Richardson to her list of powerful and conniving women. Trix characterized women as strong in their sly manoeuvring and men as weak in their resistance to the controlling female grip. Lockwood bent to Alice's will in sending the children off to strangers when they were little, and later conceded to Alice's approval of Jack Fleming as a husband for Trix, although he had little faith that the marriage would produce lasting happiness. According to Trix, Jack Fleming was influenced by his jealous and possessive sister, who wished to push Trix aside and establish herself as the primary woman in her brother's life. Similarly, Carrie Kipling, envious of Trix's special place in Rudyard's affections, was responsible for Rudyard's ill treatment of his sister—discouraging contact, destroying documents, and appropriating property. (Captain Holloway was the exception. He was kinder than his wife, and he was able to keep her evil tendencies in check while he was alive.)

Trix tended to believe that the men in her life had relinquished authority on matters that were emotionally complex or morally suspect, allowing their women to commit actions that were ungenerous and unkind. Trix never blamed Lockwood for anything. She blamed both Rudyard and Jack at various times but was always ready to make excuses for them and shift the blame away from them and onto Carrie and Moona.

Trix referred to this period as 'exile'. Her mostly blank journal, written perhaps after the dates noted, contained this one self-pitying and tragic entry to stand for the entire year of 1924.

'T'is but the shadow of a wife you see, The name—but not the thing—'.[16] Always able to remember her Shakespeare, Trix located the appropriate quotation. This line is delivered by the clever, loving, and loyal Helena, the spurned wife of the unknowing, unworthy, and unfaithful Bertram at the end of *All's Well that Ends Well*. Helena is eventually vindicated, reclaimed, and beloved—Trix's wish for herself.

---

16   Trix Kipling, Journal (1924). Carl A. Kroch Library, Cornell University.

11. Recovery and Return

In the spring of 1924, Trix returned to Jack in Edinburgh. Her mental health was not markedly different from what it had been for several years, but Jack's physical health, at the age of sixty-six, had declined. He was weaker and needier. At fifty-six, Trix was calm and quiet, as she had been for some time. Jack had recently purchased an austere Victorian mansion at 6 West Coates, somewhat outside of the centre of town, with room for Trix. The stately house was set back from the street by a wide, sharply sloping lawn. The interior of the house contained the familiar eclectic mix of Jack's Indian artifacts and Trix's few remaining prized pieces of furniture, rugs, embroidery, and art.

Trix was never completely comfortable in Edinburgh, but she was pleased to be recalled from exile in Jersey. In Scotland as before, Trix endured days and even weeks of straight, steel rain. The external weather mirrored her own, which remained dour. She was back in Jack's home, but she was not back in Jack's heart. She felt she had been allowed, but not exactly welcomed, back into the Fleming family.

The chief obstacle to Trix's happiness was Jack's older sister, Moona Richardson, who ruled the Fleming household. While Trix was nominally living as Jack's wife, she felt she was 'actually under the heel of Jack's big sister'.[1] Moona asserted her control in many ways. Her most annoying and offensive act was obliging Trix to have a companion/nurse tend to her. Moona chose the companions, although Trix protested that she found them unnecessary and often unsuitable. Trix recognized Moona's insistence on her having a companion as a strategy consciously designed to insult and humiliate her.

In addition to Moona, Jack had a younger and sweeter sister, Mary Craigie, who often visited and was available to care for her brother, but

---

1   Trix Kipling, letter to J. H. C. Brooking, 25 October 1945. Texas A&M.

her kinder nature was little felt. It was Moona whose influence prevailed, who oppressed Trix, and whom she held responsible for having set Jack against her years before. Trix believed that Moona had conspired to have Trix certified as incompetent in the past and continued, in the present, to demean her and attempt to demoralize her. Trix considered Moona tough, stubborn, and stupid, strong as a horse but without horse-sense. She claimed, perhaps with some exaggeration, that Moona told wicked lies about her, struck her, and even tried to maim and disfigure her. When Trix was disturbed by unusual sounds and movements during the night, she accused Moona of intentionally trying to frighten her. To protect herself from Moona's treachery and trickery, Trix had a heavy bolt installed on her bedroom door.

Moona lived in a large, cluttered house next door to her brother at Eglinton Crescent and often stayed through the winter months at the West Coates house. Friendless and defenceless, Trix felt fortunate to have the comfort of her two loyal servants, the prickly pear (pair) Mary and Minna, who had worked for her for more than twenty years. They were her faithful companions through her years of banishment and during her return to Edinburgh. They were her only reliable allies in her early years of her residence at 6 West Coates.

For the next eight years, Trix bravely assumed the role of a proper Scottish matron, taking up gardening, charity work, and visiting with friends and family. She enjoyed parts of this role—tending to the garden especially. She was proud of her roses, lilacs, daffodils, and periwinkles. She distracted herself by knitting socks and woollen caps. She reestablished her relationship with the psychic world by joining the Edinburgh Psychic College, but she did not resume her serious work as a medium or a writer of automatic scripts. And she did not take up her pen again to write fiction or verse. Caring for Jack, as his health deteriorated, was her main employment. She fussed over him as he complained of his lumbago, his gout, his legs, his back, his eyes, and more.

For many years, Trix longed to visit London and begged to be taken on a trip there. In the spring of 1932, Jack responded to Trix's frequent plaintive requests and arranged a brief visit. Several cousins and old friends of Trix's were invited to meet the Flemings for tea. Trix dressed and ornamented herself with extravagance, remaking several of her old dresses and rescuing her few remaining jewels. She was thrilled to be out of the gloom of Scotland and into the glare of London. She revived in the company of admiring cousins and friends over scones and clotted cream in the tearoom of a fashionable hotel. Performing for her audience, she told stories, quoted from her favourite poems and plays, and talked almost without a pause for the entire visit. Her young cousins were especially delighted with their eccentric and effervescent aunt. Jack took in the performance with some confusion, impressed by a new vision of his wife, who proved herself to be not only capable and coherent but witty and winning. In Edinburgh, Jack had adopted Moona's perspective on Trix and had seen her as barely recovered and unready to resume her role as mistress of the house. In London, she proved that this perspective was woefully inaccurate.

After dazzling her friends in London, Trix was ready for more. She persuaded Jack to allow her to make the short trip to Bateman's to visit Rudyard. Relaxed and happy after her recent success, she easily proved to her brother that she was her old self. During the visit, Rudyard found her to be delightful company—fresh and witty as ever and still beautiful, almost unmarked by time.

Letters between Rud and Trix resumed with greater frequency after this visit. Trix continued to suggest plots to Rud; he, to tell her stories. A letter from Rudyard to Trix several months after her visit to Bateman's in January 1933 recounted the story of a clever little girl, which delighted Rudyard and which he knew would similarly delight his sister. The story concerned:

> A small friend of mine, aged about seven. Fair with blue eyes and a shadow of a look of my Josephine about her.
>
> She has been suffering from some small ailment, which involved pain—in turn and so forth. Her Mother and she discussed the matter and symptoms, and by that way generally the mysteries of the human body. Then, she reflectively: 'Mummy, I cant see whats the use of the little hole in my tummy. Whatever good is it? Do we all have one?' Here I suppose Mummy said that the navel was common to all humanity. There was a little thought and then the child of the Dominant Race—I suppose it is to show that we are British.
>
> You can't—the gods themselves can't—defeat a breed like this!
>
> The conception of the God-given Trademark [...] but your imagination can fill in at leisure. Isn't it perfect?[2]

---

2 Rudyard Kipling, letter to Trix Kipling, 22 January 1933. University of Sussex.

The story displays not only Rudyard's sly humour but also his affection for children and his appreciation for their uncanny grasp of unspoken adult attitudes. Rudyard's use of the 'Dominant Race' has more than a trace of irony to it. He assumed (correctly) that his sister shared his opinions as well as his sense of irony and would appreciate the story. No doubt, she did.

Fig. 28 Trix and Jack in Edinburgh in 1932.

Back home in Edinburgh after her social successes, Trix reclaimed her role as Jack's partner, successfully displacing Moona at last. With his health deteriorating more rapidly, Jack was grateful to have Trix as an attentive caregiver. Trix was happy to be of use, and happier still to exercise her advantage over Moona. She also took pleasure in exercising her sharp tongue on Jack. Now that Jack was old and ill, and she was full of renewed life, she teased and gently tortured him. She no longer felt the need to repress her natural volubility and vindictive wit. If Jack had punished her in the past with his silence and distance, she repaid him with her acid tongue. Her terrible vitality in old age was punishment for his earlier tyranny. Colin MacInnes, son of Trix's cousin Angela Thirkell, watched as his Uncle Jack, 'that much mocked, admirable personage, the English—or—Scottish military gentleman: kind, good, honest, unimaginative and timid' was mercilessly, almost cruelly, teased by Aunt Trix 'like a cat with sharpened fangs'. MacInnes was present for a visit with the Flemings during which Trix always arrived late for meals, exasperating poor Jack. 'Her breast clattering with necklaces, her fingers glittering with rings, she talked, and talked, and darted witty shafts. She chattered on and on until he cried out in despair, like an Old Testament prophet in the depths of torment, "Oh, Woman! Woman!"' She responded to his outburst with a sweet smile and raised eyebrow.[3]

While Trix was revelling in her revived good spirits and good health, Rudyard, like Jack, was ailing. Despite being in poor health and almost constant pain, in August 1935, Rudyard began writing his autobiography, *Something of Myself*. The short book omitted large parts of his self and contained no description of his first loves, Flo Garrard and Wolcott Balestier, his marriage to Carrie, or the deaths of his children. But it did include at length the story of the childhood he had shared with Trix. That story always remained a vital source.

Shortly after completing the memoir, while on a trip to London to discuss his will, Rudyard was taken ill at Brown's Hotel. He was removed to Middlesex Hospital, where he died on 18 January 1936. His ashes were interred in Poet's Corner in Westminster Abbey on 23 January 1937. In his will, he left his wife, Carrie, in control of his real and intellectual property. He left small bequests to his daughter Elsie and her husband, George Bambridge, but the remainder of his large estate went to Carrie. He left nothing to his sister.

Trix's disappointment over this neglect is nowhere recorded. Rudyard's name and fame were fresh in the news. This wide coverage may have encouraged Trix, at the end of the year 1936, to copy out a previously written story (See Chapter VII), titled 'Ricochet or Boomerang's Return'.[4] The neat regularity of the hand-writing as well as the carefully written date on the story—12.30.36—suggest that Trix copied it out with the intention of sending it to magazines for publication. Although it is very unlikely that she wrote the story at this late date, it is likely that, at this time, she was feeling optimistic about her chances

---

3   Colin MacInnes, 'Aunt Trix', in *England, Half English*.
4   Alice Fleming, 'Richochet or Boomerang's Return', dated 12.30.36. University of Sussex.

of achieving publication. At times, Trix used her association with her famous brother to increase her chances of publication, but at other times she chose not to use what help might come from the Kipling name. At this moment, with the Kipling's death prominently in news, Trix found the opportunity especially tempting and submitted or considered submitting this old work for publication. If she did submit it, she did not receive a positive reply. The story was never published.

In early 1937, after Rudyard's ashes were buried in Westminster Abbey, Trix wrote 'A Biography'—a memorial poem for her brother based on his 'A St. Helena Lullaby'. Although it is a very close imitation of Rudyard's poem, it is nonetheless very personal, focusing, as before, on the crucial times they spent together. Below are the first two stanzas and the last two stanzas of the eight-stanza poem.

> A BIOGRAPHY 1865–1936
>
> BOMBAY 1865–1872
> 'How far is Poets Corner from a baby in Bombay?
> I can't explain, I cannot say—the paths they wind about.
> But Mother, call your son again or else he'll run away.
> (When you're full of mischief you must play it out.)
>
> SOUTHSEA 1872–1877
> 'How far is Poets Corner from a lonely bullied child?'
> A certain kind of wisdom is given when you weep:
> And though the fog is round you, your Star is undefiled.
> (How bitter is a stranger's bread, a stranger's stairs, how steep.)
>
> WESTMINSTER 1936
> 'How far is Poets Corner from a coffin 'neath the Jack?'
> So near that we may count the steps that bring you to the stone.
> 'Lest we forget, lest we forget' Tears, and a crowd in black,
> (And the choir's singing verses of your own.)
>
> ????
> 'How far is Poets Corner from a happy spirit freed?'
> Further than mind of man conceives, astronomers are dumb
> Your works will live behind you, but you are off at speed
> (To learn how solar systems work,—until The Kingdom come.)[5]

Although Trix and Rudyard had spent most of their adult lives apart, they had almost always been in contact, mostly by letter. Trix was deeply affected

---

5   Alice M. Fleming, 'A Biography', in Lorna Lee, pp. 160–61.

by this final loss, but she did not go mad over it. Gone was the person she had shared her childhood with and had continued to share her literary tastes and judgments with throughout her life. She had learned to console herself for her losses, and she managed to console herself for this one.

After Rudyard's death, Trix wrote about her relationship with her famous brother. Her recollections, 'Some Childhood Memories of My Brother Rudyard Kipling', published in the *Chambers Journal*, contained stories she (or he) had told before.[6] Like most memoirs, Trix's is a polished performance, a carefully chosen and edited excerpt of a life. Trix's recollections of her brother inevitably went back to their earliest years when they were all in all to each other. She detailed, as he had done in *Something of Myself*, their childhood years, when Rudyard was the person Trix most trusted, loved, and depended on.

In 'More Childhood Memories of Rudyard Kipling' (1939), Trix told of going to visit the house of desolation for the first time since childhood. When she was just minutes from the house where she and Rudyard had been exiled, she turned back, feeling her courage fail her. When she told Ruddy of her experience, he confessed that he had made the exact same cowardly retreat. 'I think we both dreaded a kind of spiritual imprisonment that would affect our dreams,' explained Trix. When Trix asked Rudyard later if he knew whether the house still stood, he answered, 'I don't know, but if so I should like to burn it down and plough the place with salt'.[7]

When Trix wrote about her adult relationship with her brother in her 'Childhood Memories,' she concluded, 'I married in 1889 and he married three years later and after that our paths in the world divided. He went west and I went east and the personal devil seemed to arrange that seldom the twain should meet'.[8] Except for the clever echo of Rudyard's line 'east is east and west is west', this is an especially feeble description of one of the most important relationships of her life. She did not attempt here in this memoir to explore deeply her feelings for her beloved brother. Rudyard was the person who had been closest to her in childhood, adolescence, and perhaps in life. She loved him as she loved no one else, but she emphasized that, 'although Ruddy and I were always devoted comrades there was never any Charles-and-Mary Lamb or Dorothy-and-William Wordsworth

---

6   Alice M. Fleming, 'Childhood Memories of My Brother Rudyard Kipling'.
7   Alice M. Fleming, 'More Childhood Memories of My Brother Rudyard Kipling', *Chambers's Journal*, July (1939).
8   Ibid.

(brother-sister intimacy/incest) nonsense about us'.[9] While there was probably no such intimacy between the two, there was an attachment that transcended time, space, and speech. Rudyard's lifelong dislike of Jack Fleming and Trix's similar hatred for Carrie suggest some sexual jealousy, as does Rudyard's first and most intense love—Flo Garrard, who was a friend of Trix's and served as a model for his one romantic heroine. When Rudyard wrote *The Light that Failed*, his only romantic novel, he created a young woman who was an amalgam of Trix and Flo. He longed for Flo and continued to long for her for years, even when it was clear that the relationship was impossible.

Usually reticent in speaking about Rudyard when he was alive, Trix allowed herself to speculate very little about his character after his death. She credited him with originally having his mother's sunshiny Irish nature but believed that after his almost fatal illness, Josephine's death, and John's later death, he was a sadder and harder man. Responding to suggestions made by others, she rejected the idea that his terrible childhood had completely poisoned his character in later life, and she also disagreed with those who thought he was a happy, carefree man.

When speaking or writing about Rudyard, Trix was especially touchy about any disparaging or demeaning remarks. A particularly irritating piece of gossip which seemed to follow Rudyard—that the family had black blood—disturbed her deeply. Rudyard simply shrugged the slander off. When he was accused of being '8 annas in the rupee' (not pure), a nasty racial slur, Trix vigorously refuted this slander, asserting that 'it would be difficult to find two large families so absolutely free from any connection with India as the Kiplings & the Macdonalds were in 1865—And their woodpiles were utterly devoid of any n-----'.[10] Trix often repeated an upsetting story of going to the opera in Florence, wearing a low-cut evening dress, and being insulted and offended by a woman seated behind her, who suddenly rubbed at her bare shoulders and neck with her black gloved hand. After rubbing so hard she caused Trix's skin to redden, she looked at her glove and said in a disappointed

---

9 The relationship between Dorothy and William Wordsworth particularly annoyed Trix. She wrote to Maud on 24 May 1944, 'I only love W.W. in patches —& never adored the tiresome Dorothy – unwholesome & selfish!'

10 Alice M. Fleming, 'My Brother Rudyard Kipling', *Kipling Journal*, December 1947.

voice—'Oh, it doesn't come off. I've heard so often about your brother having black blood I thought I must see if your white neck was real'.[11]

Trix, like most of the British of her time, was always especially sensitive to matters of class as well as race. She asserted forcefully that she, Rudyard, and their parents were always part of Simla's highest society, that they were invited everywhere, participated in the exclusive amateur theatrical society, dined and danced with the finest people. Back when she and Rudyard were being mistreated and humiliated by the Holloways, they maintained their senses of self by assuring each other that they were of a higher class than the Holloways, that they had breeding, culture, and family far superior to Aunty Rosa and Harry. After Rudyard's death, it remained important to Trix that he be remembered as superior to people of colour or people of a lower class, caste, or culture.

Trix mourned the loss of her brother in private. In public, she added 'sister of the late great man' to her persona, enthusiastically joining the Kipling Society when it was formed in 1937. She made herself readily available to biographers and interviewers and was happy to talk about her famous sibling.

Fig. 29 Trix at a Kipling Society Luncheon in the 1930s, with J.H.C. Brooking (the head of the Kipling Society) and Florence Macdonald.

---

11 Trix Kipling, letter to J. H. C. Brooking, 7 October 1941. Texas A&M.

After Rudyard's death, she engaged in a number of disputes first with Carrie and later with Elsie, Rudyard's daughter, over control of Rudyard's literary estate. With energy and focus, Trix fought with Carrie, who repeatedly tried to block publications and retain and control copyrights. Trix recognized Carrie's pleasure in the power of saying no and wondered how (and for how much) she had said yes and sanctioned the hideous film versions of 'Wee Willlie Winke' and 'Gunga Din'. Trix criticized Carrie's more than forty-year habit of shielding Rudyard from reporters and publicity. During his life, this might have been useful, but after his death, it was hardly necessary. When Trix tried to reason with Carrie about releasing information or documents, she was met repeatedly with the objection that Rud would have hated it. Trix responded that he wouldn't hate it now, or, if he did, he was learning not to, for he was above and beyond such worries. Trix's most damning criticism of Carrie was that she looked upon books as merchandise only. Trix claimed she had never seen Carrie read a book and doubted if she could.

While Carrie was alive, Trix kept her displeasure largely to herself, but the ill-feeling between the two smouldered just below the surface for many years. After Carrie's death in 1939, Trix allowed the embers of her animosity to flare up. Trix blamed Carrie and her influence for all that she disliked in her brother. It was Carrie who had changed him from being loving and giving to being suspicious and greedy, who had allowed his heart to shrink as his genius grew. Trix believed that the breach that occurred between herself and Rudyard during her years of exile was, if not caused by Carrie, certainly prolonged and exacerbated by her. Trix bitterly resented that Rudyard and Carrie had kept several of her old friends from visiting her during her years of banishment and was especially unforgiving of Rudyard (under Carrie's influence) for having ever considered having her declared incompetent.

Elsie, Rudyard and Carrie's one surviving child, continued her mother's battles after her death. Trix found herself again engaged in a family squabble over Rudyard's works. When Trix was invited to record her recollections of her early life with her brother to be broadcast by the BBC, Elsie blocked the transmission of the broadcast. She objected to the use of several quotations, claiming copyright infringement and threatening legal action if the broadcast were not cancelled. Her objections were considered groundless. The quotations she objected to were from unpublished poems that existed only in Trix's memory, and it was 'thought therefore that they could be regarded as her personal possessions', but the threat of legal and financial consequences caused the BBC to back away from the program. The BBC had had to bow to other objections raised by Elsie 'based on similar absurd reasons'. Elsie's objection over the copyright issue was seen 'as a blind to cover the personal one'.[12] She did not want Trix to make the broadcast. The interview was never aired but was eventually published in *The Kipling Journal*. J.H.C. Brooking, the president of the Kipling Society, concluded that Elsie was 'acting more as an enemy than as a friend of our Society', but he was unable to impeach her or request her resignation from the Society. Trix, along with Brooking and the BBC, gave in to Elsie's demands without resorting to legal recourse or personal attack. Somewhat later, Elsie claimed that Trix was no longer responsible for her actions, an accusation that Brooking flatly contradicted, citing a recent letter from Trix that was 'crystal clear'. Brooking considered Elsie unreasonable, while he found Trix not only reasonable but flexible and generous. Trix levelled the same criticisms at Elsie as she had against Carrie. She accused them both of having no literary taste or judgment. Elsie, she remembered, couldn't read until she was eight years old and, she believed, had read little since.

In her later years after Rudyard and Jack were dead, Trix battled with Moona, Carrie, and Elsie again and again. Trix disliked these three women and believed they not only disliked her, but had made repeated attempts to remove, displace, or discredit her. Trix may have intentionally or unintentionally encouraged and aggravated the envy and enmity of these women. She had the greatest contempt for women like Carrie and Elsie, who cared little for books and rarely read them. She was proud to set herself her apart and above such ignorant women.

---

12 J. H. C. Brooking, letter to Trix Kipling, not dated. Texas A&M. 'In the course of the talk, however, there were three quotations in verse – two from one poem and one from another. Both these poems were unpublished and neither had any existence except in Mrs Fleming's memory: it was thought therefore that they could be regarded as personal possessions of Mrs Fleming. Mrs Bambridge, however, through her agent, Messrs. A. P. Watt, claimed copyright in these extracts and the right to refuse permission to reproduce them, and she did in fact refuse such permission'.

She held a place in her brother's life that neither Carrie nor Elsie could ever approach, much less fill. Only her mother Alice had had literary taste and talent. Trix was worthy of envy—for her beauty, charm, and especially for her literary judgment, prodigious memory, and witty conversation. Alice had been a fair rival; but Carrie, Elsie, and Moona were beneath consideration.

The outbreak of the Second World War in 1939 did not pass Trix by, as did the First. During the war, she and Jack remained in their solid stone house in Edinburgh, although they were offered safer quarters in the country. They were prepared with sand, water, and shovels on each floor and endured the boredom of black-outs and the terror of air-raids. Trix did her share for the war effort by writing names, addresses, and figures in ration books and by doing her knitting in khaki.

One day, while drinking tea in her drawing room, Trix heard a loud booming crash, which she took for a railway accident. When Jack woke from his afternoon nap and heard Trix's account of the noise, he kindly agreed that it came from the railway, although he knew full well that it was the sound of near-by big guns. Similarly, the sight of small planes fighting in the afternoon sky, which Trix assumed was an air exhibition, was recognized by Jack as a real dog fight. Gallant soldier Jack protected his wife from the terrors of the fighting, which were often fairly close by.

Always alert to what she, as a good wife, should do, Trix cared for Jack attentively during his last long illness. When he died in 1942, it was a loss—perhaps more of structure than of affection. Over the course of more than forty years, being married to Jack, being estranged from Jack, and being reunited with Jack had shaped her life. For a decade, tending to Jack's complaints and illnesses had dominated her days and her thoughts. She was pleased that she had done her wifely duty and reported with satisfaction that, when Jack died, he was resting peacefully in her arms.

Trix also did her duty to Moona, who remained a presence in Trix's life even after her brother's death. Despite disliking and distrusting her, Trix took care of Moona when she needed companionship, nursed her after a fall, and, when she was ill, oversaw her care in a nursing home. Moona died at the age of ninety in June 1947. Three weeks after Moona's death, her younger sister, Mary Craigie, died at the age of eighty-eight. Trix was grateful to Moona for her two lovely nieces—Ethel Craigie, who married Thomas Walker Hector, and Katharine (Kit) Johnston, who married Harry Crossley. Both women later became devoted to their 'Aunt Trix'.[13]

Jack's death left Trix alone to manage by herself. Although it took some time for Jack's substantial estate to be settled, when it was, Trix discovered that the estate was left in a way that benefitted his other heirs at Trix's expense. Trix was left with an allowance and a pension sufficient for necessities, although not for luxuries, which she had always expected and enjoyed. Jack had promised to leave Trix enough for dresses and sweets, but there was actually only enough for food and expenses. Trix fretted over the rising cost of everything—her maids' wages, her gardener's fees, hotel rates in London, dresses, hats, and gloves. Nonetheless, she managed with fewer niceties and a diminished household staff and contrived, with a little management, to buy the ornaments that she had always loved.

She did not waste much time mourning, but rather allowed herself new and deserved freedoms. After Jack's death, Trix travelled, talked, and indulged herself. In 1943, venturing out into the world of commerce, she opened a gift shop, 'Gifts and Gratitude', on Roxburgh Street in Kelso, forty miles southeast of Edinburgh on the River Tweed. The shop was a fund-raising venture for the benefit of soldiers. Although she employed a manager for the store, on occasion she gamely worked behind the counter and chatted with customers.

Sloughing off the roles of proper matron, companion, and nursemaid to Jack, she became a garrulous and eccentric old lady. She happily moved about, visiting London and participating in the activities of the Kipling Society. When in London, she stayed at Bailey's Hotel or with Katherine Crossley (Moona's niece) in Streatham. When she came to London, often for a period of a few weeks, she charmed everyone she met. Novelist Angela Thirkell, Trix's cousin, and her son Colin, along with Hilton Brown, the secretary of the Kipling Society, and all the Macdonald cousins rallied around and feted her when she was in town.

She was always in high spirits in company, showing off with a ceaseless flow of conversation, dotted with quotations from Shakespeare. On one occasion, Gwladys Cox (Gwladys's husband's uncle, Ralph Richardson,

---

13   Moona had two nieces, Ethel Craigie, who married Thomas Walker Hector and Katharine (Kit) Johnstone, who married Harry Crossley.

had been married to Moona) and several others 'sat silent, while this one small, elderly lady with flashing, intelligent, deep-blue eyes talked and talked—for two solid hours. We listened spell-bound, and when she left, the place seemed empty and silent—such was the spirit of her'.[14]

The most vivid description of Aunt Trix as a determinedly eccentric, voluble old lady comes from first cousin twice removed Colin MacInnes. MacInnes was himself a writer of great charm and a shrewd, tender, and penetrating chronicler of English life. As an outsider himself—half English/half Australian and openly gay in the 1950s and 60s—he was drawn to his dramatic and flamboyant 'Auntcestress' Trix. He described a typical visit with her, 'in her spacious and frightful drawing-room, decorated with a singular mixture of Indian souvenirs of uncle Jack's, and of objects of pre-Raphaelite art belonging to her own family'. She was at the time in her seventies, he in his twenties.

> With her hands fluttering like butterflies, but with her body in repose, she would look somewhere over the top of my head, or round the side of me, as if it was my shadow, or my guardian angel, she was addressing. The most beautifully constructed, precisely enunciated phrases fell then from her lips as if she'd learned the intricate sentences by heart; and so far did she often adventure into a forest of conditional clauses, and of parenthetical embroidery, that I wondered if she would ever conclude these Proustian periods with sufficient syntactical clarity. Not once, however—rather to my disappointment—did she fail to do so. And if, as sometimes happened, the thoughts that passed so rapidly through her agile brain outpaced even her capacity for expressing them, then, while she stopped a moment to dispose her ideas in a harmonious sequence, she would utter a high-pitched 'And ...' like the sharp cry of a bird in pain an 'And...' destined to prevent me from interrupting, rather as someone leaves his hat on a seat in the train to show that, even though he's not occupying it himself, you must not. On such occasions, I found that the only way I could break in on her was to put my hands over my ears and shut my eyes. The sound would then cease; and when I looked up again aunt Trix gazing mildly at me, and hear her saying in kind, gentle tones, 'yes, dear. Have you something to say to me?' 'Aunt Trix; I want to *speak*'. 'Then *speak*, dear. Pray Speak'. This I would do; while she waited, her eyes averted and her thoughts probably elsewhere, until, when I paused for an instant, aunt Trix, in whose mind a great backlog of thought by now accumulated, would give a slight smile, say, 'Yes, dear, yes ...' and begin again.[15]

---

14 Gwladys Cox, 'Aunt Trix, Some Recollection', in Lorna Lee, pp. 73–74.
15 Colin MacInnes, p. 114.

She doted on children and loved animals. She often accompanied children to the zoo, where she entertained them by speaking Hindustani to the elephants and hippopotamuses. She had close relationships with Macaws and parrots as well. After taking two of her little grandnieces to the zoo in 1937, she reported with delight that one of them asked, after gazing at the big turtle in the aquarium, 'Where is the mock turtle?' These performances were not a form of craziness but an inspired contrivance for charming children. Colin MacInnes described a day at the zoo with her, where she addressed,

> Cynical macaws who strolled courteously along their perches to listen to her. Herself like some rare bird [...] she spoke to them [...] until a crowd of curious Scots gathered round her [...] sufficiently near to observe if the birds would bite her when she popped chocolates through the bars into their huge, slow, lazy beaks. When birds and Scots were all assembled in sufficient numbers on either side of the metal barrier, aunt Trix would turn to tell their human brethren what the birds were thinking, as if she were the interpreter between two portions of the animal kingdom.[16]Children responded by returning her love. Like her brother and others who had suffered in childhood, she retained a great affection for children and knew how to engage and delight them. She was well known for her ability 'to charm the heart out of any child and was full of amusing little tricks with handkerchiefs and finger magic to hold them by her'.[17]Trix had learned early that one sure way to gain notice and praise was by entertaining—quoting Shakespeare, reciting poetry, and singing songs. Interminable poetic quotation was the greatest flaw in her otherwise graceful social manner. All the descriptions of Trix from friends and relatives present her as sparkling, often to a blinding degree, in her conversation, full of wit, vivacity, and humour. Her scandalous talk and whimsical rhetorical flourishes, which were often ascribed to her 'fey' character, were in her conscious control. Colin MacInnes's brother Lance Thirkell said of Trix. 'There was a streak of sheer mischievous innocent and delightful wickedness which ran through her entire conversation and all her letters for those who knew her. [...] I think I might best describe Trix as having a reverent irreverence'.[18]

When her brother and husband had been alive, she had spoken little of her psychic powers; but after their deaths, when she was no longer constrained by their displeasure and disapproval, she spoke openly

---

16 Ibid.
17 Katherine Crossley, letter to Gwladys Cox. 'Some Recollections', in Lorna Lee, p. 94.
18 Lance Thirkell to Sheila Wilson, 30 January 1988.

about her psychic triumphs—conveying a message from a dead child to her grieving mother, and reassuring a lance-corporal that his mother would recover from an illness and reproving him for doubting his sweetheart. Her greatest success was a vision of sacred relics that came to her in a dream during the night when she had slept with an iron key tucked beneath her pillow. She published some of her dramatic experiences in psychometry in the *Kipling Journal* of October 1945. Trix revelled in telling stories of her second sight, describing places she had never been to, repeating conversations she had never heard, seeing spirits, interpreting dreams, receiving messages, calling up visions, etc.—but these were performances, meant primarily to surprise and delight. They were not meant to be taken with great seriousness.

Trix retained her sharp tongue and keen memory into old age. Lord Birkenhead and Hilton Brown, both of whom consulted Trix when writing their biographies of Rudyard, found her extremely cooperative and helpful. Both were awed and amazed at the power of her memory. She answered pages and pages of letters crammed with questions from Lord Birkenhead, whom she later referred to as 'Lord Woodenhead'.

When Lord Birkenhead and his assistant Douglas Rees travelled together to Southsea to visit the House of Desolation in 1946, they had Trix's description of the house in hand to check against the actual house. Rees reported, 'Everything was exactly as stated—so much so that it was not difficult to supply in imagination the dampness, the gloom, the Victorian furnishings, the texts on the walls and even the musty smells from the data which we had brought'.[19] He came away marvelling at the extraordinary accuracy of Mrs Fleming's memory.

Well into her seventies, Trix remained physically healthy and active and took some pride in this. She claimed to walk five miles a day at seventy-seven years of age, a number she considered over large. Up until the last two years of her life, her one health complaint was malaria, which returned on occasion in the hot weather and made her feel like 'chewed string'. She boasted of weighing only 101 pounds despite eating like a fool. Her weight went up and down. When thin, she felt she looked pinched. When heavier, she believed her wrinkles (some of them at least) disappeared. She remained vain about her appearance to the very end of her life, dressing in her own extravagant style whenever

---

[19] Douglas Rees, the Birkenhead papers. University of Sussex.

she ventured out. Her distant but devoted Fleming cousin, Gwladys Cox, described her at the age of seventy-seven: 'Small and slight with a perfectly chiselled, small, aquiline nose and deep sapphire-blue eyes, she is extraordinarily energetic for her years with amazing powers of conversation'.[20]

In August 1946, she was diagnosed with diabetes and put on a strict diet. She was ordered to eat three big meals and two snacks a day and to take shots of insulin. In May 1947, she suffered an attack from diabetes and ended up lying rigid on the ground, her face the colour of earth and her eyes and mouth both wide open. She was revived, dosed, and warned to be more careful about her diet. The diabetes made her feel languid, weak, and forgetful. She followed the diet and took the insulin but found 'living by rule' an unhappy encumbrance on her freedom. In the last year of her life, she suffered from the flu and spent much of her time in bed. But she felt it was ungenerous to complain as she had been free of pain and sickness for twenty-five years. She was determined to enjoy her old age, to take advantage of what little time she had left.

When Trix reflected on the almost completed span of her life, she recalled that her only happy years were between 1883 and 1889. These were the years of the Family Square in Lahore, Dalhousie, and Simla. She characterized the years of her marriage as years of strain and unhappiness. She admitted that if she had her life to live again, she would never have married Jack. She very rarely complained about the disparity of interests and energy between herself and Jack, and she never openly compared the narrow and confined life she had chosen with Jack to the artistic, intellectual, and bohemian circles she had had contact with through her parents, brother, and Macdonald relatives. When she chose Jack at nineteen, she chose what she hoped would be solid comfort and tender care. She chose (supposed) emotional stability over intellectual excitement. What she got turned out to be neither. Jack's own instability, expressed through numerous physical ailments and constant complaining, required most of his and her energy. She and Jack scarcely shared one thought or pleasure. Trix contrived to make up for this lack through her own writing and her friendships with Maud and other cultured women, her work with the Society for Psychical Research, and her visits with her exceptional family. She had, at one time, suggested that Maud write a novel about a troubled

---

20 Gwladys Cox, 'Some Recollections', in Lorna Lee, p. 71.

marriage, but, during her years of exile, she withdrew this suggestion, noting that it would make a horribly sad book. Trix's own portraits of an unhappy marriage, rendered in her George and Mabel dialogues, are comic riffs on what she recognized was a 'horribly sad' situation.

Trix never openly expressed regret for giving up her writing and rarely mentioned her early aspirations to become a novelist like her brother and her best friend. Experience had taught her that she did not possess the confidence and persistence to develop and promote her talents when confronted with difficulties and discouragements. It wasn't for lack of models that she faltered. Rudyard and Maud, two very close models of immense success, might have served as positive inspirations, or as too stiff competition. Both possibilities have been suggested, and both seem likely. Maud was, after Rudyard, the most popular Anglo-Indian writer of her generation. Her romance/adventure novels (*Captain Desmond*, 1907, *The Great Amulet*, 1908, *Candles in the Wind*, 1909, *Lilamani*, 1911, *The Hero of Herat*, 1915, *Far to Seek*, 1921, and many more up to 1940) were devoured by the female novel-reading public.

The greatest losses are the satiric novels Trix never wrote and the fierce heroines she never created. Although she had a ready store of anger to call upon in order to create a disappointed, thwarted, and bitter heroine, she could not imagine how such a heroine might recognize her own nature, use it productively, abuse it disastrously, or change it convincingly. Her two novels are flawed specifically because she could not shape her own rage into fictional form and bestow it and its consequences on her two heroines. Instead, she created heroines who were unaccountably angry at the start of the fiction, and illogically satisfied, immoderately punished, or left adrift in their conflict and confusion at the end. Trix had the insight to locate and describe many of the unpleasant realities of women's lives— pretence, imposture, resentment, discouragement, disappointment, anger, and aggression—but not courage or talent enough to shape these realities into plausible plots with appropriate rewards or punishments. Presenting women's constraints and complaints fully would have conflicted with the good manners and proper behaviour that Trix's society and family valued and that she, having internalized them herself, could never fully disown or discard.

Only as an old lady did Trix allow herself to express her anger fully in wickedly irreverent conversation. It is a great loss that she didn't take up her writing again in her sixties or seventies. She might have dipped her pen poisonously and productively into the inkpot up until her death. She might have written truly about women's needs to disguise their true selves at the end of her life when she no longer had to disguise herself.

In her old age, she said of her life, specifically of her years in exile, that it had been a waste. Certainly, it was a waste of much talent and spirit, but not at all a complete waste. She produced fine, if flawed, fiction and poetry. She contributed to the work for the Psychic Research Society. She supported and shaped the work of her friend, Maud Diver. She collaborated with and encouraged her brother, providing him with a sympathetic, like-minded, and bookish companion and correspondent throughout most of his illustrious career. She delighted all who knew her with her gift for words, not only on paper and between covers, but also in conversation. Her brilliant talk, embellished by quotations and ornamented with devilish humour, was well remembered by anyone fortunate enough to have shared her company.

Her friends lamented that she was remembered primarily for her sweet nature when young and her sharp tongue when old. They thought she ought to have done tremendous things, but was prevented by many difficulties, both internal and external. If she had been more self-assured and daring, less dependent on the approval of her conventional family, she might have been able to defy them, disobey their rules, disappoint their expectations, and express her true self. If late Victorian society had allowed women to write with anger and aggression about the repressions, humiliations, and hurts they suffered, she might have written novels that reflected her own thwarted experience and the experiences of many other women as well. That so much energy and talent wasted itself is sad, but her life could have been sadder still—she could have succumbed to the common fates of many talented and unfulfilled women of her time—madness, invalidism, and suicide—but she chose life. Again and again, she chose life.

Despite all the restrictions that bound her, she made choices. When she was embraced by the Family Square, she chose to find happiness in her family, her talent, and her beauty. She chose to marry tall and handsome Jack Fleming. She persevered for some years with her fiction writing with only scant encouragement, and she was gratified at the publication of her stories and novels. She strategized to separate from

Jack when she felt betrayed and, at the same time, devised a way to alleviate her ancient mother want. She found pleasure in making a proper home for Jack and took pride in being useful to the SPR. She delighted in entertaining and performing, especially for children. Although she often felt like an unwanted parcel, she was not without a will and wiles of her own.

Trix died at home at 6 West Coates on 25 October 1948. She had outlived her husband and her brother, but her nieces and nephews and the many others who called her 'Aunt Trix' felt her loss and remembered her with great affection and admiration. Gwladys Cox recalled, 'She was made of "spirit, fire and dew" and at 80 died young'.[21]

---

21   Katherine Crossley, letter to Gwladys Cox. 'Some Recollections', in Lorna Lee, p. 96.

Select Bibliography

Primary Sources

Baldwin Papers. The University Library (University of Sussex).

Barrett Browning, Elizabeth, *Aurora Leigh* (London: J. Miller, 1864).

Besant, Annie, *Study in Consciousness—A Contribution to the Science of Psychology* (Chennai: Theosophical Publishing House, 1907).

— *Why I Became a Theosophist* (London: Freethought Publishing, 1889).

Craig, Maurice, *Psychological Medicine* (London: J & A Churchill, 1905).

Dickens, Charles, *David Copperfield* (London: Bradbury & Evans, 1950).

Diver, Maud, 'A Brahman's Honour', in *Sunia: And Other Stories* (Edinburgh and London: William Blackwood & Sons, 1913).

— 'A Moment's Madness', in *Sunia: And Other Stories* (Edinburgh and London: William Blackwood & Sons, 1913).

— *Candles in the Wind* (Edinburgh and London: William Blackwood & Sons, 1909).

— *Captain Desmond, V.C.* (New York: G. P. Putnam's Sons, 1907).

— *Far to Seek: A Romance of England and India* (Edinburgh and London: William Blackwood & Sons, 1921).

— 'Feet of Clay', in *Sunia: And Other Stories* (Edinburgh and London: William Blackwood & Sons, 1913).

— *Lilamani: A Study in Possibilities* (London: Hutchinson, 1911).

— 'Sunia: A Himalayan Idyll', *Longman's Magazine* (1898).

— *The Englishwoman in India* (Edinburgh and London: William Blackwood & Sons, 1909).

— *The Great Amulet* (Edinburgh and London: William Blackwood & Sons, 1908).

— 'The Heart of a Maid', in *Sunia: And Other Stories* (Edinburgh and London: William Blackwood & Sons, 1913).

—*The Hero of Herat: A Frontier Biography in Romantic Form* (London: Constable & Co. Ltd, 1912).

— 'When Beauty Fades', in *Sunia: And Other Stories* (Edinburgh and London: William Blackwood & Sons, 1913).

Ferguson, Rachel, *The Royal Borough of Kensington* (London: Johnathan Cape, 1950).

Hamilton, Sir Ian, *Listening for the Drums* (London: Faber & Faber, 1944).

Hill, Edmonia Taylor, 'The Young Kipling', *Atlantic Monthly*, April 1936.

— *The Carpenter Kipling Collection: Scrapbooks, Sketches, Verses, Autographs, Photos (1880–1943)*. The Library of Congress.

Hope, Laurence (Adela Florence Cory), *The Garden of Kama* (New York: Garden City Publishing, 1901).

Huntington-Whiteley, J. M., correspondence with Barbara Fisher.

Johnson, Alice, 'On the Automatic Writing of Mrs Holland', Proceedings of the Society for Psychical Research, 20–25 (1908–1911).

Kipling, John Lockwood, *Beast and Man in India* (London: Macmillan, 1891).

— Alice Kipling, Rudyard Kipling, and Trix Kipling, 'Quartette,' *The Civil and Military Gazette*, December 1885.

Kipling, Rudyard, 'At the End of the Passage', *The Boston Herald*, 20 July 1890.

— *Barrack-Room Ballads and Departmental Ditties* (New York: M. F. Mansfield & Co., 1898).

—'By Word of Mouth', *The Civil and Military Gazette*, 10 June 1887.

— *Collected Stories of Rudyard Kipling: Introduction by Robert Gottlieb* (New York: Alfred Knopf, 1994).

— and Trix Kipling, 'Echoes, by Two Writers', *The Civil and Military Gazette*, August 1884.

— 'In the House of Suddhoo', *The Civil and Military Gazette*, 30 April 1886.

— *Kim* (London: Macmillan, 1901).

— *Letters*, ed. by Thomas Pinney, 2 vols. (Iowa: University of Iowa, 1990).

— *Plain Tales from the Hills* (Calcutta: Thacker, Spink & Co., 1888).

— *Something of Myself*, ed. by Thomas Pinney (Cambridge: Cambridge University Press, 1990).

— *The Light that Failed* (Philadelphia: Lippincott's Monthly Magazine, 1891).

— 'The Mark of the Beast', *The Pioneer*, July 1890.

— 'The Phantom Rickshaw', in *Quartette* (Lahore: The Civil and Military Gazette, 1885).

— 'The Return of Imray', in *Mine Own People* (New York: John W. Lovell Company, 1891).

— 'The Sending of Dana Da', *The Week's News*, 11 February 1888.

— 'The Strange Ride of Morrowbie Jukes', in *Quartette* (Lahore: The Civil and Military Gazette, 1885).

— special collections. *Texas A&M University Libraries*.

Kipling, Trix, 'A Journey in the Jungle', *The Pioneer*, 21 February 1897.

— 'A Little Learning', in *Plain Tales from the Hills* (Lahore: The Civil and Military Gazette, 1886–1887).

— 'A Pinchbeck Goddess', in *Plain Tales from the Hills* (Lahore: The Civil and Military Gazette, 1886–1887).

— 'At a Christmas Ball', *Black and White*, December 1892.

— 'A Woman of Seasons', *The Pall Mall Gazette,* March (1895).

— (Mrs J. M. Fleming), *A Pinchbeck Goddess* (London: Heinemann, 1897).

— 'Casual Leave', *The Pioneer*, 27 October 1892.

— (Mrs J. M. Fleming) and Alice Kipling, *Hand in Hand: Verses by a Mother and Daughter* (New York: Doubleday, 1902).

— 'Her Brother's Keeper', *Longman's Magazine*, June (1902).

— 'How It Happened', in *Plain Tales from the Hills* (Lahore: The Civil and Military Gazette, 1886–1887).

— 'Hunter on Marriage', *The Pioneer*, 22 June 1892.

— 'In Shadowy Thoroughfares of Thought', *The Pioneer*, 1 December 1892.

— 'In the Blues', *The Pioneer*, 7 May 1892.

— 'Little Pink House', *The Pall Mall Magazine*, August (1894).

— 'Love: A "Miss"', in *Plain Tales from the Hills* (Lahore: The Civil and Military Gazette, 1886–1887).

— 'Love-in-a-Mist', in *Plain Tales from the Hills* (Lahore: The Civil and Military Gazette, 1886–1887).

— 'Mrs John Brown Protests', *The Pioneer*, 19 May 1892.

— 'My Aunt-in-Law's House', *The Pioneer*, 7 September 1892.

— 'My Sister-in-Law's Alarms', *The Pioneer*, 12 May 1892.

— 'Our Own Correspondent', *The Pioneer*, 2 January 1892.

— 'Our Theatricals', in *Plain Tales from the Hills* (Lahore: The Civil and Military Gazette, 1886–1887).

— 'Richochet or Boomerang's Return', unpublished short story.

— (Beatrice Grange), *The Heart of a Maid* (Allahabad: Indian Railway Library, 1890).

— 'The Judge's Whist', *The Pioneer*, 24 November 1892.

— 'Wife in Office', *The Pioneer*, 28 April 1892.

Lawrence, Lady, *Indian Embers: The Diary of an English Novelist during the Heyday of the Raj* (Palo Alto: Trackless Sands Press, 1991).

Lee, Lorna, *Trix: Kipling's Forgotten Sister: Unpublished Writings of Trix Kipling* (Kent: Pond View Press, 2003).

Macdonald family, papers. The University Library (University of Sussex).

Macdonald, Edith, *Annals of the Macdonald Family* (H. Marshall, 1928).

Macdonald, Frederick W., *As a Tale that Is Told* (London: Cassell, 1919).

Macdonald, Helen, interview with Barbara Fisher (2004).

MacInnes, Colin, 'Aunt Trix', in *England, Half English* (London: MacGibbon & Kee Ltd., 1961).

Myers, Frederic W. H., *Human Personality and its Survival After Bodily Death* (London: Longman Green, 1903).

Nivedita, Sister (Margaret Nobel), *The Web of Indian Life* (London: Heinemann, 1904).

Norton, Charles Eliot, *Rudyard Kipling: A Biographical Sketch* (New York: Doubleday & McClure, 1899).

Office of the Superintendent of Government Printing, India, *The Quarterly Indian Army List, 1896–1912*.

Perrin, Alice, *East of Suez* (London: Anthony Treherne & Co. Ltd., 1901).

— *The Anglo-Indians* (London: Methuen & Co., 1912).

— *Star of India* (London: Cassell, 1919).

Plowden, Geoffrey, correspondence with Barbara Fisher.

Private collection of Lorna Lee.

Sattin, Anthony, ed., *An Englishwoman in India: Memoirs of Harriet Tytler, 1828–1858* (Oxford: Oxford University Press, 1986).

Savi, Ethel, *Baba and the Black Sheep* (London: Hurst & Blackett, 1914).

— *The Daughter-in-Law* (London: Hurst & Blackett, 1913).

Steel, Flora Annie, *From the Five Rivers* (London: Heinemann, 1893).

— *On the Face of the Waters* (London: Heinemann, 1896).

— *Tales of the Punjab* (London: Macmillan, 1894).

— and Grace Gardiner, *The Complete Indian Housekeeper and Cook* (London: Heinemann, 1898).

Thirkell, Angela, *Three Houses* (Oxford: Oxford University Press, 1931).

Secondary Sources

Allen, Charles, 'A Glimpse of the Burning Plain', in *A Glimpse of the Burning Plain: Leaves from the Indian Journals of Charlotte Canning*, ed. by Michael Joseph (London: M. Joseph, 1986).

— *Kipling Sahib: India and the Making of Rudyard Kipling* (New York: Pegasus Books, 2009).

— *Plain Tales from the Raj* (London: Andre Deutsch, 1975).

Ankers, Arthur R., *The Pater: John Lockwood Kipling: His Life and Times 1837–1911* (Kent: Pond View Press, 1988).

Appignanesi, Lisa, *Mad, Bad, and Sad: Women and the Mind Doctors* (New York: Norton, 2008).

Baldwin, A.W., *The Macdonald Sisters* (London: Peter Davies, 1960).

Benfey, Christopher, *If: The Untold Story of Kipling's American Years* (London: Penguin Books, 2019).

Birkenhead, Lord, *Rudyard Kipling* (London: Weidenfeld & Nicholson, 1978).

Brown, Hilton, *Rudyard Kipling* (New York: Harper & Bros., 1945).

Buckland, C.T., *Sketches of Social Life in India* (London: W.H. Allen & Co., 1884).

Carrington, Charles, *Kipling* (London: Macmillan, 1955).

Chamberlain, Kathy, *Jane Welsh Carlyle and her Victorian World* (New York: Overlook, 2017).

DeSalvo, Louise, *Virginia Woolf: The Impact of Childhood Sexual Abuse on her Life and Work* (New York: Ballantine, 1989).

Dykstra, Natalie. *Clover Adams: A Gilded and Heartbreaking Life* (Boston: Houghton Mifflin Harcourt, 2012).

Fitzgerald, Penelope, *Edward Burne-Jones: A Biography* (London: Michael Joseph, 1975).

Flanders, Judith, *Circle of Sisters: Alice Kipling, Georgiana Burne-Jones, Agnes Poynter and Louisa Baldwin* (New York: Norton, 2001).

Gardam, Jane, *Old Filth* (New York: Europa, 2006).

Gilbert, Sandra M. and Susan Gubar, *The Madwoman in the Attic* (New Haven, CT: Yale University Press, 1979).

Gilman, Charlotte Perkins, *The Yellow Wallpaper and Other Writings* (New York: Bantam, 1989).

Gilmour, David, *The Long Recessional: The Imperial Life of Rudyard Kipling* (London: Pimlico Books, 2002).

— *The Ruling Caste: Imperial Lives in the Victorian Raj* (New York: Farrar, Straus & Giroux, 2005).

Gordon, Catherine, ed., *Evelyn De Morgan: Oil Paintings* (London: De Morgan Centre, 1996).

Gould, Alan, *The Founders of Psychical Research* (London: Routledge & Kegan Paul, 1968).

Gray, John, *The Immortalization Commission: Science and the Strange Quest to Cheat Death* (New York: Farrar Straus and Giroux, 2011).

Gross, John, ed. *The Age of Kipling* (New York: Simon & Schuster, 1972).

Hamilton, Trevor, *Immortal Longings: F.W.H. Myers and the Victorian Search for Life After Death* (Exeter: Imprint Academic, 2009).

Heilmann, Ann, ed., *Feminist Forerunner: New Womanism and Feminism in the Early Twentieth Century* (Pandora, 2003).

Hitchcock, Susan Tyler, *Mad Mary Lamb: Lunacy and Murder in Literary London* (New York: W.W. Norton, 2005).

Horowitz, Helen Lefkowitz, *Wild Unrest: Charlotte Perkins Gilman and the Making of 'The Yellow Wall-Paper'* (Oxford: Oxford University Press, 2010).

Hustvedt, Asti, *Medical Muses: Hysteria in Nineteenth-Century Paris* (New York: W.W. Norton, 2011).

Johnson, Diane, *The True History of the First Mrs. Meredith* (New York: New York Review of Books, 1972).

Lapore, Jill, *Book of Ages: The Life and Opinions of Jane Franklin* (New York: Knopf, 2013).

Lee, Hermione, *Virginia Woolf* (London: Chatto & Windus, 1996).

Lee, Lorna, *Trix: Kipling's Forgotten Sister: Unpublished Writings of Trix Kipling* (Kent: Pond View Press, 2003).

Luckhurst, Roger, *The Invention of Telepathy* (Oxford: Oxford University Press, 2002).

Lycett, Andrew, *Rudyard Kipling* (London: Weidenfeld & Nicholson, 1999).

MacMillan, Margaret, *Women of the Raj* (London: Thames & Hudson, 1988).

Miller, Jane Eldridge, *Rebel Women: Feminism, Modernism and the Edwardian Novel* (Chicago: University of Chicago Press, 1994).

Mitford, Nancy, *Zelda* (New York: Avon, 1970).

Moore, Susanna, *One Last Look* (New York: Vintage Books, 2003).

Murphy, Gardner, *The Challenge of Psychic Research* (New York: Harper, 1961).

Nicholson, Adam. *The Hated Wife: Carrie Kipling 1862-1939* (New York: Short Books, 2001).

Oberhausen, Judy, 'Sisters in Spirit: Alice Kipling Fleming, Evelyn Pickering de Morgan and 19th-century Spiritualism', *The British Art Journal*, 9 (3) (2009), 38–42.Orel, Harold, ed., *Kipling Interviews and Recollections*, vols. 1 and 2 (London: Macmillan, 1983).

Ricketts, Harry, *Rudyard Kipling: A Life* (New York: Carroll & Graf, 1999).

Said, Edward W., *Orientalism* (New York: Vintage Books, 1979).

Schultz, Bart, *Henry Sidgwick: Eye of the Universe* (Cambridge: Cambridge University Press, 2004).

Scott, Paul, *The Raj Quartet* (New York: William Morrow, 1977).

Shengold, Leonard M. D., *Soul Murder: The Effects of Childhood Abuse and Deprivation* (New Haven, CT: : Yale University Press. 1989).

Shloss, Carol Loeb, *Lucia Joyce: To Dance in the Wake* (London: Bloomsbury, 2003).

Showalter, Elaine, *The Female Malady: Women, Madness, and English Culture, 1830–1980* (New York: Pantheon Books, 1985).

Spurling, Hilary, *Paul Scott: A Life of the Author of the Raj Quartet* (New York: W.W. Norton, 1990).

Stirling, A. M. W., *William De Morgan and His Wife* (New York: Henry Holt & Co., 1922).

Strouse, Jean, *Alice James: A Biography* (Massachusetts: Harvard University Press, 1980).

Taylor, Ina, *Victorian Sisters: The Remarkable Macdonald Women and the Great Men They Inspired* (Maryland: Adler & Adler, 1987).

Trombley, Stephen, *All that Summer She Was Mad: Virginia Woolf: Female Victim of Male Medicine* (New York: Continuum, 1982).

Washington, Peter, *Madame Blavatsky's Baboon: Theosophy and the Emergence of the Western Guru* (London: Secker & Warburg, 1993).

Wilson, Angus, *The Strange Ride of Rudyard Kipling* (London: Secker & Warburg, 1977).

Wilson, Edmund, *The Wound and the Bow: Seven Studies in Literature* (Oxford: Oxford University Press, 1965).

Wilson, Frances, *Dorothy Wordsworth* (London: Faber & Faber, 2009).

Woolf, Virginia, *A Room of One's Own* (London: Hogarth Press, 1929).

— *Mrs. Dalloway* (London: Hogarth Press, 1925).

— *Three Guineas* (London: Hogarth Press, 1938).

Index

'A Biography' 218
'A Christmas Minstrel' 156
Allingham, William 37, 83
A Pinchbeck Goddess 81–82, 113, 124–125, 130, 134–137, 139, 141
  publication 136
  reviews 136, 141
  writing process 124
'A Sympathetic Woman' 156
Aunty Rosa. *See* Holloway, Sarah
automatic writing 158, 160, 168, 171, 176, 181–183, 190, 192, 194–195, 202
  mediumship 39, 172, 189–190, 192–193, 214
  'Medusa' 158
  'The Valley of Shadows' 159
'A Woman of Seasons' 122

Baldwin, Alfred 10, 21, 34, 36, 39, 146, 180
Baldwin, Louisa (née Macdonald) 10, 34, 36, 39, 180
Baldwin, Stanley 10, 34, 39, 44–45, 47, 54
  relationship with Trix 44, 47
Balestier, Wolcott 109, 217
Balfour, Gerald 169, 181
BBC 222
Bielby, Elizabeth 78–79
Bikanir House 58, 61, 78
Blavatsky, Helena 68, 170
Boer War 161–162
British Raj 3, 59, 84, 110, 115
  child-rearing 13, 33
  cultural segregation 33, 66, 115, 185
  memsahibs 111, 116
  social life 68, 81, 115
Brown, Hilton 225, 228

Burne-Jones, Georgiana (née Macdonald) 4, 27, 34–35, 37, 39, 50–51
Burne-Jones, Philip 34, 51

Clouds 180, 200
Coates, Redney 184
Colenso, Robert 146–148
collaboration between Trix and Rudyard 22, 63, 74, 82
  ambiguous authorship 75, 81–82
Cox, Gwladys 225, 229, 232
Craigie, Ethel 224
Craigie, Mary 213, 224
Craig, Maurice 205
Craik, Georgiana 50, 53
Craik, Mary 50
crystal-gazing 7, 68, 158, 160, 168, 171, 181, 192, 194

de Morgan, Evelyn 157–160, 171, 184
de Morgan, William 157, 184
Diver, Cyril 118, 124, 142–143, 188
Diver, Maud (née Marshall) 49, 54, 66, 75, 78, 116–119, 121, 124–130, 135–137, 139–143, 150, 184–188, 195, 204, 208–209, 229–231
  correspondence with Trix 116–118, 121, 126, 135–137, 139, 142, 185–186, 188, 208
  critique from Trix 130, 186–187, 209
  first encounter with Trix 54
  marriage 116
  publications 129, 186–187, 230
  writing process 117, 140, 186
Dudwell Farm 207–208

Echoes, by Two Writers 63, 79
  'Hope Deferred' 63
  'Jane Smith' 63

Edinburgh 1–3, 103–106, 143, 145, 179, 189–190, 197, 208–209, 213–216, 224–225
Edinburgh Psychic College 214
education 17, 20–21, 49, 54, 76, 79, 130
  Hope House School 17
  Notting Hill High School for Girls 49, 116
  Sunday school 18
  university prospects 54
  Westward Ho! 48–49

First World War 205–206
Fleming, John Murchison
  alleged infidelity 147, 204
  career 84, 95, 112, 188–189
  conflict with Rudyard 2, 85, 89, 199, 204
  conflict with Trix 99, 108–109, 142, 147–148, 173, 177, 188, 203, 206, 208, 216
  death 224
  engagement to Trix 85, 91, 95
  estate 225
  health 96, 108, 141, 182–183, 213–214
  marriage 91, 95
  rejection by Trix 85, 88
  separation from Trix 147, 165
Freud, Sigmund 191–193
  transference 193

Gables, the 124, 148, 150, 179, 189–190, 197–201
Garrard, Florence 49, 63, 86, 108, 217, 220
George and Mabel sketches 113–114, 151, 153, 157, 230
  'A Cheerful Giver' 155
  'Character Delineated' 156
  'Keeping a Diary' 155
  'The Joys of Camp' 156
  'The Pleasure of his Company' 156
Gifts and Gratitude 225

Golding's Farm 43
Grand, Sarah 127
Grange, the 10, 18, 27, 51
Gurney, Edmund 174, 176, 191

Hand in Hand 151, 163–164
  'Love's Derelict' 152
  'Love's Murderer' 151
  'Memory' 153
  'Where Hugli Flows' 151
Healey, Sibyl 116, 141
Heinemann 127, 135–136
'Her Brother's Keeper' 149–150
Holloway, Harry 12–17, 20, 23, 25, 49, 221
Holloway, Pryse Agar 9, 12–14, 36, 211
  death 14
Holloway, Sarah 9, 12–29, 33, 36, 43, 47–49, 53, 119, 122, 211, 221
  abuse 14, 19, 23, 27
  affection for Trix 14, 18, 27, 48
  religion 20, 29, 53
Holt, Winifred 205

imposture 6, 132–133, 230
India
  Bombay 10–11, 13, 27–28, 38–39, 41, 57, 62, 69, 130, 182, 185, 218
  Calcutta 110–111, 115, 117, 121, 139, 151, 165, 167, 176, 182, 185, 188
  caste 19, 60, 110–111, 119, 221
  Dalhousie 61, 63, 65–66, 116, 187, 229
  Mussoorie 111, 121, 125
  Simla 61, 65–70, 74–78, 86, 90–91, 93–95, 111, 116, 124, 131, 133, 136, 155, 182, 221, 229
Indian Rebellion of 1857 59
Italy 159, 189
  Florence 159–160, 171, 220

Jack. *See* Fleming, John Murchison
James, Alice 160
James, William 160, 169, 172, 189, 192

Johnson, Alice 167–168, 172, 174–179, 181–182, 189–191, 195, 205–206
  research conclusions 179, 181, 190
Johnston, Katharine 225

Kipling, Alice Macdonald
  ambition to become a nurse 79, 82
  birth 4
  childlessness 6, 119, 143, 188
  depiction by Rudyard. *See* Kipling, Rudyard: 'Baa Baa, Black Sheep'
  depiction by Rudyard's biographers 2–3, 26
  identity as a writer 64, 114, 125, 157, 184, 209, 230
  literary influences
    Aurora Leigh 31, 64
    Charles Dickens 21–22, 26, 128
    contemporary novels 127–128, 184
    Shakespeare 6, 21, 49, 69, 114, 183, 211, 225, 227
  marriage. *See* Fleming, John Murchison: marriage
  nicknames
    Beatrice Grange 100
    Ice Maiden 76
    Rose in June 66, 75, 155
    Trix 5
  performance 2, 6, 22, 69, 160, 215, 227
  suitors 69, 78, 83–84
  unfinished stories 137–139
Kipling, Alice (née Macdonald)
  career 62, 69
  death 197
  psychic experience 68
  psychic experiences 170
  relationship with Trix 11, 28, 33, 35, 37, 53, 61, 73, 145–146, 148–149, 164, 190
  suitors 37, 83
Kipling, Caroline (née Balestier) 109–110, 121, 125, 198, 201, 206–207, 209–211, 217, 220, 222–224
  alleged destruction of Lockwood's will 201, 211
  care for Trix 207, 209
  control of Rudyard's literary estate 222
  influence on Rudyard 109, 210, 222
Kipling, Elsie 217, 222–224
Kipling, John Lockwood 5, 28–29, 34–35, 38–41, 50–51, 54, 58–59, 61–62, 67–69, 76, 79, 83–86, 89–90, 95, 100–101, 121, 124, 148, 157, 163–164, 189–190, 197–201, 205, 211, 237
  career 28, 40, 68, 121
  death 200
  estate 201, 205
  marriage 38–39
  relationship with Trix 5, 40, 61, 85, 198–199, 211
Kipling, John (son of Rudyard) 205–206, 220
Kipling, John (third child of Alice and Lockwood) 33
Kipling, Josephine 148, 215, 220
Kipling, Rudyard
  'Baa Baa, Black Sheep' 16–17, 26, 30, 37
  death 217
  estate 222
  fame 2–3, 107, 121, 184, 209, 217–219
  opinions on psychic research 2, 171, 202
  relationship with Trix 2, 6, 19, 23, 25, 46, 53, 63, 65, 71, 77, 85–86, 146, 198, 201, 207, 210–211, 215, 218, 222
    conflict 198, 201, 222
  romantic interest in Flo Garrard. *See* Garrard, Florence
  Something of Myself 26, 217, 219
  supernatural stories 170
  The Light that Failed 220
Kipling Society 221, 223, 225

Lahore 2, 27–28, 41, 54, 57–58, 61, 63, 65–66, 78–79, 88, 90, 95–96, 107, 110–111, 121, 229
Lodge, Oliver 169, 180–183, 194
  Life and Matter 182
  relationship with Trix 180–181, 183
London 10, 18, 37, 40, 45–46, 48, 50, 82, 104–109, 124, 145–148, 163–164, 167, 172, 179, 182, 190, 194, 198–199, 204–205, 214–215, 217, 225, 250
Lord Birkenhead 26, 228
Lord Clandeboye 77
Lord Dufferin 68–69
Lorne Lodge 12, 14, 18, 24, 28–30, 36, 43, 48–51
  arrival 9
  Jane 15, 18, 20
  return 48

Macdonald, Edith 10, 34, 39, 182
Macdonald family
  bohemianism 18, 52, 229
  religion 29, 37, 40, 180
  traditional values 39, 52
Macdonald, Frederick 38–40
Macdonald, George 37–38
Macdonald, Hannah 10, 35, 37
Macdonald, Harry 37–39
MacInnes, Colin 216, 226–227
Mackail, Margaret (née Burne-Jones) 34, 49, 51, 78, 85
Marshall, Violet 75, 116
'More Childhood Memories of Rudyard Kipling' 219
Morris, William 18, 37, 180
mother want 31, 61, 64, 134, 149, 197
Myers, Frederic 167–169, 172, 174–176, 178, 181, 191–195
  Human Personality and its Survival of Bodily Death 167, 172, 195
'My Rival' 73

New Woman 126, 136
numerology 185

'Odes for the Coronation' 161
  'If' 162
  'The Milenders' 161
  'The Pavement Stand of Westminstree' 161

Piper, Leonora 172, 189–190
'Plain Tales from the Hills' 80–82, 114, 121, 130
  'A Little Learning' 81–82
  'A Pinchbeck Goddess' 81
  'How it Happened' 81–82
  'Love: A "Miss"' 82
  'Love-in-a-Mist' 81–82
  'Our Theatricals' 82
Plowden, Edith 3, 35, 51, 53, 199
Poynter, Agnes (née Macdonald) 34–35, 39, 182
Poynter, Ambrose 34, 36
Poynter, Edward 34–35, 39, 180, 182
psychiatric treatments 3, 146–147, 149–150, 192, 194, 199–200, 203, 205–206, 209
  certification as incompetent 203, 205, 214, 222
psychic research 2, 6, 168, 171, 173, 192, 202
  cross-correspondence 181, 189
  impact on mental health 160, 171, 191, 195, 202

Rees, Douglas 228
Richardson, Moona 108, 209–211, 213–216, 223–226
  influence on Jack 210–211, 213, 215–216
'Ricochet or Boomerang's Return' 123, 141, 217
Robinson, Kay 77, 80, 84, 88
Rudyard Lake 38, 84
Ruskin, John 18, 37, 169

Saturday Club 183
Savage, George 147, 203, 205
Second World War 224

Society for Psychical Research 3, 167, 169–170, 172–176, 180, 183–184, 190–191, 193–195, 229
  founding 168
'Some Childhood Memories of My Brother Rudyard Kipling' 219
Sorabji, Cornelia 185
St. Andrew's 108
Survey of India 84, 91, 95, 188

Taylor, Caroline 104, 108
The Civil and Military Gazette 59, 62–63, 69, 80, 112
The Family Square 2, 61–62, 66, 71, 78, 83, 107–108, 110, 121, 229, 231
'The Haunted Cabin' 71
The Heart of a Maid 71, 93, 98–100, 123–124, 129–130, 133–135, 138
  publication 100
  writing process 93–95, 98
'The Little Pink House' 121
theosophy 68, 170
The Pioneer 68, 83, 112–114, 125, 135, 140, 153, 157
  'A Journey in the Jungle' 140
  'Casual Leave' 113
  'Hunter on Marriage' 113
  'In Shadowy Thoroughfares of Thought' 113
  'In the Blues' 114
  'Mrs John Brown Protests' 113
  'My Aunt-in-Law's House' 113
  'My Sister-in-Law's Alarms' 113
  'Our Own Correspondent' 114
  'The Cry of the Mother' 125
  'The Judge's Whist' 113
  'Wife in Office' 113
the prickly pear 206, 214
The Retreat 86, 88
'The Smuggler's Cave'/'Old Mother Midnight' 184
Thirkell, Angela 216, 225
Thirkell, Lance 227
'Through Judy's Eyes' 30
Trix. *See* Kipling, Alice Macdonald
Tweddell, Augusta 83

Verrall, A. W. 172–173, 175, 179, 181, 184, 189–190

'Waiting for Cargo' 123
Walburga, Lady Paget 160, 171
Warwick Gardens 50, 52–53
Webb, Nettie 116
Weyhill House 199–203
White Town 111, 183
Wilden 10, 34, 47, 108, 180
Wilde, Oscar 51–52
Winnard, Hannah 50, 52
Wyndham, Percy 180
  The Souls 180

About the Author

Barbara Fisher graduated from Bennington College with a B.A. and received her M.A. and Ph.D. degrees in English Literature from Columbia University. For many years, she taught 18th and 19th Century English Literature, mostly at Eugene Lang College, the undergraduate college of the New School University in New York City. She has also been a book reviewer for major U.S. newspapers including the *The New York Times*, *The Washington Post*, and *The Boston Globe*, for which she wrote a book column every other Sunday for fifteen years. This is her first book as an independent scholar. She is currently working on a biography of mid-20th Century cultural and literary critic Lionel Trilling.

About the Team

Alessandra Tosi was the managing editor for this book.

Annie Hine and Adèle Kreager proof-read this manuscript. Annie compiled the index and created the Alt-text.

Jeevanjot Kaur Nagpal designed the cover. The cover was produced in InDesign using the Fontin font.

Cameron Craig typeset the book in InDesign and produced the paperback and hardback editions. The main text font is Tex Gyre Pagella and the heading font is Californian FB.

Cameron also produced the PDF and HTML editions. The conversion was performed with open-source software and other tools freely available on our GitHub page at https://github.com/OpenBookPublishers.

Jeremy Bowman created the EPUB.

Raegan Allen was in charge of marketing.

This book was peer-reviewed by two referees. Experts in their field, these readers donated their time to help ensure the academic rigour of our books. We are grateful for their generous and invaluable contributions.

This book need not end here...

Share

All our books — including the one you have just read — are free to access online so that students, researchers and members of the public who can't afford a printed edition will have access to the same ideas. This title will be accessed online by hundreds of readers each month across the globe: why not share the link so that someone you know is one of them?

This book and additional content is available at:
https://doi.org/10.11647/OBP.0377

Donate

Open Book Publishers is an award-winning, scholar-led, not-for-profit press making knowledge freely available one book at a time. We don't charge authors to publish with us: instead, our work is supported by our library members and by donations from people who believe that research shouldn't be locked behind paywalls.

Why not join them in freeing knowledge by supporting us:
https://www.openbookpublishers.com/support-us

Follow @OpenBookPublish

Read more at the Open Book Publishers BLOG

You may also be interested in:

Breaking Conventions
Five Couples in Search of Marriage-Career Balance at the Turn of the Nineteenth Century
Patricia Auspos

https://doi.org/10.11647/obp.0318

Eliza Orme's Ambitions
Politics and the Law in Victorian London
Leslie Howsam

https://doi.org/10.11647/obp.0392

William Sharp and "Fiona Macleod"
A Life
William F. Halloran

https://doi.org/10.11647/obp.0276

www.ingramcontent.com/pod-product-compliance
Lightning Source LLC
Chambersburg PA
CBHW040903250426
43673CB00064B/1949